MAY

J

Depression and Suicide in Late Life

Depression and Suicide in Late Life

by

Diego de Leo
Department of Psychiatry, University of Padua

René F. W. Diekstra
Department of Clinical and Health Psychology, University of Leiden

Hogrefe & Huber Publishers
Toronto • Lewiston, NY • Bern • Göttingen • Stuttgart

Library of Congress Cataloging-in-Publication Data

Depression and suicide in late life / Diego De Leo, René F. W.
Diekstra.
p. cm.

1. Depression in old age—Treatment. I. De Leo, Diego, 1951—
II. Diekstra, R. F. W.
[DNLM: 1. Depressive Disorder—in old age. 2. Depressive
Disorder—therapy. 3. Suicide—in old age. 4. Suicide,
Attempted—prevention & control. WM 171 S958]

RC537.5.S85   1990   618.97′68527—dc20   90-4428 CIP

Canadian Cataloguing in Publication Data

Main entry under title:
Depression and suicide in late life
Includes bibliographical references

1. Depression in the aged. 2. Depression in the aged—Treatment.
3. Geriatric psychiatry. I. De Leo, Diego, 1951–   II. Diekstra, R. F. W.

RC537.5.S86   1990   618.97′68527   C90-093861-7

© Copyright 1990 by Hogrefe & Huber Publishers

P. O. Box 51
Lewiston, NY 14092

12–14 Bruce Park Ave.
Toronto, Ontario M4P 2S3

ISBN 3-456-81822-X
ISBN 0-920887-66-X
Hogrefe & Huber Publishers
Toronto • Lewiston, NY • Bern • Göttingen • Stuttgart

Printed in Germany on acid-free paper

To our affectionate (and patient!) wives, Cristina and Nelly

TABLE OF CONTENTS

Foreword

Sadness is a normal state of mind brought about by adversity; depression is a *disorder*. There is a substantial zone of overlap, yet for mental health workers, it is essential to determine on which side of the border a client/patient is operating.

- Depression is a *mood disorder*—and much more: Many other psychological functions are affected, such as drive, motoricity, hedonic functioning, sleep, and appetite.

- Depression is a *frequent disorder*: With a lifetime prevalence of approximately 8%, it exceeds by far the frequency of such disorders as schizophrenia and Alzheimer's disease.

- Depression is a *life-threatening disorder*—a major precursor of suicidal behavior. In a group of 100 patients hospitalized for suicide attempts, we found definite signs of depression in 83% of them in the 2 months preceding the attempt (van Praag, 1982). Severe depression leads to suicide in 10–15% of cases. In the United States, the rate of suicide is 0.12‰, the approximate rate of attempted suicide 2–4‰. Recognition of an underlying depression is essential, because frequently that condition is treatable.

- Depression is a *costly disorder*. The total direct costs, i.e., the expenditures for diagnosis, treatment, and rehabilitation in the United States is estimated to be $2.1 billion per year. The total indirect costs, i.e., the costs incurred for lost productivity from mortality and morbidity, totals approximately $10 billion and $4.2 billion, respectively. That amounts to a total economic loss of $16.3 billion yearly (Stoudemire et al., 1986). The losses in terms of quality of life, for both patients and those near to them, are immeasurably high.

The decision to terminate one's life is rarely unequivocal, at least not in attempted suicide. (The antecedents of completed suicide are, of course, much less known.) It is ambivalent behavior par excellence. There is the will to die and at the same time the will to live—albeit under more favorable conditions. Attempted suicide is an attempt to die as well as a means to achieve support felt to be otherwise unattainable. It is no wonder, then, that we could demonstrate that severe anxiety is common in the weeks prior to an attempt, often attaining panic proportions. I avoid the term "para-suicide," because it plays down too much the self-destructive component of a suicide attempt. Recognition of the help-seeking component is equally essential in view of the planning of adequate therapeutic interventions.

Attempted suicide is always the result of two interacting factors: a stressful event and a concurrent mood state that lowers resistance to stress. The event can be overwhelming or ostensibly minor, though for a given individual devastating. The concurrent, underlying mood state is variable as well. Shame may be the predominant tone, or guilt, or hopelessness, or disappointment, or sense of failure. Yet, traumatic event and mood state are not enough to explain suicidal behavior. Many experience adversity: "Permissive mood states" are known to many, yet suicidal behavior is relatively uncommon. In other words, a third force has to be operating, i.e., disposition or suicide vulnerability. Suicide threshold-lowering factors might be psychological in nature. Personality traits such as dependency, impulsivity, and low frustration tolerance, for instance, can count as such. Sociological risk factors have also been extensively studied. As an example, I recount that the destitute, the underprivileged, the underdog seems to be at greater risk of suicidal acts than the upper echelons of society. Until quite recently, suicide had been hardly studied from the biological point of view; attempts to do so were even bitterly contested by antipsychiatrists. Today, the issue whether brain dysfunctions can predispose to suicide in a stressed individual is a legitimate scientific concern. The finding that disorders in the functioning of the neurotransmitter serotonin seems to correlate with suicidal behavior—and that across diagnoses—even raises hopes that in the future pharmacology could begin to contribute to suicide prevention.

Both depression and suicide have been extensively studied in adults and more recently in adolescents. Curiously, the elderly have also in this respect suffered from neglect, in spite of the high frequency of both conditions in that age group. The Norwood-Montefiore Aging Study (Kennedy et al., 1989, 1990), for instance, revealed that 17% of the elderly experience significant levels of depression. The suicide rate among the elderly is the highest of all age categories. Perhaps depression is frequently missed in the aged and held for early dementia or considered as "mere" sadness caused by social isolation, physical illness or disability, or perceived meaningless of life. Suicidal tendencies could be easily "rationalized" as being generated by similar forces.

Evidence to substantiate that view is lacking, but even if it were to be shown correct, therapeutic nihilism would be unjustified.

For all those reasons, the book of De Leo and Diekstra is more than welcome. It brings together much of the available data on depression and suicide in the elderly and does so in a lucid, succinct, yet comprehensive and imminently readable manner. This is a true state-of-the-art work and makes for essential reading for all (mental) health workers involved with the elderly. It contains all the elements of a "classic," and I am quite confident it is bound to become one.

Herman M. van Praag, M.D., Ph.D.
Department of Psychiatry
Albert Einstein College of Medicine/
Montefiore Medical Center
New York, New York

REFERENCES

Kennedy, G. J., Kelman, H. R., Thomas, C., Wisniewski, W., Matz, H., & Bejier, R. (1989). Hierarchy of characteristics associated with depressive symptoms in an urban elderly population. *Am. J. Psychiatr. 146*, 220–225.

Kennedy, G. J., Kelman, H. R., & Thomas, C. (1990). Emergence of depressive symptoms in the community elderly: Importance of declining health and increasing disability. *J. Comm. Health 15*, 95–105.

Stoudemire, A., Frank, R., Hedemark, N., Kamlet, M., & Blazer D. (1989). The economic burden of depression. *Gen. Hosp. Psychiatr. 8*, 387–394.

van Praag, H. M. (1982). Depression, suicide and the metabolism of serotonin in the brain. *J. Affect. Dis. 4*, 275–290.

Acknowledgements

Thanks are due to Prof. Luigi Pavan (Department of Psychiatry, University of Padua) for his constant encouragement. Gratitude should also be expressed to Dr. Guido Magni (Wyeth-Ayers, Paris) for years of stimulating collaboration and specific assistance with Chapters 1 and 11. We are also indebted to Prof. Michiel Hengeveld (Department of Psychiatry, University of Leiden) for carefully reviewing the manuscript, to Dr. Leonid Prilipko (World Health Organization) and to Prof. Paul Kielholz (Department of Psychiatry, University of Basel) for their important suggestions.

Introduction

The progressive increase in the elderly population has obliged the medical profession to pay increasing attention to geriatric problems. However, many doctors are still undeniably ill-prepared to tackle many of the specific problems related to aging. In general, there is a strong tendency to use diagnostic nomenclatures conceived for younger subjects and to use the same procedures of treatment—without any particular distinction for age group. There is also a strong underlying prejudice according to which many pathological conditions in the elderly are the result of an irreversible degeneration, a belief that has strongly influenced the therapeutic attitude of doctors.

Disorders of mood are the clinical phenomena most frequently found in elderly subjects. The numerous loss events inevitably accumulating in the later part of life provide a partial explanation—in psychosocial terms—of the greater prevalence of depression in this age group. Moreover, age-related biological changes may in some way predispose the subject to the onset of a depressive episode, and may perhaps also partially explain the tendency toward chronicity found in affective as well as organic disease in the elderly. However, the mechanisms through which biological factors interact with social and psychological factors are not yet fully understood, although it seems reasonable to believe that a greater biological vulnerability may increase susceptibility to the effects of stressful life events.

Regardless of etiological considerations, it is vital to modify the attitude of resignation so often characterizing the clinical approach to psychiatric disturbances in the elderly. One of the aims of the psychogeriatrician—and of this volume in particular—could be to instill a more optimistic attitude with regard to the treatment of depression in the elderly subject. There are in fact no constitutional reasons why biological, psychological, or social therapeutic approaches in the elderly should necessarily be futile or ineffective. Once correctly identified, the clinical problems of depression are equally accessible to treatment in both young and old subjects.

Thus, this book is addressed mainly to those involved in the care of the elderly—geriatricians, psychiatrists, psychologists—but also to social workers and to all who want to learn more about course and cure of depression and related problems in the elderly.

- Chapter 1 describes prevalence data on depression in the elderly, given the general lack of findings on incidence. The main methodological problems in epidemiological studies are also discussed, and particular emphasis is laid on the differences between data from studies based on rating scales and those using clinical interviewing.

- Chapter 2 reports on the main characteristics of depressive profiles in the elderly, considering not only the "major" disturbance, but other disorders typical in the elderly such as organic mood disorders, "masked" depressions, pseudodementia, and the frequently difficult distinction between depression and dementia. The disappearance from modern nosography of "involutional melancholy" is also examined. This chapter also treats the new techniques of brain imaging and their contribution to new insights into the physiopathology of depression.

- Nowadays it appears evident that psychosocial factors play an important role in the mental and physical health of an individual, especially in the elderly. Chapter 3 focuses on those problems as the one more closely associated to depression: loss of social support, bereavement, relocation, retirement. Recent insights coming from psychoimmunology are also examined.

- Neurochemical changes in the brain correlated with aging are discussed in Chapter 4, in which the main neurotransmitter systems and the possible connections between alterations in these and the affective disorders are examined in some detail.

- The contribution of the new noninvasive diagnostic techniques is taken up again at some length in Chapter 5, which is concerned with depressive profiles possible linked to alterations in brain blood flow. Particular attention is paid to post-stroke depression and site of lesion. A section is also devoted to the outcome of carotid endarterectomy operations, especially to its repercussions on the well-being and affective sphere of the individual.

- An affective profile that may be considered typical of the elderly is that connected to Parkinson's disease, discussed in Chapter 6. Parkinson's disease is frequently accompanied by depressive symptomatology whose dynamics are still *sub judice*; it is not yet clear whether the affective disorder is a reaction to the disease or a direct effect of it in the sense of a symptom.

- Chapter 7 is concerned with mania and hypomania: distribution, age of onset, main characteristics, and evolution. The numerous difficulties encountered in the definition of the principal characteristics of mania in the elderly are discussed at some length.

- Chapter 8 deals with the pharmacological treatment of mood disorders and their peculiarities. Pharmacodynamic and pharmacokinetic problems typical of the elderly organism are discussed, together with the side effects of the various categories of drugs. Particular attention is paid to drugs that have proved effective in elderly subjects, including lithium and carbamazepine. This chapter also examines the common interactions between drugs.

- In Chapter 9, reference is made to the treatment of some disorders that are particularly frequent in the elderly: the "minor" depressions, the dysthymias, and adjustment disorders. The discussion here mainly centers on benzodiazepine treatment, psychotherapeutic treatment being considered in the last part of the chapter.

- The latter is discussed at greater length in Chapter 10, which is organized according to theoretical orientations. The possibilities of psychoanalysis in the elderly are examined, together with a discussion of the various different psychotherapeutic schools, including the psychodynamic, cognitive, and behavioral schools, "life review therapy," etc. Group psychotherapy and unstructured psychological supports are also considered. A section is dedicated to the important and peculiar aspects of transference and countertransference relationships with the elderly.

- Following a review of the available findings on the evolution of the affective disorders, Chapter 11 reports an experimental study conducted on a population of patients passing through the outpatient service of the Psychiatric Clinic in Padua, Italy. This study substantially confirms the results of previous studies by Murphy, namely, that outcome still remains poor in a high proportion of cases.

- Chapter 12 deals with the most typical elements of suicidal behavior in the elderly: socio-demographic characteristics, associations with physical and psychological disorders, means of suicide, distribution. Particular emphasis is placed on the differences between prevalence data in different nations and continents, using data collected by the World Health Organization.

- Chapter 13 describes possible treatment of suicidal elderly persons with particular reference to currently feasible strategies of prevention.

- Finally, Chapter 14 summarizes some of the unresolved debates in the study of mood disorders in the elderly. Emphasis is placed on problems relating to the identification of "cases," drug trials with specific protocol for elderly populations, and the design of new rating scales.

PART ONE:
GENERAL ISSUES

CHAPTER 1
Depression in the Elderly: Epidemiological Aspects

- Mood disorders are the most common psychiatric disturbances present in old age. This chapter examines relevant studies concerning the epidemiological dimension of the problem. Issues related to methodological problems, such as determination of "cases," correct utilization of rating scales, and identification of different subtypes of depression, are also presented.

- Despite the uncertainties surrounding the etiological nature of the different interactions and the role played by psychological factors, it seems possible to state that depression is more frequent in the elderly than in the young, especially minor mood disorders. Moreover, it would appear that many conditions typically linked to advanced age, particularly physical disease, may be accompanied by depressive symptoms that, while not severe enough to qualify as a proper clinical pathology, may be disabling.

Over the last few years, increasing interest has been given to the problems of old age, especially to those relating to the emotional and cognitive spheres. This may be explained by the increasing number of people involved in attempts to improve medical and health-care services, as well as the increasing concern for quality of life. Emphasis is being placed not only on prolonging life, but on rendering it pleasant and worthwhile.

Taking a simple numerical point of view, it may be said that while the world population stood at approximately 4 billion in the 1970s, by the end of this century it will have risen by about 50%. This estimated increase is mainly the result of the reduction of mortality at the two extremes of the human biological cycle, in infants and the elderly. As a consequence, the elderly will constitute an ever-increasing proportion of the total population, the number of persons over 65 probably doubling over the next 50 years.

At present, people aged 65 years or over make up, for example, about 12% of the population of the United States and 13.2% of the population of Italy. The importance and dimension of the problem becomes even clearer if we consider that the risk of suicide increases with increasing age—for males over 65 years of age the suicide rate is about three times higher than for the general population [110]—and that depression is closely linked to suicide [25].

Despite increased concern about the elderly and their problems over the last few years, our society continues to "cultivate" certain stereotypes of the elderly that frequently have a very negative effect on their well-being [157]. For example, there is a widespread opinion that the mental faculties of the elderly are so weak that they are no longer able to look after themselves. Yet in the United States, as an example, less than 5% of persons over the age of 65 ask for residential care [96].

The underrating of the capacities of the elderly in a society that privileges youth and dynamism may generate a lack of incisiveness in the treatment of mental disorders in the elderly, even when these are curable and reversible. On the other hand, the tendency to think of aging as a *disease* may lead to the correlation of symptoms such as apathy, asthenia, memory disorders, and deterioration in physical conditions to the aging process itself, when these symptoms may in fact be the result of a depressive situation. Confirmation of the deleterious effects of these erroneous convictions is given by the fact that recognition of depression in the elderly is often rather poor: Only 25% of depressed elderly persons receive adequate medical treatment [349]. Diagnosis of depression seems to be particularly complex in the elderly with medical problems, given that most of the depressive symptoms experienced by the patient are attributed to the aging process, the disease, and organic disturbances of the central nervous system [61]. However, it is worth noting that the presence of atypical symptoms (which may be found in other age groups, but are particularly frequent among older subjects), of a high incidence of chronic physical diseases (80% of the geriatric population is affected by at least one chronic disease [500]), and of the simultaneous use of one or more pharmacological products may combine to create real problems for proper diagnosis [160].

Furthermore, depression is probably the most frequent of all psychiatric disturbances in both adult and elderly subjects [686]. It has been reported that there is an approximately 10–20% risk of developing an episode of major depression in the course of a lifetime [91], and that the incidence of depression rises with increasing age [379]. It has also been found that the onset of most first episodes of depression occurs during the second half of life. In absolute terms, depression is one of the most common psychiatric diagnoses in individuals over the age of 60 [680], while the diagnosis of cerebral organic syndrome seems to be prevalent in those over 80 years of age [477].

METHODOLOGICAL PROBLEMS IN THE IDENTIFICATION OF "CASES"

Despite the well-documented findings reported above, the true incidence and prevalence of depression in this age group is still not sufficiently clear. Generally, the estimates reported by various research projects vary considerably according to the type of population examined, the instruments, and the criteria employed in diagnosis, etc.

Table 1 shows the percentage prevalences in some countries as reported in international literature. One of the most influential variables in the estimates provided by the various investigators is whether the evaluations were conducted on the basis of clinical interview or standardized scales, which are often self-rated. As can be seen, studies based on scales report far higher percentages (at least in the case of research on general populations). Percentages are also markedly higher in high-risk populations such as residents of homes for the elderly and patients affected by organic diseases.

While a good deal of research is available on the prevalence of depression in the elderly, almost no work has been done on the incidence of affective disorders in this age group. The evaluation of this variable in fact requires a more complex research design including two separate assessments, the second of which serves to determine the number of subjects who were not considered a "case" at the first assessment but had developed the disorder subsequently.

Returning to Table 1, we may now analyze some of the problems connected to the evaluation and redesignation as "cases" of subjects preliminarily categorized as being at the "borderline."

Table 1. Prevalence of depression in the elderly.

Studies carried out with rating scales	Studies carried out with clinical interview
5.8% (Enzell, 1983)	0.008% (Munijaya, 1973)
9.5% (Golberg et al., 1985)	0.06% (Linn et al., 1980)
14.7% (Blazer & Williams, 1980)	0.9% (Hasegawa, 1985)
16.7% (Frerichs et al., 1981)	1.76% (Bollerup, 1975)
16.9% (Murrel et al., 1983)	1.7% (Weissman et al., 1985) (Major D.)
	2% (Soresens & Stromgren, 1961)
	5.3% (Maule et al., 1984)
	6.8% (Weissman & Myers, 1978)
	10.2% (Kay et al., 1985)
	2.2%–5% (New Haven) (Meyers et al., 1984)
	1.2%–3.1% (Baltimore) (Meyers et al., 1984)
	0.5%–3.1% (St. Louis) (Meyers et al., 1984)
On medical outpatients	
20% (Kukull et al., 1986)	
On nursing home residents	
38% (Mann et al., 1984)	
On medical inpatients	
42% (Magni et al., 1985)	38% (Magni et al., 1985)
	42.7% (Magni et al., 1986)

From De Leo and Magni [157].

Feelings of sadness, disappointment, and loss are normal aspects of human existence we have all experienced. But when these aspects persistently influence daily activities of work, study, family life, etc., and especially when they are accompanied by suicidal ideation, the result is frequently depression. But at what point does something that may be considered a normal variation in the affective sphere become pathological? This distinction is important from the clinical point of view in deciding, for example, whether or not to treat an elderly person with drugs. But it is also important in medical research, when disorders of a similar etiology, course, and prognosis must be delineated. In order to resolve this problem, numerous classifications of depression based on clinical criteria have appeared over the last 10–15 years [7], though only the recent development of diagnostic criteria such as the DSM-III [11] has permitted the definition of clear operational guidelines for affective disorders. These guidelines offer—at the least—a standard point of reference for research on the affective disorders.

Nevertheless, the problems of defining the borderline between normality and anomaly persist, and will probably remain with us for some time to come.

At present, many of the self-rating scales suitable for use with the elderly (including the *Zung Self-Rating Depression Scale* [715], the *Beck Depression Inventory* [42], the *Geriatric Depression Scale* [711], etc.) provide the means for calibrating the intensity of depressive symptoms, and the cut-off values are useful indicators of an important clinical symptomatology. (In drug trials, for example, the cut-off values are used as a criteria for inclusion.) Yet it is important to remember that the self-rating scales cannot be used as the sole basis for diagnosis, and their employment as a screening method is often improper.

As there is no laboratory test that reliably distinguishes depression, the main source of evaluation of this disorder to date has been what we may generically term "the interview," which is subdivided into a clinical evaluation based on the clinical examination of psychiatric tradition, and a psychometric evaluation rooted in psychological tradition. Each of these systems has its advantages and drawbacks, which will now be briefly examined.

The validity of clinical evaluation depends largely on the ability and experience of the evaluator in examining the subject and reducing the possible errors of measurement. Even with the use of precise and rigorous criteria such as those contained in the DSM-III-R, however, the validity of the data obtained is not always good. A recent study conducted in Denmark has, in fact, revealed that difficulties are involved in the use of these diagnostic criteria [38]. Six or seven expert psychiatrists evaluated 35 patients with depression, excellent agreement being found in the diagnosis of major depression. Clear discrepancies emerged in the classification of the sub-type with melancholy, however: Only 9 of the 35 patients were diagnosed as melancholic by all the examiners, and there was considerable disagreement about the diagnosis of another 9 subjects.

When we consider that the psychiatrists involved in this study all had a good level of experience, were working full time in an academic setting, and had worked together for many years in the field of affective disorders, it is clear that validity (and, consequently, interrater reliability) in the diagnosis of depression is still extremely problematic, even when rigorous criteria are employed. It is, moreover, likely that the validity of clinical diagnoses is considerably lower in other settings, for example, general medical or nonpsychiatric specialist wards.

Unlike clinical examination, many of the tests for depression are based on closed response items (often of the "yes/no" or "a little/fairly/very/extremely" type), which leave the selection of response to the patient. This considerably reduces the "examiner effect," through which some of the phenomena observed are inevitably affected by the way in which they are seen by the person examining them, for example, by previous experience, beliefs etc. On the other hand, responses to self-rating scales tend to be multideterminate: The motivations to the response to a single demand (for example, "Do you often feel depressed?") may vary from individual to individual in a way that has no direct connection to the item really being measured, but rather may depend on other factors of interference, for example, the way in which the different subjects interpret the word "depressed."

Scales for the evaluation of depression are generally composed of 15–30 items and may hence give a fairly precise idea of at least the overall situation, even if "errors" do occur in particular items. Moreover, most of these scales have been carefully examined for validity and reliability. However, validation is usually performed in only a few specific populations characterized by precise sociodemographic boundaries, and an instrument that is valid in one setting (e.g., in younger adult subjects) is not necessarily valid in others (e.g., elderly subjects or children).It should be remembered that these scales also include items relating to somatic symptoms, given that one of the spheres in which depression manifests itself is the "soma."

Since elderly subjects are clearly more at risk for organic disease and are more likely to be suffering from chronic disturbances that are being treated with a variety of drugs, they are hence more likely to score high on these specific items. This increased score may raise the subject's score above the cut-off point and lead to classification as a "case" even though the subject is merely suffering more than others from certain organic disturbances.

Another aspect requiring attention is the type of population for which the scale was originally designed. Questions valid for psychiatric patients are not necessarily so for another group, such as a general population. Thus, measurement tests, although they permit a greater objectivity in the observation of a given phenomenon, must be carefully calibrated for the population under study. This is why they should not be used as screening or diagnostic instruments.

One last limit to the use of such tests is connected to the degree of fidelity of the patient's response. Some subjects will deny having experienced a certain symptom or affect, and in others reporting of the symptom may be modified by unconscious mechanisms. The clinical interview has a clear advantage with respect to this problem, as there is direct contact and the relationship that is inevitably established between the examiner and the patient often (though not always) helps to overcome this difficulty.

However, the two different approaches briefly described here are not in contrast; it is reasonable to assert that they may be used in combination in the identification and diagnosis of a case. The self-rating scale may permit a relatively simple and inexpensive assessment of a given population. As each scale has its own cut-off point, the one that is most sensitive for the specific purpose should be selected. Individuals designated as "depressed" on the basis of test scores might then be interviewed by an expert clinician using one of the valid instruments available, such as the *Schedule for Affective Disorders and Schizophrenia* (SADS) [630] or the *Diagnostic Interview Schedule* (DIS) [555]. These are structured interviews that permit the evaluation of affective disorders according to the Research Diagnostic Criteria (RDC) [198] or the *Diagnostic and Statistical Manual of Mental Disorders, 3rd ed., Revised* (DSM-III-R) [11], which have been shown to overcome some of the reliability problems connected to the use of unstructured clinical interviews.

They have also been designed to provide the detailed description of both psychopathology and functioning necessary for the evaluation of prognosis and overall severity of the disturbance [588].

Over the last years, the use of this kind of structured interview has become widespread. This certainly represents a step forward in research, ensuring a greater standardization and accuracy in clinical evaluation. However, in the field of psychogeriatrics, it should be noted, the problem of clinical differentiation between depression and dementia remains open. And while the importance of this problem in clinical practice is clear, its relevance for community populations is even greater. A partial solution to this may be offered by the introduction of instruments designed for the evaluation of cognitive functions, such as the

Mini Mental Status Examination [208]. But this latter test still fails to differentiate between dementia and pseudodementia, an apparent decline of cognitive function consequent on depression [688] which will receive further attention in the following chapter.

EPIDEMIOLOGICAL FINDINGS

Returning to the epidemiology of depression in the elderly, interesting data have been obtained in the United States in a study entitled *Epidemiologic Catchment Area Program* (ECAP) [538], probably the largest study existing to date in the field of the epidemiology of psychiatric disorders in the elderly. The research examines 2,588 noninstitutionalized subjects aged 65 years and over and resident in Connecticut [687]. This population represents 77% of the original sample, 23% having refused to collaborate. All the subjects were interviewed with the *Diagnostic Interview Schedule* (DIS)—the most recent version of which permits the formulation of psychiatric diagnoses according to the criteria of the DSM-III—and the *Mini Mental State* (MMS), which, as we have mentioned, allows a relatively rapid screening for the presence of dementia or other disorders causing alterations in cognitive function.

The prevalences of affective disturbances reported by these authors over a 6-month period are 1.7% for major depression, 0.1% for bipolar disorder, and 2.4% for dysthymic disorder. Some 3.4% of the respondents presented severe alteration of cognitive capacity and 12.7% a slight alteration. In their discussion, the authors correctly stress the low prevalence of psychiatric disorders (6.7%), about half that found in the population under the age of 45 years in the same research program [482]. Even when severe cognitive disturbances are added to the psychiatric disorders, the morbidity percentage (10.8%) was still lower than that for the population under 45.

These data seem at least partially to overturn the conventional view of the extent of functional psychiatric disorders in the elderly and stress the importance of the cognitive disturbances. However, some considerations should be made here. First, the data relate only to persons living within the community, to the exclusion of institutionalized subjects. This may have lead to a positive bias in the population, with the exclusion of the more "disturbed" subjects. The authors of the article take this problem into account, though they report that in their catchment area, the institutionalized population represents only 5% of subjects aged 65 years or over, and their exclusion could have had no appreciable effect on the results. From Table 1 it may be seen that subjects in institutions are in fact considerably more at risk than those living in the community, and it is hence possible that their exclusion may have lead to at least a small effect on the results.

A second consideration once again relates to the selection of the population. Although the 77% overall response is good, still approximately one-fourth of subjects did not participate in the study. It is possible—though not demonstrated—that the noncollaborating group may have been those with the worse physical and/or mental health conditions.

A third consideration concerns the diagnosis of affective disturbance. Neither atypical depression nor adjustment disorder with depressed mood in fact appear in the tables or in the text of the paper. A recent study employing the criteria of the DSM-III for the evaluation of the prevalence of affective disturbances in a group of elderly subjects with general medical pathologies revealed that these two disturbances represent about 29% of the affective disorders found in the study population [416]. In an even more recent survey on general medical inpatients in a geriatric hospital for whom psychiatric consultation had been requested, the number of "minor" depressions (including dysthymic disorders, atypical depressions, and adjustment disorders with minor depression) was ten times greater than the number of major affective disorders [174]. It is thus probable that the inclusion of these diagnostic categories appreciably increases the prevalence percentages.

Lastly, it should also be noted that about 62% of the subjects in the population studied were enjoying good or excellent conditions of health and another 27.5% fairly good health. This finding is somewhat in contrast with the findings of other studies that describe the elderly as being at high risk for physical disease. Indeed, subjects aged 65 and over make up 12–13% of the population but consume 25% of the total drug production [655]. This would seem to indicate that a large proportion of them in fact do not enjoy very good health—if good health is taken to imply not taking drugs. A recent epidemiological study conducted in Saskatchewan, Canada, showed that subjects aged 60 and over, although comprising only 16% of the population, accounted for fully

42% of all drugs prescribed, and that more than 50% of individuals in this age group were consuming drugs [589].

On overall analysis of these findings, it would appear that the elderly are not more at risk for severe depressive states, such as major depression, than other age groups. In effect, various authors [327, 485, 513] have found percentage prevalences for the affective psychoses (a category embracing the current concept of major depression) which are fairly similar to those found in other phases of life, ranging from 1% to 1.5%. According to Clayton [119], for example, risk for bipolar disturbance drops by more than 90% in subjects over the age of 60 years. A study by Gurland et al. [263], using the *Comprehensive Assessment and Referral Evaluation* (CARE), also found that the prevalence of major depression in subjects aged 65 and over is similar to that found in younger subjects, while other clinically relevant depressive disorders appeared to increase in frequency to over 13%. These observations appear to confirm the biological nature of the major affective disorders [7], whose overall phenotypical expression occurs in earlier phases of life.

The minor affective disorders, on the other hand, increase in frequency in the elderly, and it may be affirmed that the greater overall prevalence of depression in old age depends largely on this sort of disorder [145, 477].

Another factor to be taken into account is that the longer a person has lived, the stronger is the possibility that he or she will have suffered from psychiatric disorders: A greater number of depressions that may be defined as secondary may have occurred.

The widespread use of drugs and psychotropic drugs in these subjects [423] seems to depend, on the one hand, on their being more at risk for physical diseases and, on the other hand, on a large number of persons with minor psychiatric disorders (especially minor depressions) receiving a preeminently pharmacological treatment. This tendency has a negative consequence in the onset of side effects that are sometimes worse than the disorder or symptom for which they were originally prescribed.

Another important consideration relates to physical disease. As we have seen, the ECAP population was on the whole made up of relatively healthy subjects. This is not concordant with other findings in the literature presented here [157, 423, 589, 655], from which it may reasonably be deduced that the health conditions of the elderly are generally worse than those of adults. This point is particularly worth stressing, as the factor most constantly associated with depression in the elderly in the various epidemiological studies is, in fact, ill health. The studies presented in Table 1 clearly demonstrate that the presence of physical disease is an extremely significant variable in the context of depression.

Other factors associated with depression are disability, expressed as days spent in bed or away from one's usual activities, and the loss of an organ (amputation) [133, 214, 321]. The "Research Report" by Hafner and Riecher on Mannheim [265] asserts that the rate for psychiatric morbidity in elderly people with intermediate and severe physical impairment was approximately six times higher than that found among physically healthy elderly individuals. Other experiences [420] in a group of patients with general medical pathologies showed that physical diseases involving the CNS and muscular-skeletal apparatus are more predictive of depression than diseases involving, for example, the cardiovascular, respiratory, or urinary apparatuses. The most disabling disorders are, in fact, disturbances of the CNS and muscular-skeletal apparatus, which are most likely to render the subject dependent on others. As the social network of the elderly subject is generally smaller than that of the younger adult, disturbances creating disability are particularly distressing.

FURTHER OBSERVATIONS ON THE PREVALENCE OF DEPRESSION

Some other factors associated with depression in the elderly merit brief attention here.

The elderly subject is exposed to many situations of stress linked to old age. Zung [716] notes that geriatric subjects experience a greater number of loss events. Besides ill-health, these events may relate to the death of family members or friends as well as work, income, and housing conditions. Other authors emphasize the importance of loss of role, consequent on retirement or job-loss through ill-health [226]. More generally, it may also be said that "losing" one's youth and the approach of death may itself constitute a stress-provoking situation compounding those noted above.

In our society, the elderly often find themselves isolated from a functioning support network. This renders them more vulnera-

ble to the destabilizing effects of stressful life events than younger subjects. Recent clinical studies [267, 389] have confirmed this
hypothesis and have also shown that the type of stress-provoking
situation most frequently associated with depression differs between men and women. Women, whom many studies have found
as presenting more depressive symptoms than men [61, 110, 119,
263, 355], appear to be more sensitive to lack of social relations,
financial problems, and the fear of death, while men are more
disturbed by not being involved in an activity they perceive as
interesting [355, 389].

It should be noted, however, that while a great deal of information is available on the beneficial influence of social support
on the mental health of the general population, little work has
been done with specific regard to the elderly [287]. The so-called
buffering effect of social structures and significant interpersonal
relations remains largely hypothetical as far as the older age
groups are concerned. In any case, it seems likely that stress-provoking situations and negative changes in life conditions may
give rise to a loss of self-esteem in both young and old, and this
sort of event is considered the most frequent psychodynamic
mechanism underlying the onset of depression in the elderly
subject.

Yet it should not be forgotten that, except in relation to poor
physical health and female sex, the literature is by no means
unanimous—in fact there is frequently open disagreement. For
example, according to Hafner and Riecher [265], social isolation
accounts for only a small part of variance. Certain individuals are
able to live an extremely retiring life without experiencing distress, whereas others live alone but maintain contacts with relatives and friends.

One last aspect worthy of discussion relates to the possible
role of other cultural and social factors in the explanation of the
discrepancies in the figures for prevalence reported in Table 1.
For instance, Hasegawa maintains that the low percentage of
prevalence he found in Tokyo [275], confirmed by other Japanese
authors working in other regions of this country, depend to a
large extent on differences in family structure as compared to
western countries. Approximately 42% of the Japanese population is, in fact, made up of three-generation families, while the
corresponding figure for the United States is only 3%. According
to this author, family life not only precludes loneliness but also
has beneficial effects on the preservation of mental health.

The sociocultural factors playing a significant role in the ECAP study are evident from the study itself. The differences between the various centers that participated in the study are in many cases extremely clear. In the case of affective disorders in the elderly, a previous investigation by the same authors found that the prevalence percentages for these disorders in New Haven were double those for certain other cities, such as Baltimore and St. Louis [538].

It is likely that over the next few years the ECAP study as well as other studies in other regions of the United States and elsewhere will be able to furnish a more precise picture of the epidemiology of affective disorders in the elderly. One may hope that they will also provide information about the sociocultural factors underlying the data obtained and an etiology of these problems in late life.

CHAPTER 2
Characteristics of Depression in the Elderly

- In this chapter, we review the most common characteristics and forms of depression in old age. Also, we discuss the disappearance from recent classification of involutional melancholia, a disease in which hypochondria and somatizations should be "typically" present. In fact, depression in older persons may be difficult to detect because it can be "masked" by organic disease and, furthermore, could be easily considered as "merely" secondary and consequently left untreated. Also, distinguishing depression from dementia may be difficult especially when so-called pseudodementia is involved.

- Certain modern objective biological tests such as DST and THRT are easily performed, and a lower REM latent period (used only when a specific laboratory equipment is available) can help us to diagnose depression.

- Finally, the possible relationship between depression and sexual function are considered and also how they can reciprocally affect older persons who are often falsely judged as being sexually inactive.

DEPRESSIVE PROFILES IN THE ELDERLY

As we have seen in Chapter 1, the word depression refers to a variation in mood along a spectrum ranging from normal to pathological. Feelings of sadness and regret are part of our daily lives, but they are particularly present in the elderly, who, for instance, are more frequently called to cope with the loss of persons dear to them, physical disease and often disability, changes in social status, etc.—situations that may cause a drop in mood in *any* individual. When such a switch in affectivity is directly linked to a life event, the depression may be defined as "reactive," or, in the more precise terminology of the DSM-III [10], as an "adjustment disorder." If the depression develops in a subject already affected by a severe physical disease or other mental disorders, it is defined as "secondary." This form of depression may be considered as a sense of desperation linked to the unpredictable and recurrent relapses of the primary disease and to the restrictions, risks, and negative social and interpersonal implications that accompany it.

If the primary disturbance is physical, the depressive effect may be caused directly by alterations of the endocrine metabolism, the central nervous system, etc., rather than indirectly, as a psychological reaction to the disease itself. Such kinds of depression may be identified today in the "organic mood disorder." Other frequent forms of depression, today defined as "dysthymia" or "depressive neurosis," seem to appear in predisposed personalities (especially in neurotic types) and have a tendency to become chronic (lasting at least 2 years) with occasional brief periods of normal mood. Lastly, major depression (which may be unipolar or bipolar according to whether there is also history of mania) is now considered a psychobiological disturbance, with affective, cognitive, and somatic symptomatological manifestations. The affective state found in the depression is similar to that of sadness, but is longer lasting (at least 2 weeks), more profound, and pervasive for the individual experiencing it. In some cases, the predominant characteristics may be irritability and loss of interest. Changes occur in the cognitive sphere, with patients giving idiosyncratic interpretations of themselves and their experiences. For example, patients may consider themselves inadequate and undesirable, and attribute unpleasant experiences to physical or mental defects. In general, the manifestation of major depression in the elderly is similar to that in younger subjects, although on some occasions it may have rather particular characteristics and pose serious clinical problems. A good description of the characteristics of an episode of major depression may be found in the DSM-III, now in its revised version [11], to which the reader is referred. Here it is sufficient to describe the main peculiarities of this pathology in the elderly.

There is rarely an increase in appetite with a consequent substantial increase in weight; hypersomnia is also rare, while psychomotor agitation is probably more frequent than its contrary [91]. Other typical symptoms of a major depression are tiredness and loss of energy, isolation, and lack of sexual interest. Suicidal desires and the wish to be dead are also frequent. In this context, it should be remembered that suicide rates among the

Table 2. DSM-III-R diagnostic categories of mood disorders and adjustment disorders with depressive features.

Bipolar disorders
	Bipolar disorder
296.4	manic
296.5	depressed
296.6	mixed
296.70	Bipolar disorder NOS
301.13	Cyclothymia

Depressive disorders
	Major depression
296.2	single episode
296.3	recurrent
300.40	Dystymia (or depressive neurosis)
311.00	Depressive disorder NOS

Adjustment disorders
309.00	With depressed mood
309.28	With mixed emotional features
309.40	With mixed disturbance of emotions and conduct

---

elderly are higher than in any other age group in almost all societies [171, 289] (see elsewhere in this volume).

The fundamental importance for clinical practice of correct diagnostic identification cannot be emphasized too strongly, as the decision to prescribe pharmacological treatment in an elderly person should never be taken lightly. The diagnostic categories defined in the DSM-III-R are shown in Table 2, which also shows the adjustment disorders that, as mentioned above, represent a theoretical evolution of the concept of reactive depression. In the DSM-III, the adjustment disorders are defined by many different clinical profiles; Table 2 shows only situations characterized by a depressive component, which are frequently also accompanied by emotional expressions of anxiety.

This brings us to a further borderline of uncertain definition: the distinction between depressive and anxious states. According to Murphy [477], a rule of the thumb is that the diagnosis of depression has precedence over that of anxiety. If the depressed mood appears concurrently with symptoms of anxiety, the primary diagnosis should generally be of depression. Naturally, this diagnostic rule may be complicated by situations in which, for example, the depression appears in a personality with anxiety traits or in a subject suffering from chronic anxiety. Furthermore, it is not uncommon for residual anxiety to persist for some time after resolution of a depressive episode [477]. These elements of diagnostic confusion have contributed to the persistence of the option in clinical practice for the much abused diagnosis of "anxious-depressive syndrome." It should not be forgotten that disorders with a sizable anxious component, such as the so-called minor depressions (especially dysthymic and adjustment disorder with mixed emotional features), are particularly common in the elderly, occurring at least five times more frequently than the major depressions [262].

MAJOR DEPRESSION

The type of disturbance normally manifesting in a depressive situation may be different among older persons. In this age group, there is, for example, a higher incidence of states of psychomotor restlessness, hypochondriac fears, feelings of loss of self-esteem, delusions of ruin and poverty, and suicidal ideation [702]. While clinical situations of psychomotor delay seem to be more frequent in younger subjects, the greater frequency of restless depressions in the elderly has been interpreted as an adjustment disorder of the beta-adrenergic system [91].

Profiles of confusions and "pseudodementia" are almost exclusively found in elderly subjects. One last phenomenon frequently encountered in the elderly is that of depression "masked" by somatic symptoms (we will return to this type of situation later). Kiloh and Garside [341] report that after the age of 45 depression is most frequently manifested with psychotic and/or endogenous type symptoms, and Perris [509] maintains that elderly patients with unipolar depression are subject to a greater number of episodes of illness, which tend to be more severe and persistent. However, Cole [122] has recently shown that subjects with primary depression and onset after the age of 60 tend to present a better course than subjects with earlier onset. Blazer [59], on the contrary, found no substantial differences between young and old subjects for the duration and severity of the depressive episodes. These discrepancies lead us to surmise the frequent presence in the elderly of a complex interaction between psychosocial and organic factors, the latter including the entirety of biological modifications implicit in the physiological and pathological process of aging.

In a study on 41 elderly subjects compared with 50 healthy subjects, the use of computerized axial tomography (CAT) permitted the identification of a subgroup of patients with ventricular enlargement and cerebral atrophy. These subjects presented late onset of the symptomatology (after the age of 60 years) and had more endogenous symptoms. None of the patients participating in the study had been diagnosed as affected by dementia or presented initial signs of dementia [305]. It should be stressed that in the above-cited study by Cole [122], which reported a benign prognosis for late onset cases, the patients were affected by primary depression and did not present severe organic diseases or signs of deterioration of mental faculties. It is hence possible that subgroups of subjects with and without initial organic CNS disorders may be identified among subjects with late onset of depression.

In conclusion, it may be affirmed that:

1) Elderly patients without signs of CNS alterations, without serious concomitant diseases, and with late onset of depression appear to have episodes of illness similar to those in younger subjects. They respond fairly well to pharmacological treatment and have a better prognosis than patients with onset prior to the age of 60 years.

2) Elderly patients with slight or modest alterations of the CNS and in a state of compensation present a chronic symptomatology, respond less to pharmacological treatment and have a worse prognosis than patients of whatever age of onset with an undamaged CNS. (For a wider discussion of the prognostic variations in the major affective disturbances, see the specific chapter in this volume.)

INVOLUTIONAL MELANCHOLY

Involutional melancholy was long believed to be the form of depression typical of old age. However, since its initial identification as a separate clinical manifestation of manic-depressive psychosis [350], involutional melancholy has been the subject of lively theoretical debate. According to Kraepelin, the characteristics of this disorder are the following: late onset of the disorder, absence of previous episodes of affective disturbance, fear symptoms, resignation, and hypochondriacal delusions (assuming extreme connotations in Cotard's syndrome). The disorder is further distinguished by its prolonged course, unfavorable prognosis, and the likelihood of progressive deterioration. Kraepelin maintained that the disorder was an acquired rather than endogenous condition [350]. About 30 years later, Titley [645] described the possible salient traits of the underlying personality as follows: great moral rigidity, few interests, difficulty in adjustment and in interpersonal relationships, obstinacy, and constant anxiety. For Titley, the personality of the involutional melancholic might be considered closer to normal than that of the manic depressive. In the DSM-II (1968), this disorder was considered as a problem presenting in the involutive period and characterized by feelings of worry, anxiety, restlessness, and severe insomnia. These symptoms might often be accompanied by guilt feelings and hypochondria, sometimes assuming the characteristics of delusion.

More recently, Gurland [261] affirmed that depression in the elderly may be distinguished from that in younger subjects by a preponderance of anxious aspects, somatic preoccupation and hypochondria, loss of concentration, and difficulties of recollection. However, after careful evaluation, the category of involutive melancholy was removed from the DSM-III because of the inconsistency of the pathognomic traits involved [682]. Nevertheless, various authors have continued to support the nosographic validity of this type of disturbance. Pichot and Pull (cited in [84]), for example, considered that the elimination of the psychiatric nomenclature of involutional melancholia was premature, maintaining that much research remained to be done into the effect of the aging process on depressive symptoms as well as into the influence of the age of onset of a depressive episode on later manifestations. Brown et al. [84], in a 1984 publication on 60 subjects with early onset of depression, report that a subgroup of 31 subjects affected by major depression with late onset presented significantly more somatization and hypochondria and less loss of libido, guilt feelings, suicidal ideas, and family history of depression. Although the clinical and experimental evidence for the recognition of involutional melancholia as a distinct clinical entity is admittedly insufficient, these authors reasonably conclude that many depressive profiles in the elderly may present characteristics very different from those found in younger subjects.

BIPOLAR DISORDER

The bipolar disorder usually first manifests between the ages of 20 and 30, and continues as recurrent episodes. Some authors have asserted that mania is rather rare in old age, while others report that the presence of manic symptoms in the depressed elderly subject is quite common, and that there is a marked increase in the frequency of this pathology after the age of 60–70 years [628]. We felt this argument justified separate treatment in a chapter presented later in this volume. However, as for the unipolar disorder, we here present a brief summary of the salient aspects of the bipolar disorder:

1) Patients with bipolar disorder and concurrent impairment of CNS functions tend to evolve toward chronicity, but the symptomatology is prevalently manic. According to Himmelhoch et al. [285], these subjects are rather unresponsive to treatment with lithium, while other authors [612] maintain that lithium should be considered a useful preventive and therapeutic measure.

2) Patients without neurological alterations are not distinguishable from young patients and respond adequately to treatment.

DIFFERENTIATION BETWEEN DEMENTIA AND DEPRESSION

An important aspect in need of clarification concerns differential diagnosis between depression and senile dementia. Many elderly depressed subjects come to the general practitioner with cognitive disorders that are frequently attributed to dementia type situations. This same "attitude" has been observed among American, Canadian, and English psychiatrists [188].

It should be remembered that most depressed elderly subjects do not present signs of cognitive impairment; although they frequently complain of forgetfulness, their performance on tests for short-term memory is not different from that of nondepressed subjects of a similar age [527].

In any case, differential diagnosis with dementia should be performed, bearing in mind that the latter disorder usually has insidious onset and manifests with progressive deterioration, confusion accompanied by disorientation, intellectual impair-

Table 3. Characteristics of depression and senile dementia.

	Depression	Senile dementia
Depressed mood	++++	++
Disturbance in sleep and appetite	+++	++
Suicidal ideation	++	+
Anxiety	+++	++
Ostility/irritability	++	+++
Emotional unstability	+	+++
Confusion	++	++++
Disorientation	+	++++
Short-term memory disorders	+	++++
Diminished vigilance	++	++++
No sociality	++	++++
No cooperation	++	++++

+   = very few characteristic
++ = few characteristic
+++ = slightly characteristic
++++   = very much characteristic
(adapted from Salzman & Shader, 1979)

ment, disorders of short-term memory, and sometimes hallucinations. The depressive episode, on the contrary, is not characterized by progressive intellectual deterioration and may be accompanied by guilt feelings and self-reproof. Table 3 shows some of the criteria for differential diagnosis described by Salzman and Shader [583a].

PSEUDODEMENTIA

A further source of diagnostic complication is given by the possibility of pseudodementia. This syndrome is characterized by alterations in memory, orientation, and intellectual function, symptoms that may give rise to the suspicion of organic impairment, but are in fact a different expression of depression in the elderly [575].

Delusional ideas may also appear; a depressive situation, although mild, is nearly always present. It is estimated that approximately 12% of all elderly subjects diagnosed as having dementia are in fact affected by a pseudodementia deriving from an underlying depressive disorder [606].

The concept of pseudodementia has given rise to considerable debate as to whether or not the syndrome actually exists. Recent observations by Bulbena and Berrios [88] indicate the existence of at least two subtypes of pseudodementia, one associated with depression (depressive pseudodementia) and another "associated" with delirium—in the sense that in this latter case the most probable diagnosis is, in fact, delirium. The authors, however, do not exclude the possibility that severe depressive situations may present with "behavioral phenocopies of delirium."

Diagnosis of pseudodementia is based on a careful case history (often collected with the help of family members); particular attention should be paid to previous depressive episodes and relatively rapid appearance of the current symptomatology. Pseudodementia often responds satisfactorily to treatment with antidepressants or ECT. A tendency to relapse and/or the development of sequelae of various kinds has also been noted [88]. Table 4, adapted from Finlayson and Martin [206], may be useful in differential diagnosis between pseudodementia and organic dementia. A further handy diagnostic aid in this context is Wells' 22-item checklist [688] in which the presence/absence of various symptoms defines the disease in one sense or the other. It is worth emphasizing that the finding of "cortical atrophy" on CAT examination is not, on its own, conclusive in the differential diagnosis.

Table 4. Differentiating dementia from pseudodementia.

Pseudodementia	Dementia
Onset quite abrupt	Onset insidious
Progression usually rapid	Progression usually slow
Patient aware of deficits	Patient not as aware
Complaint of memory loss	Patient tries to hide loss (confabulates)
Global responses ("I don't know")	Patient emphasizes accomplishments
Impairment not usually worse at night	Usually worse at night
Depressed mood	Patient is typically "happy"
Vegetative symptoms	Nonvegetative
History of psychiatric disturbance common	Not common
Suicide risk considerable	Suicide risk much lower

(adapted from [206])

MASKED DEPRESSION

Frequently, depressive disorders in the elderly do not present with all the classic symptoms described (affective, cognitive, and somatic), but rather with only some of them, most usually the somatic. The term "masked depression" is used in such cases to indicate a state in which the typical loss of mood tone is masked by other symptomatological manifestations considered by the patient to be the principal disorder. Such "masks" are not limited to somatic symptoms (such as chronic pain of various location, gastrointestinal and genito-urinary disturbances, etc.), but may also appear as behavioral alterations and, in the elderly, as hypochondriacal fears [206, 416, 583]. Research carried out on a population of 10,000 general practitioners showed that approximately 10% of the patients consulting them were depressed, about half of them presenting with masked depression [338].

These findings give a clear indication of the extent of the problem. The fact that many patients manifest a depressive condition of this type depends on numerous factors relating to the individual and social spheres, some of which are known, whereas others still require clarification. For example, for some people the expression of an affective state of sadness is far more threatening than speaking of a somatic disturbance of some type. The manifestation of depression through physical symptoms may offer elderly subjects relief from the responsibility of their depressed feelings—and at the same time provide the means to direct their anxiety and guilt feelings against themselves as in a form of self-punishment. The diagnosis of masked depression [415] should be reached on the basis of a series of positive elements, namely:

1) Depressive spectrum disorders (depression, alcoholism, and sociopathy) are present in the family history.

2) The patient may already have experienced one or more clear depressive episodes in the past.

3) The symptoms often tend to present in a periodical manner. There may be an alternation between depressive episodes and somatic disturbances; a circadian rhythm is frequently detectable in the symptomatology.

4) The patient's strong focus on the somatic sphere pushes any affective type symptoms that may be present into the background. However, the autonomic signs of depression, includ-

ing insomnia, anorexia, constipation, etc., can nearly always be detected.

5) The subject's attitude during the examination appears adequate, attention being mainly focused on the organic level. If questioned, the patient tends to deny or minimize intrapsychic or interpersonal difficulties, considering them irrelevant to the theme of the interview. Even direct questioning, for example, about whether he or she has felt sad or down over the previous days, are often met with rapid denials from subjects who are in fact clinically depressed. In such cases, it may be a good idea to direct the discussion to changes that may recently have occurred in the subject's life and to his or her feelings in relation to them.

However, sometimes one can overcome the patient's resistance. The symptom then acquires a more precise meaning in psychodynamic and relational terms: It may be the response to a loss or an attack on the patient's self-image, and at the same time may represent a defence against depression.

ORGANIC DISEASE AND DEPRESSIVE SYMPTOMS

Many physical diseases may also present with depressive symptoms—psychiatric sequelae that are nowadays defined, as we noted earlier, with the term "affective organic disorder." These include Parkinson's disease, malignant tumors (especially of the pancreas), iron, folic-acid or vitamin B12 deficiency anemias, thyroid disorders (especially hyperthyroidism) and adrenal disorders (Addison's and Cushing's diseases), hyperparathyroidism, and infections of various types. Furthermore, all physical diseases, whether slight or severe, always give rise to psychological reactions of some sort [163]; they are often accompanied by feelings of anxiety, sadness, and discouragement. Diseases implying a level of disability or pain may give rise to appreciable loss of self-esteem, dependence and clear depressive situations. These reactions may often satisfy the criteria of the DSM-III for major depression.

The prevalence of depression in patients admitted to the hospital with medical complaints is much higher than in the general population, ranging, in most studies, between 20% and 36% [465, 670]. In a study by ourselves [420], we evaluated for differences between geriatric and adult patients in emotional responses to physical disease. Two groups of consecutive patients, made up respectively of 178 elderly patients and 201 adults, were tested with the *SCL-90-R* and the *Zung Self-Rating Depression Scale*. Emotional responses to the disease and to hospitalization proved to be rather different in the two groups, responses being prevalently depressive in the elderly group and prevalently anxious in the adult group. The disease hence appears to assume a meaning of "loss" in the geriatric group and of "threat" in the adult group. The prevalence of depression was 20.39% in the adult subjects and 42.13% in the elderly. Multiple regression analysis revealed that the factors most predictive of depression in the elderly are female sex and the presence of a disabling physical disorder. These results confirm the high prevalence of depression in elderly subjects with physical disease and provide an explanation for the high percentages of secondary depressions found in elderly subjects [61, 495].

The use of common drugs such as reserpine, methyldopa, propranolol, indometacine, etc., may be associated with depression or even trigger depression in some individuals [417]. Since the elderly are more likely to present concomitant medical pathologies and use proportionally more medicaments than other age groups, it is clear that these subjects are particularly at risk for depression. The foregoing explains the difficulties sometimes encountered in the formulation of a correct diagnosis. It is vital that the doctor should not *a priori* dismiss symptoms such as loss of strength, irritability, loss of interest, etc., simply as expressions of the aging process. Rather, it should always be borne in mind that somatic symptoms may often represent the manifestation of a masked depression, a diagnosis that may be facilitated by the use of the above-cited criteria. Once a depressive situation is suspected or ascertained, the possible organic causes reported above should be excluded; it will also be necessary to collect a detailed list of all drugs recently used by the patient.

The reasons for improving the identification of depression are self-evident. In the case of the somatized forms, iatrogenic risk is not uncommon: The affective disorder is frequently recognized only after expensive, lengthy, and occasionally dangerous (in the case of surgical exploration, for example) diagnostic and therapeutic procedures. The difficulties of correct diagnosis are clearly illustrated by the fact that many depressed patients in whom psychological distress has in fact been recognized are then treated—both by the general practitioners and in the hospital setting—with minor sedatives that have no effect whatsoever on mood [160, 423, 685].

BIOLOGICAL CONFIRMATION OF THE DIAGNOSIS OF DEPRESSION

In addition to precise clinical criteria and rating scales, biological tests are now available for the confirmation of major depression. These may also be useful for the evaluation of the patient's response to the treatment implemented and for the formulation of a prognosis. The most thoroughly studied of these prognostic-diagnostic tests, and the one that has so far given the most reliable results in major unipolar depression, is the failure to suppress the secretion of cortisol after administration of dexamethasone (DST) [104]. This test is able to identify approximately 50% of patients suspected of having major unipolar depression. The test also appears to have important therapeutic applications, as results normalize after adequate response to treatment.

Another test currently considered useful is the response of thyroid-stimulating hormone (TSH) to the administration of thyreotropin-releasing hormone (TRH). This test is known by the initials TRHT [237]. After administration of TRH, patients with major unipolar depression show an initial maximum peak of serum TSH of less than 7 µU/ml (the normal response is 17 µU/ml); patients with other forms of depression or normal subjects do not show this response. The possibility of false positivity seems to be relatively low. For this test, as for the DST, an alteration persisting after treatment may help to identify those patients in whom relapse may be expected in the short term.

The associated use of both the tests described above permits a good overall level of diagnostic reliability, identifying approximately 80% of melancholic type major depressions [236]. However, currently available studies on the use of these tests in the elderly are few, and there are considerable discrepancies in the results. Carroll et al. [104] have published findings on 39 elderly subjects affected by melancholy confirming the applicability and usefulness of the dexamethasone suppression test in the diagnosis of depression in geriatric subjects. Similar results were recently reported by Spar and La Rue [626], while Brown [85] found that elderly subjects may present abnormal responses to the DST even in the absence of a depressive syndrome.

In recent studies by ourselves [422], the DST was used in a population of geriatric patients admitted to the hospital for organic disorders. Thirty-eight were diagnosed as depressed and 18 as nondepressed according to the criteria of the DSM-III. Only 11% of the controls and 11% of patients affected by dysthymic disorders displayed an abnormal response to the DST, compared to 73% of the patients with major depression. The sensitivity of the test for this pathology and in this setting was 73% and the specificity 89%, thus confirming its potential applicability and usefulness in elderly subjects. But both the DST and the TRHT may play a useful role only when associated with a careful clinical and case history examination, without which they can have no diagnostic function.

The biological factors connected to depression brought to light in scientific research are by no means limited to the DST and TRHT. Other available tests worthy of mention here include the assay of GH response to hypoglycemia or clonidine, urinary MHPG assay, COMT activity in the erithrocytes, blood platelet affinity for imipramine, etc. However, little information is available about the use of these tests in geriatric populations, and for this reason we have excluded them from our discussion here.

DEPRESSION AND SLEEP ALTERATIONS

Sleep disturbances are a practically constant symptom in dysthymias, although the extent of the disturbance may vary.

In depressive disorders, sleep patterns are disturbed both quantitatively and structurally. There is almost always a lengthening of sleep latency as well as frequent and prolonged periods of wakefulness during the night with early final wakening, total sleep time thus being considerably reduced.

From a structural point of view, the most important modification appears to be a reduction in delta sleep [363, 474] and in particular in its deepest component (Stage IV sleep).

While modifications in REM sleep are generally slight, onset is nearly always early (i.e., REM latency is reduced). This finding, reported by various authors, is considered specific to the depressive disorders [363, 444, 668] and even a biological marker of these disturbances [362]. It is, in fact, present in all patients with primary depression (whether unipolar or bipolar) not taking pharmacological treatment as well as in mania and schizoaffective disorders. It persists until the depressive state begins to improve and is dependent on age, pharmacological treatment and other sleep patterns [654]. Patients with primary depression have greater REM activity and intensity than patients with secondary depression [472].

It has been observed that the greater the suppression of REM sleep (in terms of increased latency and percentage of total sleep) induced by treatment with tricyclics, the better the prognosis for treatment with this drug [364]. According to Kupfer et al. [365], an increase in REM latency and a reduction in sleep latency associated with the administration of amitriptyline is a more efficacious predictor of response to treatment than the clinical evidence itself.

Sleep influences hypothalamus-hypophysis regulation and hormone production; the sleep disturbances correlated with depression probably imply changes in cerebral monoamine metabolism (serotonin and perhaps catecholamines), and possibly also in the opioid receptors [472]. We have already seen that sleep disturbances improve with amelioration of the depressive state. The biological implications of sleep and of its alterations in the depressive syndrome largely make up the theoretical presuppositions of "sleep deprivation" in the treatment of endogenous depression [517]. In any case, sleep deprivation (SD) has generally produced only temporary antidepressive effects [658]; some studies have reported an increased vitality on the day after return to normal sleep [472]. Antidepressants appear to prolong the effects of deprivation, preventing relapses [472]. Cole and Muller have also affirmed the efficacy of SD in depressed elderly subjects [125]. It has also been reported that partial sleep deprivation (awakening at 0.30) is just as effective as total deprivation, but more practical [593]. Lastly, a temporary improvement in depression after a night of SD seems to be a good index of responsiveness to tricyclic treatment [705].

With the sole exception of the study by Cole and Muller [25], the published findings generally refer to sleep in depressed adult subjects. However, it should be noted that largely similar results have been obtained in depressed elderly subjects [543], although the currently available studies on the interactions between age, sleep patterns, and depression are by no means numerous.

Maggini et al. [413] observed that the differences in sleep patterns between depressed subjects under and over the age of 60 years are negligible, ". . . as if the depression tends to mask age-related modifications . . ."

Ulrich et al. [654] found a positive correlation between age, first REM latency and delta sleep: their results reveal that the characteristic sleep patterns of major depression appear to be correlated with age, in the sense that elderly depressed subjects seem to present a greater reduction of REM latency than do young or adult depressed subjects.

More recently, Maggini et al. [414], in a continuation of research into the relationships between age and depression, observed that sleep patterns in elderly depressives (over the age of 60) are significantly different from those of younger depressed subjects (under 45 years), showing a higher incidence of Stage II sleep and a reduced REM sleep as well as more frequent reawakenings during the middle of the night; in patients over the age of 75, Stage IV sleep appeared to be virtually absent.

In conclusion, the most constant sleep disturbances in both depression—regardless of age—and senility appear to be the same: a structural alteration in the depth and continuity of sleep, represented by a reduction in Stage IV sleep and in first REM latency. Depression and age hence appear to act synergically on the same physiopolygraphic parameters: in the elderly depressed subject, the alterations related to the depressive pathology are compounded by those occurring naturally with increasing age, so that sleep is more severely disturbed than in younger subjects.

DEPRESSION AND SEXUAL PROBLEMS

Depression is the mental disorder that most frequently causes sexual problems. The most common clinical symptom of depression is in fact a reduced interest in sexual life (loss of libido). There is generally a reduction in the frequency of sexual relations and, in males, the onset of secondary impotence. Less frequent are cases of increased sexual activity. Some depressed patients may report an increased frequency of sexual relations or masturbation to enhance relaxation or combat insomnia [155]. As in other somatic symptoms of depression, the characteristics and intensity of sexual problems may vary from person to person or vary in one individual in the course of the disease. They may also appear to vary with the duration and severity of the depression. Despite the "natural" tendency in the elderly toward chronicity of all symptoms, it seems that sexual symptoms may often be readily be modified if the depressive situation received adequate treatment. If the loss of sexual interest and/or impotence persists after the disappearance of the psychiatric symptomatology, support therapy may prove necessary [352, 353]. The underlying depression frequently remains unidentified, however. For example, it is often thought to be a reaction to the sexual symptom itself. In cases such as these, the depressive symptoms initially responsible for the sexual disorder may remain untreated, aggravating the sexual symptoms. Hence, the anxiety, worry, disquiet and general feelings of inadequacy that are the most important components of a depressive syndrome—especially in the elderly—complicate and perpetuate the patient's sexual problem.

Once the presence of other symptoms of depression has been established, the next step is to determine whether the sexual dysfunction is the cause or the consequence of the depression, as therapeutic strategies may vary widely according to the etiology of the problem. For example, the problems of sexual impotence, a common medical situation with a variety of possible causes, may be approached with very different forms of treatment.

The collection of the patient's sexual history is essential—and no more difficult than the collection of anamnestic data for the diagnosis of depression. A few questions are generally sufficient to identify the problems falling under the heading of sexual dysfunctions: impotence, alterations in orgasm, early or late orgasms, dyspareunia, loss of sexual desire.

Differential diagnosis may be performed on the basis of some typical questions:

1) acute depressive syndrome with "symptomatic" sexual dysfunction (whether or not in the presence of conflict with partner);

2) chronic depression with "symptomatic" sexual dysfunctions (whether or not in the presence of conflict with partner);

3) sexual dysfunction correlated with conflict with partner (and consequent reactive depression);

4) sexual dysfunction independent from marital problems;

5) periods of sexual disinterest followed by hyperexcitability (bipolar disturbance).

While in acute and chronic primary depression sexual dysfunction is never present in isolation, but is always associated with other depressive symptoms, sexual problems associated with marital conflict may sometimes create diagnostic uncertainties. However, symptomatic origin can be excluded when there are no autonomic signs of depression and when insomnia, loss of appetite, weight loss, and suicidal thoughts are not present to a clinically relevant extent.

Sexual problems independent of marital tensions may include primary impotence, primary orgasmic alterations, ejaculatio praecox, etc. These situations are not accompanied by clinical signs of depression.

Changes in libido and sexual drive are commonly encountered in bipolar disturbances and usually do not present difficulties for diagnosis, given their typical symptomatology. It may be particularly difficult in the elderly to distinguish between a drop in sexuality because of individual characteristics (i.e., from the aging process) and an absence of sexual life arising from depression. It should be noted, however, that the decline in libido and sexual activity consequent on aging is gradual and never total, while loss of sexual interest and activity as a result of depression is relatively sudden and persists throughout the course of the disease.

A study by De Leo et al. [147], in which *Zung's Depression Scale*, modified for the detection of sexual symptoms and administered to 150 residents of an retirement home, revealed a strong correlation between depression and sexual symptoms. No significant correlations were found in either men or women between scores for sexual symptoms and age, probably because the subjects were all of similar age [147].

Although an association between sexual problems and depression is frequently encountered in clinical practice, very few studies have so far attempted to clarify this relationship. The link between loss of libido and depression in old age is hence unclear and certainly requires further investigation.

CHAPTER 3

Psychosocial Factors, Ill-Health, and Disease in the Elderly

- Several studies have shown that psychosocial events play an important role in the mental and physical health of an individual, especially in the elderly. Despite this, it is not very clear which approaches are to be adopted to alleviate these harmful effects in terms of mortality and morbidity. It is obvious that, in this context, the identification of "psychosocial problems" and possible interventions are particularly difficult for a number of reasons, since it involves a certain kind of population with numerous untreatable conditions. Moreover, those difficulties are not common to all.

- Although individual characteristics in influencing the impact of a single event on the well-being of a subject are important, the available literature shows that it is possible to identify some more frequently encountered cluster of problems [296], namely, (1) loss of social support; (2) bereavement; (3) relocation; (4) retirement.

- Obviously, even these cluster of problems, personal factors, and individual aspects can partly or completely modify the impact the event has and the reaction of persons involved. However, no matter what the emotional reaction to the occurrence is, these events considerably affect the person's psychophysical equilibrium, and considering the precarious condition of the elderly, these can represent some of the many factors involved in the development of suffering. The complex relationship between psychosocial events and health was shown in many instances even if it is still difficult to establish the interaction modalities between psychophysical features and the event, especially when specific preventive measures are being considered.

- Moreover, recent demonstrations that these factors affect the immunologic and neurochemical system present new and stimulating problems both on a cognitive and on a operative level.

LOSS OF SOCIAL SUPPORT

Many research projects were aimed at studying the relationship between social and physical health in the elderly. The evaluation of these issues presents several conceptual and methodological problems. First, we must define the term "social support," which usually is practically evaluated by considering the frequency, duration, and intensity of interactions. Besides the need to evaluate the qualitative aspects, particular attention must be given to the "perception" the subject has of this "support unit."

According to Wortman [708], the following features must be considered in order to achieve the above:

• expression of a positive effect;

• acknowledgement of trust and understanding;

• encouragement to openly express trust and feelings;

• offering advice and information;

• offering material help.

Social support can be differentiated into tangible and intangible elements, and thus its efficacy can be assessed though its objective and subjective features. The lack of social support related to psychophysical health of the elderly was principally considered a cofactor that can only indirectly have more or less negative impacts on other stressing events.

Table 5. Lack of social support and physical health of the elderly.

Reference	Main finding
Linn et al. [388]	Significant correlation between lack of social support and diseases (especially psychiatric)
Berkman & Syme [49]	Lack of social ties was a significant predictor of mortality in a longitudinal study of over 6000 adults
Schaefer et al. [590]	Perceived social support was a significant predictor of health status
Snow & Crapo [623]	Worsening of life satisfaction in relation to emotional bondedness
Blazer [59]	Lack of social support was a significant predictor of 30-month mortality
Asher [20]	Social network was a predictor of some general health outcomes but not of specific illness

Adapted from [296].

According to other authors [59], social support would also be involved in establishing (independently from specific events) possible dangerous behaviors for the subject. We must also remember that most studies carried out regarding this topic concern the general population. Probably once we specifically study an elderly population, the importance of social support in the context of health can be rather different. Overall, the literature shows an objective and a subjective relationship between loss of social support as well as increase of morbidity and mortality.

Thus, this loss is not only a psychosocial problem with obvious affects on the well-being of the elderly, but also a *risk cofactor* whenever it worsens the impact of any other event.

RELOCATION AND WELL-BEING OF THE ELDERLY

Especially for the aged, relocation can represent a very stressful event because of the changes it causes in various practical and affective aspects of their lives. In fact, it may involve "losses" especially of social and emotional contacts.

Studies regarding this topic concentrate on the effects of relocation both as a "subjective experience" and as an objective evaluation in terms of decreased activity or increased morbidity and mortality rates. Most studies demonstrated as a result of relocation an increased incidence of disease or a worsening of functional deficits. When the elderly are relocated into nursing homes, there is a stronger impact for evident reasons. In certain cases, there was an increase in mortality rates, especially during the first months [6]. Kasl [322] observed more negative consequences in subjects who were obliged to be institutionalized because there was no other alternative. Conversely, those who "freely chose" a nursing home had less drastic consequences. Moreover, the unpredictable nature of the change is surely a factor that negatively affects the acceptance of relocation. In this study, the presence of depression and social isolation are identified as predictive factors for an increased mortality risk.

Bourestom and Tars [70] pointed to a marked increase in the mortality rate during the 3 months prior to the relocation in subjects who accepted it as a "radical" and "lethal" change compared to the rates found in already institutionalized subjects.

Some authors [717], instead, showed an improvement of well-being in those who are "prepared" for the relocation and in those

Table 6. Relocation and physical health of the elderly.

Reference	Main finding
Costello & Tanaka [131]	High morbidity rates (38%) during the first 6 months following admission.
Lieberman [386]	High mortality rates during the first year of institutionalization.
Ferrari [201]	Higher post-relocation mortality in those who were forced to move into an institution in comparison to those who decided to enter institutional life.
Kasteler et al [323]	Adverse effect on health after "forced" relocation.
Lawton & Yaffe [375]	No average effect relocation may be adverse to some elderly people and beneficial to others.
Lawton & Cohen [376]	Adverse effect of "forced" relocation on health over a year.
Bourestom & Tars [70]	If relocation implies a radical change (e.g., remote institution), the more pessimistic is subject about his health following relocation, the greater is the deterioration.
Kasl et al. [322]	Elderly who were forced to move had significantly more hospitalization events.
Lawton et al. [377]	A modest improvement in well-being was observed when the move was toward smaller dwellings.

Adapted from [296].

accepted in centers that have preventive plans to help them to accept and adjust to their new environment. This indicates that both the type of change and degree of freedom are essential features for the well-being of the elderly.

RETIREMENT

Here, it is difficult to detect the specific effect on physical health both because of the various aspects of the previous occupation and its association with many other features, especially organic diseases. Research has often produced contradictory results not only for purely methodologic factors.

In many instances, retirement depends on the subject's health since he or she can anticipate retirement age—which then becomes an "obliged" choice. In other cases, the specific aspects of

Table 7. Retirement and physical health of the elderly.

Reference	Main finding
Thurst et al. [652]	No effect on life expectancy. Morbidity measures showed an improvement in health after retirement.
Haynes et al. [277]	Elevated death rates in 4–5 years post-retirement period. Social factors other than retirement were not significant predictors of survival rates.
Ekerdt et al. [192]	Retirement was not found to be a significant predictor of physical health.
Ekerdt et al. [193]	Half the retirees claimed no change in health status 2 years or more after retirement (38% claimed an improvement)

Adapted from [296].

the previous occupation affect the evaluation considerably, even if not in a systematic fashion.

Some factors were observed to be particularly important for these evaluations:

- *Type of occupation.* This obviously refers not only to the type of job, but especially to what the subject thinks of it. Also important is the environment in which work takes place.

- *Period between retirement and detection.* Retirement can be conceived as an adoptive process and thus something that evolves with time into a true acceptance or adaptation. For instance, Atchley [8] defines a preretirement stage as one in which "stress is anticipated," a "honeymoon" stage filled with great satisfaction of what has occurred, a phase of disillusionment after a latency of 1–2 years when problems arise and when a rise in the morbidity and mortality rates occurs.

- *Socioeconomic class.* The effect of this factor on the impact of retirement is often clear even if it appears especially difficult to extrapolate from the general situation. In the case of workers, although we noticed an improvement of well-being after they stop working, the mortality rates and life expectancy remain worse than those of higher socioeconomic classes [296].

- *Possibility of choice.* Even in this case, the freedom of choice appears to be considerably important. In fact, anticipated-forced retirement appears to have worse effects on the health of involved individuals than a gradual and an adequate preparation to this life change.

Obviously, many other variables, especially personal ones can be important, and perhaps only until recently have the complex relationships between retirement and well-being been properly considered. It is hoped that this correlation also with other variables, such as occupation, health condition, and general contentment, emphasize the role personal variables and subjective perception play in this event.

BEREAVEMENT

Bereavement is an experience of loss that, because of its consequences on the psychomedical morbidity, can be considered the prototype of stressful events with possible devastating effects on the psychophysical equilibrium.

It is still difficult delimit a "normal" and a "pathologic" bereavement reaction. Several studies have contributed to identifying the group of symptoms that accompany this reaction, but they have particularly demonstrated the heterogeneous nature of individual reactions both with regard to their intensity and their duration. Thus, personal, cultural, social, and biological variables can influence one's reaction to a given loss. It was also observed that morbidity and mortality risks related to this situation cannot be generalized, but rather must specifically be evaluated together with the individual characteristics of the subject [280]. Thus, we can understand the complexity and difficulty in detecting subjects and situations at risk.

Various studies have been carried out to identify the factors directly involved in bereavement. However, it was difficult to establish clear cause-effect relationships because of methodologic problems and the heterogeneous nature of the situations.

Zisook et al. [714] believe the bereavement reaction has a more negative course when the following factors are present:

- previous depressive states;
- long period of stress prior to the loss;
- stressful relationship with the lost person.

Even if the manifestation of bereavement strictly depends on personal, cultural, and social factors, many works have shown a close relationship with neurobiologic systems especially immunologic ones, partly verifying the hypothesis that an increase of mortality depends on immunodepression or an alteration of immune regulatory systems [406]. This would explain both the heterogeneity and complexity of the consequences as well as the increased incidence of some diseases such as infective or immunologic disturbances.

From a strictly psychiatric point of view, the "loss effect" was observed in many assessments, even if we must consider the difficulty in evaluating the effects of a single event in complex situations, as is the case with the elderly population.

Following bereavement, the quality of life degenerates in various ways. Clayton [117] reports a 35–45% incidence of depression during the first year which becomes qualitatively and quantitatively worse in subjects with a previous psychiatric his-

Table 8. Bereavement and physical health of the elderly.

Reference	Main finding
Young et al. [712]	Significantly higher risk of mortality in first 6 months after bereavement.
Parkes [505]	Significant increase in G.P. visits for both somatic and psychiatric complaints in the 6 months following bereavement.
Rees et al. [537]	Significantly higher mortality rate, especially in widowers, during the first year of bereavement.
Bunch [89]	Increase in suicidal rates, especially in males, during the first year of bereavement.
Clayton [117]	High rates of depression (35–45%) during the first year of bereavement.
Bartrop et al. [36]	T-lymphocyte function was significantly depressed approximately 8 weeks following bereavement.
Mellstrom et al. [454]	Significantly higher mortality risk increased by 48% in males and 22% in females during the 3 months following bereavement (in age group 70 to 74).
Thompson et al. [643]	Significantly higher number of new or worsening illness, two months post-bereavement. Use of modifications was increased.
Irwin et al. [300]	Natural killer (NK) cell activity diminished during the 3 months following bereavement.
Irwin [299]	Increased levels of cortisol and norepinephrine—usually higher in the plasma of seriously distressed persons—could mediate the reduction of NK cell activity during bereavement.

Adapted from [296] and [406].

tory [118]. Moreover, an increase in alcohol and drug abuse and consequently in hospitalizations (especially in psychiatric clinics) was observed.

Usually, instead of an increase of specific pathologic patterns, heterogeneous symptoms were detected. This was probably due to the prominence of depression or the relative lack of early signs of illnesses that later clearly manifest themselves, such as cardiovascular and neoplastic diseases [412]. Mortality rates increase especially in 55–74-year-olds most frequently because of violent causes such as accidents, suicides, and homicides [636]. More specifically, the risk of suicide is especially high during the first year among males, but once the event becomes accepted this incidence tends to return to normal values [89]. Kaprio and Koskenvuo [319] reported a peak in the pattern with clearly higher values in males. In the following period, male and female rates become similar even if values greater than the average are observed.

The above points out the possibility of detecting links between the experience of a loss and psychophysical consequences especially through a biopsychosocial and physiopathologic interpretation of the phenomenon. Research carried out with this aim, although relatively scarce, led to considerable results.

The relationship between stress and disease shown by many studies, follows two trends of interpretation:

- A stressful experience itself changes the life style and this can directly affect health.

- A stressful event indirectly affects the psychophysical well-being by altering the endocrine, immunologic, and central nervous systems.

Regarding the changed life-style, drinking, smoking and psychodrugs consumption [714] increase after a loss, and subjects often lack the desire to take care of their health [43]. Moreover, once the spouse dies, widows or widowers admit they do not wish to live long, which could be related to the reported suicide incidence [319]. Even accidental deaths and those from unknown causes could result from slow self-destructive processes or from a decreased interest toward oneself [250]. Thus, all these tendencies could explain the overall qualitative worsening of life-style and related consequence regarding the psychophysical conditions of these individuals.

The psychoendocrine response to stress was shown immediately after the "loss," though no specific single relationship was found with successive psychic and physical complications. The similarity demonstrated between bereavement and depression with regard to the increased adrenocorticoid function and the sympathetic nervous system and the possible changes of prolactin and GH levels, is not directly ascribable to the presence of successive pathologic features [714].

Today, the most interesting hypothesis regarding a direct relationship between bereavement and diseases is an immunologic explanation of increased mortality following infections, neoplastic, and autoimmune diseases [594].

In a study to assess lymphocytic response to stimulation with mitogens (phytohemoagglutinin and concanavaline A), Bartrop [36] could show no difference from controls immediately after the loss, whereas after 2 months the bereaved group had a clearly lower than normal response even if no qualitative differences of T- and B-lymphocyte populations were observed. In a subsequent project, Schleifer et al. [595] assessed subjects before and after the loss, and confirmed a reduced response to mitogens after 2 months and intermediate values (between pre- and postbereavement) after 1 year.

Other research [632] has attempted to establish a correlation between immune-depressive and cortisol serum levels, though without reaching any final conclusion. This would agree with the common hypothesis regarding the role of hypercortisolemia in the development of a reduced immunologic function [632]. According to Linn [390], immunologic disturbances from stress are quite variable in different subjects and would represent a differential trait depending on the presence of depressive symptoms. Irwin [300], for instance, has shown that the activity of natural killer (NK) cells decreases 1–3 months after bereavement; this can be correlated with the level of depression.

He also stressed the reduction of Ts cells (suppressors) and an increase of Th cells (helpers), a phenomenon compatible with the high incidence of autoimmune diseases in these subjects [426]. Currently, evaluations of reported immunologic abnormalities cannot fully explain whether they result from the loss event or the subsequent depression. For instance, Locke [403] reported that the low cytotoxic activity can be predictive of psychiatric symptoms, but it is not retrospectively differentiated from certain distressing situations such as bereavement. In addition,

Irwin [299] suggested that during bereavement hormones and neurotransmitters can mediate regulation of the immune system especially the decreased cytotoxic activity of NK cells. For instance, serum cortisol and noradrenaline can increase in subjects who have experienced various types of stress, and decrease in vitro the activity of NK cells.

Moreover, the recent discovery of adrenergic, cholinergic, and histaminergic receptors or the surface of lymphocytes [571] is interesting as a possible interrelationship between psychoendocrine and immunologic disturbances. These are potentially responsible for some frequent lesions found during bereavement. Thus, reports show the relationship between stressful event and "abnormal regulation" of the neuro-endocrino-immunologic systems—leaving unanswered, however, the question as to whether the event in itself, the depressive reaction, or both are responsible for this.

In the elderly, bereavement plays a primary role especially when we consider the direct and indirect consequences that develop in real life following certain events:

- In the elderly this event generally occurs after long periods of living together isolated as a couple, so that "total isolation" of the surviving partner develops.

- The surviving partner who remains alone becomes a high risk subject for institutionalization.

- An older person, especially if male, who remains alone is usually at risk regarding morbidity and mortality.

Some research aimed to evaluate the health of the bereaved elderly on a short-term level found a risk increment for morbidity and thus an increased utilization of health services as well as a rise in mortality rate especially among males.

Norris [490] demonstrated that the "loss" represents more a psychologic than a physical stress, felt more during bereavement, but absolutely independent from previous stress levels. Moreover, the most acute somatic problems and reactions are more frequent in situations of sudden and unexpected loss. Many studies have reported contradictory evaluations of the possibility of differentiating bereavement from depression. Breckenridge et al. [75], for instance, stressed that the key symptoms of depression are not present during the first phase of bereavement. In addition, no abnormal effect is observed with long-term preparation for the loss. In fact, although they were aware of the serious condition of their spouse, 70% of subjects did not foresee death as imminent or inevitable.

Moreover, in the evaluation of the impact of bereavement on the well-being of the elderly, certain procedural problems make results scarcely reliable. Nevertheless, it is possible to outline an overall pattern to explain the possible effects of a loss reaction:

- new diseases or worsening of already present illnesses;
- more serious diseases than those found in control groups;
- increased use of drugs and/or abuse of alcohol;
- worse self-evaluation of one's health condition.

Of the most recent studies, the hypothesis regarding a psychoimmunologic involvement in the increased susceptibility to develop diseases appears to be quite stimulating. This interaction, applicable to any stressful event, cannot yet be specifically related to the event itself compared to the subsequent depression. This introduces a new research field that can define the modalities of the interaction. Moreover, it stresses the possibility of identifying biological markers capable of differentiating "normal" from "abnormal" (or at least "risky") stressful conditions. Bioendocrino-immunologic hypotheses currently represent the most concrete possibilities for understanding the problem (even if the psychological interpretation must not be forgotten) and possibly for planning practical preventive measures.

FINAL REMARKS

Psychosocial factors are important and at times essential to the psychophysical well-being of an individual. They represent a topic of great interest that, however, can only theoretically explain certain conditions and cannot lead us to concrete expression of scientific-operative interpretations. Already, the identification of "events" considered as "factors of psychological disturbance" requires a selection and a subsequent generalization that must attempt to detach itself from specific features of the involved subject and the environment in which the subject lives. Specifically regarding the elderly, obviously the social factors constituting highly influential elements for their well-being involve many various aspects of their lives, and thus instead of being specific, they only generically define the problem, depending and interacting with other variables. However, it has been possible to detect types of "events" that, because of their frequency and features, are particularly involved in giving rise to a psychophysical equilibrium and/or malfunctions. These events often represent a "route," making the subject become continually more isolated and excluded from reality, especially when there is no possibility and/or capacity to react, accept, modify, or actively participate in what is occurring. In fact, the various types of events are the usual experiences that nevertheless can be given broader meanings in the elderly because of the substrate of action that considers both the "psychological features" and the environmental/physical "objective" reality.

As we have observed, it is, for instance, difficult to give an exact evaluation regarding "social support." In fact, it can scarcely be quantified or qualified both objectively and subjectively. The same can be said of "retirement," which as we have observed, cannot be simplified as a monomorphic factor, but rather must be considered a "unit of factors" that together can determine the event itself. Thus, within these two aspects, the correlation between event and psychophysical consequence is not easily obtained. They require a more detailed study in order to detect which factors are "decisive" both theoretically and practically.

The understanding of relocation is somewhat better, especially if we consider its importance in the "institutionalization" of the elderly, which obviously plays an important role.

The event that can perhaps be considered the "prototype" in the interaction between stressful experience and psychophysical equilibrium of an individual is bereavement. Besides being one of the most critical experiences of an individual, in the elderly it has a relevant impact because of its psychological and practical meaning. As outlined, many studies have analyzed the impact loss has on individuals. However, although a series of negative effects were detected, it was not possible yet to identify whether they originate in the event itself or in the subsequent depressive reaction. These demonstrations have, however, focused the attention on the possible relationships between "loss event" and physiopathologic consequences especially regarding endocrino-immunologic system. This latter today appears to be the most interesting and promising hypothetical interpretation.

The possibility of detecting how interaction occurs between a psychic event and biological "reactive" changes has introduced the need to classify and generalize, as much as possible, both theoretical and practical aspects regarding this topic. In fact, even if many psychosocial factors regarding morbidity and mortality have been known for a long time, it was not possible yet to concretely hypothesize modalities and/or operative strategies. Present interest in a psychoimmunoendocrinologic explanation of the increased susceptibility to physical and psychic diseases could represent a qualitative improvement concerning the possibility of identifying "risk conditions" and help not only to "support" patients, but possibly to "present" these disturbances.

These considerations, applicable for individuals in general, become of greater value when we consider the poor psychophysical condition of the elderly in whom the above-mentioned events can have a more "decisive" impact both because of their greater vulnerability and a series of practical interrelated implications that should not be forgotten.

Thus, without underestimating the importance of specific personal features, it is hoped that classifiable and generalized facts will be obtained in this area of study in order to plan aimed preventive measures and minimize negative effects on the psychophysical well-being of patients, especially the elderly.

CHAPTER 4
Neurochemistry of Aging and Depression

- This chapter describes the most important neurochemical changes in cerebral aging and depression. It is not yet known whether the modifications strictly connected with aging are also somehow linked with greater incidence of depression in the elderly or perhaps with greater proneness to becoming chronic or long-term.

- The answer to the first question appears to be negative since available data do not indicate that biological or "major" diseases are more frequently observed in old age. Moreover, a biologic link for minor disturbances has yet to be demonstrated, so that even in this case it seems that modifications associated with aging probably do not contribute to depression in the mood of the elderly. A stronger possibility is the relationship to the longer duration of depression in old patients (see also the chapter on the prognosis of depression in this volume). Perhaps more reliable information can be obtained from a wider application of new brain imaging techniques, which, besides clarifying further the real mechanism of action of many psychotropic drugs (including antidepressants), might also better distinguish the much debated border between "organic" and "functional" forms.

Any discussion of the neurochemistry of aging in humans must begin with the study of senility as a "normal" biological process— distinct from other forms such as dementia, which, though age-related, are pathological processes [187].

Old age is always accompanied by rather profound modifications of the structural and functional organization of the central nervous system, and this organization is based on the correct interaction of the synapses connecting the numerous neurones making up the nervous system. Deficiencies involving various different synaptic neurotransmission systems have been observed in physiological aging and in pathological aging associated with diseases of the central nervous system: Parkinson's disease and Alzheimer's disease are two well-known examples. Studies on healthy elderly humans and animals have demonstrated the deteriorative modifications of various cerebral functions, including, among others, the cognitive, mnemonic, perceptive, emotive, etc. [496, 581].

The last few years have seen a growing interest in the possible role of the free radicals (FR) in pathology and in particular in cerebral aging [273].

The brain is particularly susceptible to aggression by radicals by reason of its high content of lipids, polyunsaturated fatty acids, and easily oxidizable molecules such as the catecholamines, as well as because of the relative lack of enzymes and other scavengers, with the exception of vitamin C.

Observed cellular damages include peroxidation of the membrane and alterations to proteins, enzyme systems, and nucleic acids [273].

Peroxidation of the membrane lipids in particular leads to the formation of hydrophilic hydroperoxides within a notoriously hydrophobic structure, bringing about an increase in permeability and an inhibition of pumping mechanisms, with the consequence of alteration or even death of cellular functions [534].

Furthermore, considering that the cross-links between the unsaturated lipids of the cellular membrane are the preferential target of the FRs, it may be hypothesized that peroxidation in these sites could cause a loss of membrane fluidity and damage to the receptor structures, culminating in a more or less severe loss of functions of interaction with hormones and neurotransmitters [409].

The alteration of the equilibrium between the production and destruction of FRs and its consequences are currently thought to be one of the mechanisms implied in the physiopathology of cerebral damage, and in the theory of aging interpreted as an accumulation of elementary lesions that may evolve into the more complex degenerative forms characteristics of this age group [273].

Whatever the role of the free radicals in aging, the senile brain shows both morphologically demonstrable alterations—such as senile plaques and neurofibrillary degeneration (forms that are among the most common aging processes)—and alterations of synaptic conduction and neurotransmitter systems, characterized by a reduction in the activity of these functions, detectable via sophisticated laboratory investigations. The last few years have in fact seen an increase in the number of studies in the field of cerebral neurochemistry, thanks to the development of new laboratory research techniques such as the subcellular fractionation of specific regions of the brain or the possibility of using cultures of neuronal tissue and other invasive and noninvasive procedures [101].

Certain basic problems of definition should be born in mind in the development of an experimental approach to the study of the "normal" elderly brain:

1) Even today there is no established temporal limit considered valid by all investigators for the definition of old age in humans.

2) Marked variations still exist in the neurochemical assays of different laboratories. Among other problems, it is difficult to achieve a precise evaluation of the relationship between the situation prior to death and modifications occurring in the agonic or postmortem period.

3) There is not always agreement among investigators in the comparison of the findings emerging from studies on laboratory animals and research on the physiological aging process in humans. It would be useful, for example, to establish with more precision the age at which each of the species of experimental animals used might be called senile from all points of view.

Despite these difficulties, it is clear that some modifications of physiological function observed in the elderly (reduced sleep time, reduction in motor activity and intellectual acuity, endocrine modifications and mood fluctuations, etc.) have a corresponding neurochemistry: variations in the metabolic activity of the enzymes responsible for the synthesis and catabolism of certain neurotransmitters and quantitative alterations in these latter.

The following offers an up-to-date account of recent insights into this field, in order to give an account of how and to what extent the neurochemical systems are modified in the human brain over the life span.

NEUROTRANSMITTER SYSTEMS

The essential properties for the definition of a neurotransmitter are the following:

• synthesis within the neurones;

- release into the synaptic "pocket" on arrival of the stimulus;
- the ability to modify the potential of the postsynaptic membrane (Figure 1).

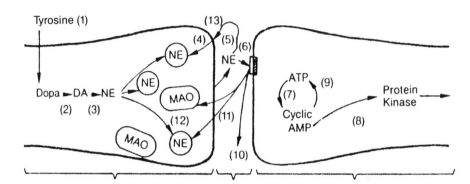

Figure 1 Norepinephrine synapse. (1) Tyrosine hydroxylase and biopterin; (2) Decarboxylase and vitamin B6; (3) dopamine ß-hydroxylase; (4) storage vesicles; (5) presynaptic release of norepinephrine; (6) receptor site (beta-noradrenergic) containing adenylate cyclase; (7) enzymatic production of cyclic AMP from ATP; (8) activation of protein kinase and transmission of neuronal message; (9) destruction of cyclic AMP by phosphodiesterase; (10) metabolism of norepinephrine in synaptic cleff; (11) reuptake of norepinephrine; (12) either storage of norepinephrine for future release or metabolism by MAO; (13) presynaptic (alpha-2) receptor that inhibits further release of norepinephrine. DOPA: dihydroxyphenylalanine; DA: dopamine; NE: norepinephrine; MAO: monoamine oxidase; ATP: adenosine triphosphate; cyclic AMP: cyclic adenosine triphosphate.

Since the passage of the signal to the postsynaptic neurone requires the complex action of various different neurotransmitter substances, different molecules have recently been distinguished and studied. These are called respectively neuromodulators, neuromediators and neurohormones. Each has peculiar interactions with the pre- and postsynaptic cell membranes [448]. The neurotransmitters identified to date include relatively simple molecules such as amino acids (GABA, glycine) or amines of a rather more complex structure (acetylcholine, catecholamine, etc.) or, again, polypeptides such as the endorphins and enkephalins. The best known of the substances usually identified as neuromediators are

- catecholamines (dopamine, noradrenaline),
- serotonin,
- acetylcholine,
- amino acids (GABA, glycine),
- histamine,
- peptides (endorphine).

Experimental research has provided a considerable body of information about the activities of synthesis, transport, storage, and release of the neuromediators at the level of the presynaptic neurone, while the mechanisms underlying the translation of the signal supplied by the neurotransmitters to the postsynaptic neurone remain largely unknown; in many cases, it may be hypothesized that a role is played by the so-called "second messenger" (the principal one being the cyclic nucleotide AMP), produced by the activation of the respective cyclase by the "first messenger" neurotransmitter [581].

Another known and demonstrated system of translation of the signal to the postsynaptic neurone is instead directly regulated by the interaction of the neurotransmitter with specific receptor sites—without, however, the activation of particular enzyme pathways. After its release into the intersynaptic space, the neurotransmitter may be recaptured at the level of the presynaptic neurone and re-stored in the synaptosomes of the end plate, or it may be transformed, by means of distinct catabolic routes, into other more or less active compounds by enzymes present both within the presynaptic nerve ending and on the neurone membranes immediately adjacent to the ending itself. These latter two phases of nerve transmission, the re-uptake and catabolic degradation of the neuromediator, are also two very important moments in the passage of information, and given the existence of significant reactions with available neurotropic drugs, they involve both the clinical and pharmacological spheres.

Particular neuronal pathways may also be identified and named on the basis of the "primary" neurotransmitter synthesized by the complex of neurones considered. Since a single neuromediator may be present in several different neuronal pathways with different functions, the precise relations between the various cerebral tasks and relative specific neurotransmitters remain, in many cases, unknown. Currently, an extremely important role is attributed to some neurotransmitters responsible for the regulation of mood, and their quantitative modification has been related to certain disorders of affective and cognitive functions in the elderly [581, 448].

The studies considered here have focused on the age-related modifications occurring in five neurotransmitters of the central nervous system: dopamine (DA), noradrenaline (NE), serotonin (5-HT), acetylcholine (Ach) and gamma-aminobutyric acid (GABA). There follows an overall picture of each of these molecules, with general definitions of their distribution, metabolic pathways, and presumed or demonstrated functions. Later we review the studies that have examined age-related variations in the quantity and the activity of each neurotransmitter and the enzymes concerned in its metabolism.

CATECHOLAMINERGIC SYSTEMS

The catecholaminergic neurotransmitters, dopamine and noradrenaline, are synthesized and metabolized in the so-called adrenergic neurones of the nervous system.

The main dopaminergic pathways regulate each of the different cerebral functions. The first, the nigrostriatal tract, belongs to the pyramidal system and controls muscular movements and posture. A reduction in the quantity of the neuromediator along this pathway causes the rigidity, tremor, and lack of motor coordination characteristic of Parkinson's disease. A second dopaminergic pathway, the tubero-infundibular tract, regulates the production and release of prolactin, while less is known about the third pathway, the meso-limbic tract, that, however, seems to be implicated in the development and course of psychotic disorders. Other dopaminergic pathways, about which little is known yet, are presumed to exist in relation to memory functions and regulation of mood and autonomic functions.

The neuronal pathways, whose mediator is noradrenaline, are even less understood. These appear to act on the central nervous system regulating mood and expression of emotions as well as maintaining the circadian sleep-wake rhythms [581]. Recent studies on age-related modification of the catecholaminergic system have given rise to interesting results.

Age-Related Modifications

Catecholamine Levels

Most studies in humans have shown a reduction in the catecholamine content of the brain of the elderly. Nearly all of these recent studies indicate, in particular, a reduction in dopamine with increasing age. We note here, in order of publication, the studies of Bertler et al. [51] and of Carlsson et al. [100], which have demonstrated a significant reduction of dopamine levels in the caudate and putamen. In vitro studies on the density of dopamine receptors failed to show an increase with age, while a relative decrease was found in the caudate nucleus [605]. There is some discrepancy between these results and those of Robinson et al. [558], who were unable to find any quantitative differences in dopamine levels in the caudate, the globus pallidus, and in the substantia nigra, but did indicate a lower quantity of the neuromediator in other cerebral areas such as the thalamus and the hypothalamus. As well, in a study by Mackay et al. [410], no significant correlation was found between age and dopamine levels in 20 cerebral areas of 10 brains from subjects in an age range of 46 to 74 years. The McGeers [447, 448], in research on catecholamine levels conducted in a more numerous sample of human brains of different ages, affirmed that there was an appreciable reduction in dopamine, which was more marked in certain areas such as the putamen, the accumbens nucleus, the amygdala, and the globus pallidus. Research on cerebral variations in noradrenaline levels have also given rise to somewhat discrepant findings. According to Robinson et al. [558], this neuromediator is reduced in all the areas indicated by McGeer and McGeer as having reduced dopamine levels [448], and especially in the hippocampus and hypothalamus, with exclusion of the substantia nigra. The above-cited study by Mackay et al. [410] affirms that the variations in noradrenaline and its metabolites were the same as those reported for dopamine.

As to studies on animal models, we would like to to note the studies by Finch [230] on cats; by Joseph et al. [315] and by Simpkins et al. [616] on rats; and by Samorajski and Rolsten [587] on monkeys, which give an overall picture of a reduced dopamine and noradrenaline content in various areas of the central nervous system in the animals examined.

A recent study by Carlsson [102] hypothesizes that the age-related neurone loss, mainly in the dopaminergic system, might be offset by an increased activity of the remaining neurones through a feedback stimulation having the ultimate effect of increasing receptorial sensitivity. This would suggest that some pathologies, especially in the elderly, may result from a defective compensatory mechanism.

Catecholaminic Enzymes

All the enzymatically catalyzed transitions may undergo variation with increasing age, resulting in an overall reduction of the available pool of neurotransmitters. The enzyme tyrosine-hydroxylase, which catalyzes the phenylalanine-tyrosine and tyrosine-L-dopa reactions, regulates the rapidity of the production of the two catecholaminic neuromediators. In various studies on the human brain, it has been observed to diminish—both in quantity and activity—with increasing age, especially in those areas having the greatest concentrations of dopaminergic endings, such as the caudate, the putamen, and the accumbens [101]. An analogous tendency has been found in various studies on decarboxylase, on dopamine-beta-hydroxylase and on catechol-0-methyltransferase, while studies on the activity of the enzyme monoamine oxidase seem to have ascertained that this substance increases with age.

- Tyrosine Hydroxylase (TH)

From studies conducted on human brains [101, 410], it has emerged that there is a significant age-related decline in the activity of the tyrosine-hydroxylase enzyme in at least three cerebral regions: the amygdala, the putamen, and the caudate.

In a study on the human brain, Cotk and Kremzner [132] found a reduced TH activity not only in the above-cited regions, but also in the substantia nigra. However, other authors [558, 257] were unable to find any reduction in the activity of this enzyme with increasing age. It is probable that this last finding results from the fact that, in the latter studies, the subjects examined were over 30, while the most rapid decline in enzyme activity seems to occur in the first three decades of life [556, 557].

- Dopamine Decarboxylase (DOC)

A decline with age in the activity of this enzyme has been observed in numerous cerebral areas. The caudate, the septal area, the substantia nigra, the amygdala—among the regions that play a significant physiological role—show a decrease in the action of this enzyme [101, 399]. Yet other studies [558] failed to confirm the existence of a significant correlation between age and DOC activity.

• Dopamine-Beta-Hydroxylase (DBH)

Also with this enzyme there is some controversy over the possible variations occurring in the course of aging. DBH is in fact a very unstable enzyme in the postmortem period; moreover, it is difficult to find a general trend, given the existence of considerable interindividual variation. Its activity has been evaluated in several studies [558, 257] that have attempted to measure its diminution in subjects aged from 33 to 74 years. These studies did not find a significant age-related variation. Studies on animal models were also unable to provide significant confirmation of any reduction in DBH in senility. For example, an extensive study by Reis et al. in 1977 [541] examined dopamine-beta-hydroxylase levels in various regions of cat and mouse brains aged between 4 and 26 months, but found no evidence of any significant correlation between the activity of this enzyme and the age of the animals.

• Monoamine Oxidase (MAO)

The existence of two types of MAO, the A and the B, differentiated on the basis of substrate specificity and a characteristic pharmacological inhibition, has been conclusively demonstrated. Despite numerous and recent studies, it is still not clear which of the two forms of monoamine oxidase is most directly correlated to the aging process—or even whether both are influenced [103]. The activity of the MAOs present on the external surface of the mitochondrial membrane increases with age both in the brain and in some peripheral organs in a large number of animal species. In humans, too, an age-related increase in monoamine oxidase activity has been known for many years [102, 496, 557]. The activity of this enzyme, and especially of the MAO-B type, has been demonstrated as increasing at the level of the locus niger, pallidus, and hippocampus, particularly in women after the onset of menopause [557]. In animal studies, some of the reported findings are discordant with those described above: Whilst some investigators have confirmed an increased MAO activity with increasing age in whole rat brains [247,320], others found no appreciable modifications [366].

- Catechol-0-Methyltransferase (COMT)

Various authors have reported an increase in the activity of this enzyme with increasing age [101, 616]. However, this finding is contradicted by other investigators, for example, Grote et al. [257], who arrived at the conclusion that there is no evidence for a relationship between the activity of COMT, age, and sex. Studies by Robinson et al. [558] also failed to find any alteration in this enzyme in the brain of the elderly subject, with the exception of the hippocampus, where a significant decline of COMT activity with increasing age was found.

Receptorial Activity

In addition to the beta postsynaptic receptor site, both dopamine and noradrenaline also bind to a presynaptic receptor called alpha 2, which regulates the release of the neurotransmitter itself. Some investigations appear to have demonstrated that age-related modifications occur in these phases of neurotransmission as well [533]. The most detailed biochemical findings concerning the catecholamine receptors refer to the postsynaptic receptor sites, which are easy to mark and study in experimental research. The receptor of a specific transmitter may also be studied indirectly, through evaluation of the activities of an enzyme that is linked to it, for example, adenyl-cyclase, or directly with methods based on the use of radioactive neurotransmitters or selective drugs.

- Beta Postsynaptic Receptors

The existence of two distinct postsynaptic receptor sites for dopamine has now been demonstrated: D1 and D2. The age factor does not seem to influence the activity of this second type of receptor, while research on the D1 receptor in animal models seems to suggest a marked reduction in the number and sensitivity of the receptor sites of adenylate-cyclase [102].

Measurement of the "binding capacity" of some receptors has become a very widespread technique in the evaluation of the presence and activity of the receptor sites. Over the last few years, two laboratories have published findings indicative of an approximately 40% reduction in specific receptor sites for 3-H-haloperidol and 7-H-spiroperidol on the striatal membranes of adult rats [251, 315].

Other research also conducted on the adult rat has shown that the density of the beta-adrenergic receptor—measured using the binding agent 3-H-dihydrohalprenolol—is significantly reduced in the pineal gland, in the corpus striatum, and in the cerebellum [230]. Similar studies on humans have not yet been conducted, but since the number of beta-adrenergic receptors has been shown to diminish at the lymphocyte level [598], various investigators have suggested that the phenomenon of the reduction of these receptors with increasing age is a general one and not limited to specific organs or specific areas of the brain.

• Presynaptic Receptors

A reduction in the activity of these receptor sites has been demonstrated in the noradrenergic nerve endings of the central nervous system of adult animals [101], while no data are available about the activity of the presynaptic receptor along the dopaminergic pathways in the elderly brains of either animals or humans.

SEROTONIN

It appears that serotonin has a peculiar activity in the regulation of the sleep-wake rhythm (REM stage) and a regulating action on mood tone. The presence of serotonin has also been demonstrated in structures linked to extrapyramidal motor activity and autonomic functions, including the regulation of the pain stimulus [102]. Some investigators hypothesize that serotonin also plays the role of "pacemaker" in the human aging process itself [496].

Age-Related Modifications

Serotonin Levels

Relatively few studies have attempted to evaluate the influence of age on serotonin levels, and there are considerable discrepancies in the results of these studies. For example, a study [558] on human nerve tissue sampled from the pons, hypothalamus, substantia nigra, and amygdala of 19 brains from neurologically normal individuals from 46–74 years showed a significant inverse correlation between age and serotonin levels in the areas considered, while—surprisingly—there was no evidence of variation in the levels of other neurotransmitters (dopamine, noradrenaline, and their metabolites), which are notoriously sensitive to increasing age [558]. Other studies have reported a reduction in serotonin with increasing age, although this was slight [557]. On the other hand, the same research team [488] was later unable to detect any modifications in brains from individuals aged 25 to 70 years. In confirmation of this latter finding, other authors [5, 532] have indicated that serotonin levels in humans remain unchanged, while 5-hydroxyindoleacetic acid increases. This finding is attributed to an alteration during old age of the mechanisms of excretion of the metabolites of serotonin and is in agreement with experimental findings [608] of an increase in fluid levels of homovanillic acid and 5-hydroxyindoleacetic acid.

More recently, other studies have revealed an increase in serotonin concentrations with respect to dopamine and noradrenaline levels in many areas of the brain of laboratory animals [496]. A similar situation may be hypothesized for humans, as these findings may be read as being indicative of a relative stability of serotonin levels in advanced age against an effective and proven reduction in the other two neuromediators. In fact, the current view is that serotonin levels remain more or less unchanged in the elderly human brain [370, 644].

Enzyme Activity

The enzymes involved in the synthesis of serotonin are tryptophan-hydroxylase and 5-hydroxytryptophan-decarboxylase. Some important technical problems are encountered in the study of the serotonergic system in humans, including, for example, the high enzymatic instability of TRH in the postmortem period, which makes it nearly impossible to demonstrate its presence in brain tissue.

For information on the catalytic enzyme monoamine oxidase, the reader is referred to the section on this enzyme.

Receptorial Activity

There are two types of serotonergic receptors in humans: the 5HT1 and the 5HT2.

A study by Shih and Young [608] appears to demonstrate variations in the number and properties of the serotonin receptor sites of the cerebral cortex of humans. Particularly noteworthy in this study are the modifications found in different stages of aging. In the cortex, for example, two types of receptor sites have been demonstrated in subjects aged 23 to 29 years, while only one type of receptor is found in subjects between 61 and 70 years of age. Furthermore, although the total number of receptor sites is greater in the elderly population, serotonin showed less affinity even at presumably physiological concentrations.

A recent study on 5-HT receptors in patients with major affective disorders revealed an increase in postsynaptic receptor activity that might be interpreted as a consequence of diminished availability at the presynaptic level [450].

ACETYLCHOLINE

Acetylcholine (Ach) is without doubt one of the most important CNS neurotransmitters. Current knowledge about the distribution in the brain of this neurotransmitter permits us to affirm with certainty that it is present in higher quantities in the extrapyramidal and limbic system. In the latter, acetylcholine has the function of controlling and processing memory functions. It has hence been the object of particular interest as its specific deficiency has been observed in Alzheimer's disease [35, 102, 140]

From an overview of all studies conducted in this field it may be said that there is an impairment of the cholinergic system in the course of aging.

Age-Related Modifications

Acetylcholine Levels

Acetylcholine disappears rapidly from the human brain in the postmortem period, so that a correct and direct quantitative evaluation of its presence in the various districts of the brain is impossible. The only indices of the functionality or impairment of the cholinergic neurones are the enzymes involved in its synthesis and degradation.

Enzyme Activities

It has been demonstrated by several investigators that increasing age brings a depression of the activity of both transferase and acetylcholinesterase in various regions of the brain [186, 448, 511], although it should also be noted that some studies on humans [410] and animals [541] failed to demonstrate any age-related modification in these enzymes.

A reliable finding emerges from the study by McGeer and McGeer [447] on 28 brains from neurologically normal individuals aged between 5 and 87 years. These authors found that at least one-third of the areas considered showed a marked age-related depression in CAT activity. Unlike in the case of other enzymes such as tyrosine-hydroxylase, dopadecarboxylase, and above all glutamic acid decarboxylase, this reduction also involved the cortex areas and, to a lesser extent, the extrapyramidal system and rhinencephalon. These authors had previously demonstrated a depression in cholinoacetyl-transferase activity at the limbic level [446], a finding confirmed by Perry et al. [511], especially in the hippocampus. McGeer and McGeer [446] report that the behavior of the enzyme acetylcholinesterase is rather similar to that of the synthesizing enzyme, though not all investigators are in agreement: Numerous studies have in fact affirmed the absence of any age-related quantitative modification in this enzyme [102, 186, 410].

Receptor Activity

With reference to postsynaptic cholinergic activity, which may be evaluated in terms of variations in affinity for the neurotransmitters and in the number of receptors, we note the studies by White et al. [693], which report a reduction in the binding ability of the muscarine receptors; and by Norberg and Winbland [489], in which these receptors were instead reported to decrease numerically, especially in the anterior sections of the hippocampus.

Further confirmation of this comes from studies conducted by Bowen [71], which report that the binding capacity of the muscarine receptors in individuals over the age of 90 years is 70% of that found in subjects aged 70 years.

It seems likely that the cognitive and memory disorders characteristic of certain elderly subjects may be attributed to this impairment of the cholinergic system; however, it is less easy to link these alterations to behavior disorders or, more specifically, to alterations in mood.

GAMMAAMINOBUTYRRIC ACID

Of the amino acids that have been shown to have the property of neurotransmission, gamma aminobutyric acid (GABA) is the best known in terms of biochemical characteristics, localization, and age-related variations.

Its activity is linked, from a pharmacological point of view, with the activity of the benzodiazepines: Some receptors for gamma aminobutyric acid are in fact closely linked to other receptors that seem to recognize only the benzodiazepine molecule. The concentration of GABA in the central nervous system has been found to be altered in some neurological diseases such as Huntington's chorea, and it has been suggested that it plays a role in Parkinson's disease and in late dyskinesia [102].

Numerous studies on animals have attempted to identify modifications of the neurotransmitter GABA in advanced age. But the findings are somewhat discordant, some studies finding an increase in total GABA content, some a reduction, and others still an increase or reduction of the specific receptor sites for this neurotransmitter [401].

A large problem in fact exists for the evaluation of the enzymatic activities of decarboxylase (GAD) in human brains since this enzyme is particularly sensitive to conditions of antemortem coma. Nevertheless, various studies appear to have demonstrated a depression of the activity of the enzyme GAD in elderly persons, especially in the thalamic areas and some regions of the cortex and rhinencephalon [301, 581]. However, on the basis of these studies it would appear that this reduction does not significantly involve the basal ganglia.

With regard to the behavior of the GABAergic receptors, their reduction has not been confirmed in the senile human brain [648]. Such a reduction has, however, been found in research on animals, especially in the substantia nigra and hypothalamus [401].

In humans, a final and interesting finding emerges from studies by Bowen [71], who reports an overall increase in GABAergic receptor sites, particularly in the temporal lobe.

Lastly, some authors hypothesize that the overall functional impairment of the GABAergic system may be responsible for the difficulties of elderly subjects in integrating the multiple information received from the outside.

BRAIN IMAGING AND DEPRESSIVE ILLNESS

Although in vitro and postmortem studies have yielded interesting information, better insight into brain neurotransmitters in normal and pathological aging will probably have to await the advent of more accurate in vivo methods of investigation. An important contribution to such developments will certainly be given by the new techniques of brain imaging, although much work remains to be done before the diagnostic potential of these techniques may be fully realized.

Positron Emission Tomography (PET)

Perhaps the most important of these methods, which have the great advantage of being noninvasive, is Positron Emission Tomography (PET). As this technique offers both structural and functional analytical images, it may permit the in vivo study of neurochemical reactions in the brain. PET utilizes tracer quantities of biologically active compounds labeled with positron-emitting isotopes and thus does not disturb the ongoing physiological processes [600]. It is expected that PET techniques can be used to investigate specific functions through the measurement of the turnover of proteins, fatty acids, neurotransmitters, drugs, and markers [121]. The technique has already been use in studies on neurotransmitter receptors, for example, in vivo binding with spiperone, a high affinity dopaminergic antagonist, and has confirmed previous knowledge of the distribution of the DI and D2 receptors [33].

Other studies on animal models have revealed alterations in the phosphorilation processes in the glial cells consequent on a diminished utilization of glucose at constant oxygen consumption. These alterations may be interpreted as typical to the aging process [33].

In the field of psychiatry, studies with PET have shown a reduction of cerebral metabolism of glucose in the supratentorial structures of patients with bipolar disturbances and its increase in patients with unipolar disorders. Other studies have shown an anteroposterior decrease in depressed and schizophrenic patients as compared with healthy controls [600].

In a study on poststroke depression [503], the severity of the depressive situation was correlated to the site of the lesion and interpreted as a consequence of neurotransmitter depletion or altered sensitivity of the postsynaptic receptors. Here, PET showed an asymmetrical increase of the sensitivity of serotonin receptors in the ipsilateral cortex [503].

In the future, PET may permit dynamic study of brain neurochemistry through in vivo imaging of the interactions between receptors and neurotransmitters as well as investigation of the kinetics and biological effects of drugs [121].

Single-Photon Emission Tomography (SPET)

Like PET, this technique gives tomographic images after administration of a radio-pharmaceutical. The latter is labeled with single-photon radionuclides such as 133Xe, 123I or 99Tc. SPET is much less expensive than SPET as the radionuclides are longer-lived and there is no need for a cyclotron. However, it also has many disadvantages: lesser spatial and temporal resolution, much less accurate quantification, and the very limited number of available radiopharmaceuticals. In normal aging SPET has been able to show the diminution of regional brain blood flow (rCBF) [609]. SPET also permits the imaging of specific cerebral receptors, though much less efficaciously than PET. There is a widespread belief that the inability of this technique to provide precise quantification may hinder its future development [33].

Nuclear Magnetic Resonance (NMR]

This is a relatively new radiological technique offering extremely fine morphological resolution and quantification of functional change. The images are visually similar to those generated by CAT scans, but are of a totally different nature. While in CAT imaging the tissues are passive, attenuating the X-rays to varying extents, in magnetic resonance they are stimulated and emit a signal containing a great deal of information on the chemical and physical characteristics of the atoms and molecules making them up. NMR has numerous advantages over other imaging

techniques. First, it does not use ionizing radiation, thus eliminating the risk of biological damage for both patients and opera-
tors. Moreover, endovenous contrast media are not used, avoiding
the problem of the severe allergic reactions these substances may
provoke. The possible applications of NMR in the study of normal
and abnormal aging of the brain remain largely to be explored,
although they already appear extremely interesting [74, 53]. It
may be presumed that NMR will provide an important contribution in the study of many clinical and psychiatric syndromes
[223], challenging the traditional dichotomy between functional
and organic states.

Computerized Axial Tomography (CAT)

Computerized axial tomography is today still the most common
means of investigation of the brain. Many studies have reported
that the incidence of cerebral atrophy increases with age, especially in male subjects [55]. However, in a study by Laffey et al.
[368] on more than 200 elderly subjects of both sexes, only 15%
showed signs of ventricular enlargement and sulcal widening.
Furthermore, although CAT studies have shown that cerebral
atrophy is significantly associated with dementia [305], the correlation between scan indices and scores on cognitive performance tests is poor [522]. It has hence been suggested that loss of
glial cells—and not of neurones—may be responsible for the atrophy, i.e., the determining factor in mental deterioration is the
quality, and not the quantity, of the loss.
    It appears that the affective disorders bear no direct relation-
ship with atrophy, but rather are connected to regional cerebral
density, which in depressed subjects appears to be intermediate
between normal and demented subjects [322]. In a recent study,
Dolan et al. [185] hypothesized that ventricular widening could
be a predisposing factor in depression.

BIOLOGICAL GENESIS OF THE AFFECTIVE DISORDERS IN SENESCENCE

The most important hypothesis concerning the biological origin of
the affective disorders was formulated more than 20 years ago. It
implicates an altered functionality of one or more monoamines
acting as neurotransmitters or as regulatory neurohormones at

the level of the nerve endings of the CNS [26]. This hypothesis is based on the observation that monoamine depletion in humans may cause a depressive state indistinguishable from the idiopathic major depressions. Furthermore, the tricyclic antidepressants and the monoamine oxidase inhibitors—both efficacious antidepressants—increase the synaptic concentrations of the monoamines themselves [640]. With the exception of GABA, the amines implicated in the genesis of depression are the same as those cited in the previous section: serotonin [659], noradrenaline [592], dopamine [618], and acetylcholine [308]; the modifications occurring in these substances with increasing age have already been described.

Synaptic dysfunction in a nerve circuit may give rise to clinical symptoms. Following the scheme proposed in the previous paragraph, it may be affirmed that a disorder may derive from:

1) an alteration in the quantity and activity of a neurotransmitter at the synaptic level;

2) modifications in the number and sensitivity of the receptor sites;

3) an altered sensitivity to the neurotransmitter of the postsynaptic enzymes.

Increasing age may influence synaptic dynamics in at least two ways, reducing neurotransmission at both

1) *the presynaptic level:* the quantity and availability of a given neurotransmitter are reduced (with the possible exception of serotonin) because of reduced synthesis or more rapid metabolism;

2) *the postsynaptic level:* neurotransmitter binding and the sensitivity of adenylate-cyclase, phosphodiesterase, and protein-kinasis may be reduced [371].

All of these biological events may increase susceptibility to depression and at least partially explain the greater frequency of affective disorders in elderly subjects [102]. Table 9 summarizes the main modifications occurring with age.

It is known that the tricyclic antidepressants as well as some new generation antidepressants increase the availability of monoamines at the synaptic level. It is presumed that this action forms the basis of the therapeutic antidepressant effect. More precisely, this effect may be realized by means of two distinct mechanisms: the first based on the re-uptake of noradrenaline, serotonin, and dopamine, thus increasing their availability in the

Table 9. Age-related changes in the central nervous system.

Neurotransmitter or enzyme	Age-related change in humans	Location
Tyrosine hydroxylase	Decreases	Amygdala
		Putamen
		Caudate
		Globus pallidus
		Nucleus accumbens
		Substantia nigra
Dopamine	Decreases	Globus pallidus
		Caudate
		Putamen
Dopa decarboxylase	Decreases	Amygdala
		Putamen
		Caudate
		Globus pallidus
		Nucleus accumbens
		Septum
		Substantia nigra
Dopamine ß-hydroxylase	Increases	Septum
Monoamine oxidase	Increases	Hindbrain
Norepinephrine	Decreases	Hindbrain
Catechol-o-methyltransferase	Decreases	Caudate
	Increases	Frontal cortex
Homovanillic acid	Increases	Cerebrospinal fluid (CSF)
	Decreases	CSF of senile patients
5-Hydroxytryptamine (serotonin)	Unchanged	Hindbrain
5-hydroxyindoleacetic acid	Increases	Hindbrain
	Decreases	CSF of senile patients
Acetylcholinesterase	Decreases	Cortex in Alzheimer patients
Choline acetyltransferase	Decreases	Hippocampus
Cyclic AMP	Decreases	Cortex
Protein kinase	Not known	Not known
Glutamic acid decarboxylase	Decreases	

(adapted from Salzman, 1984)

intersynaptic space; the second (yet to be fully investigated) involving an alteration of the sensitivity of the postsynaptic receptor site (and perhaps also of the presynaptic receptor) which enhances noradrenergic, serotonergic, and dopaminergic neurotransmission [398, 699].

An increase in the availability of the above-mentioned neuromediators may also derive from a block of their metabolism by monoamine oxidase inhibitors. Since, as we saw above, the activity of the MAO-B increases in elderly subjects, presynaptic metabolism also increases, resulting in a reduced availability of neurotransmitters. Hence, the MAO inhibitors may be very useful antidepressants in elderly subjects.

The cyclic antidepressants (like the neuroleptics) block the postsynaptic acetylcholine receptors, causing a reduction in cholinergic neurotransmission. The antidepressants may thus produce marked side effects, including confusion, disorientation, and loss of memory; externally to the CNS, the blockage of the cholinergic receptors determines dry mouth, constipation, and urine retention. All of these side effects may be particularly serious in the elderly, as cholinergic neurotransmission is progressively reduced with increasing age [102].

The action of lithium on the central nervous system may involve various neurotransmission systems. Noradrenergic transmission may be reduced as lithium inhibits the noradrenaline-adenylate cyclase linkage and hence the successive formation of AMP-cyclic; serotonergic and GABAergic neurotransmission may also be reduced. On the other hand, it has been hypothesized that the elderly show an increase in receptorial sensitivity to many drugs, resulting in a possible enhanced response—but also in an increased risk of toxicity. This hypothesis, which still requires a better definition, derives mainly from the observation of an increased response to lithium and benzodiazepines in the elderly [102]. In fact, the therapeutic effects of both lithium and the benzodiazepines are achieved at considerably lower doses in the elderly than in the young and adults.

An increased sensitivity of the receptors may also explain the particular susceptibility of the elderly to the anticholinergic effects of the cyclic antidepressants. Bearing in mind that cholinergic transmission is also reduced in these subjects (see above), it is understandable that the receptor involvement of these drugs may give rise to a much more intense response than would "normally" be expected.

The quantity of baroceptors [204], i.e., those receptors contributing to the regulation of pressure, also appears to diminish in the elderly. This finding may provide further support for the hypothetical increase in receptor sensitivity in the elderly brain. It is in fact known that the elderly are much more susceptible to the hypotensive effects of the cyclic antidepressants (and also to those of the neuroleptics) [102].

Despite discrepancies in the findings of various studies [666], the age-related modifications in the neurotransmission systems permit us to draw at least one precise indication: Both therapeutic and toxic responses to the psychotropic drugs are enhanced in the elderly. Consequently, there is an increased liability to side effects in this age group, so that prescribed dosages should be lower in the elderly than in younger subjects.

CHAPTER 5
Alterations of Cerebral Blood Flow and Depression

- In this chapter, we discuss how mood disturbances can be correlated with blood flow. Flow-imaging techniques have shown hypoactive and especially "hypofrontality" areas in medically untreated depressed subjects. These functional markers quickly disappear once normal mood is reestablished.

- Depression, especially in its major form, is a sequela in perhaps more than 50% of stroke patients. Moreover, it appears that the closer the anterior margin of a left hemisphere lesion is to the frontal pole, the more severe is depression. This also has extremely important consequences for the patient's rehabilitation, since obviously the more depressed one is, the greater is one's motivation for rehabilitative exercise. Unfortunately, even rehabilitation colleagues are not sufficiently aware of the concomitant depression, being convinced that "proper" retraining by itself can restore normal mood. Thus, they believe depression is simply a reaction to the stroke and thus does not need any psychiatric treatment.

- No matter what the origin of depression is, it should be understood that a subject whose mood is psychologically and/or pharmacologically supported is better prepared for rehabilitation. Moreover, a slower or decreased blood flow in the brain might be associated with mood disturbances in addition to a certain degree of impairment of cognitive functions. This seems deducible from a series of observations in subjects who underwent carotid endarteriectomy.

- Unfortunately, the reestablished feeling of well-being and improvement of cognitive performances observed at a short-term level do not last long. In fact, medium- and long-term follow-ups indicate these patients return to preoperative conditions, probably because of arterialization of the grafted patch with subsequent detachment of new microemboli and progression of the disease from the untreated carotid. However, we still cannot fully explain this problem and do not know how to prevent this unavoidable worsening.

The recent development of new techniques for in vivo investigation of cerebral activity has given rise to new insights into the relationships between the structures and functions of the brain in normal conditions and in various psychopathological situations [501]. The high incidence of vascular and degenerative brain pathologies in the elderly on the one hand, and of psychopathological manifestations in the form of cognitive and depressive disorders on the other, seems to suggest a need, particularly in the field of psychogeriatrics, for increased integration of neuroscientific progress and clinical psychiatry.

Studies on the relationship between cerebral blood flow and depression are currently developing along two main research lines, one with a prevalently clinical approach and the other more specifically concerned with laboratory and instrumental examination procedures. The latter field includes research using radioactive markers for the measurement of cerebral blood flow and metabolic activity, while studies of the former type have focused on depression following stroke and on mood alterations in subjects submitted to carotid endarterectomy.

CEREBRAL BLOOD FLOW IN DEPRESSION

Most current techniques for the measurement of regional cerebral blood flow (rCBF) [548, 457] employ Obrist's Xenon 133 inhalation method [492], which, on the basis of Fick's principle and using multiple external scintillation detectors, permits separate calculation for grey and white matter of blood flow in the cerebral areas underlying the detectors. This two-dimensional recording system for CBF is especially reliable in the measurement of blood flow in the cerebral cortex. However, it is also possible to measure CBF in deeper cerebral structures (three-dimensional recording) by means of PET (positron emission tomography) and SPET (single-photon emission tomography).

In normal young subjects, in waking conditions, and in psychosensorial rest, rCBF follows a distribution pattern characterized by "hyperfrontality" in both hemispheres, cortical flow being markedly higher in the frontal regions than in the postcentral, temporal, and occipital regions [298, 549]. This pattern shows preferential modifications in relation to the functional activity of the cortex during different cognitive performances and in relation to the intensification of these activities in response to incentivation tasks [248, 674, 675, 372]. In the normal aging process, there is a progressive decline in resting cortical blood flow in both hemispheres and in all regions, though more marked in the frontal regions. Normal rCBF persists, however, during cognitive activities and incentivated performance [457, 675, 453]. This tendency toward reduction of the normal pattern of "hyperfrontality" of the rCBF in the elderly subject has a metabolic parallel in an analogous progressive reduction in the utilization of glucose— which is also more marked in the frontal regions—detected in tomographic studies using radioactive fluorodeoxyglucose [360].

The research conducted to date on rCBF in depression has given rise to somewhat varied results, perhaps because of a certain lack of methodological uniformity, the use of different diagnostic criteria in the selection of patients, and the possible existence of different rCBF distribution patterns in the vast spectrum of the depressive disorders.

In patients with major depression submitted to 2 weeks of drug washout, Mathew et al. [438, 439] found a bilateral hemispheric reduction (more marked in the left hemisphere), the degree of which was inversely correlated with the severity of the depression. A reduction—this time symmetric—in resting rCBF was also found by Warren et al. [674] in patients admitted to hospital with depressive disorders: These subjects conserved the normal "hyperfrontal" pattern of rCBF and response to cognitive activation and incentivation.

Different results were obtained by Chabrol et al. [109] in 20 depressed adolescents not undergoing pharmacological treatment. Here, mean hemispheric CBF did not differ from that of the control group, and the flow distribution pattern was characterized by a clear relative hyperfrontality, which was more intense in the subgroup with major depression. In subjects with major depression and undergoing various forms of pharmacological treatments, Uytdenhoef et al. [656] found left frontal hypervascularization associated with right posterior hypervascularization, while Gur et al. [260], correcting rCBF values for pCO_2, found a normal resting rCBF and anomalies in activation patterns during cognitive performance. In a study conducted with labeled fluorodeoxyglucose (18FDG) and PET on subjects with bipolar depression after a pharmacological washout of more than 2 weeks, Buchsbaum et al. [86] found a reduction in frontal cortical utilization of glucose with reduction of the normal anteroposterior gradient (which was evaluated at 2.7 in the normal controls and 0.2 in the depressed patients). Using the same technique (PET and 18 FDG), Phelps et al. [519] found subjects with bipolar depression with an overall cortical glucose hypometabolism and a subgroup of subjects with unipolar depression with marked hypometabolism in the left frontal cortex. The latter anomaly was corrected in subjects showing positive clinical response (euthymia) to the administration of methylphenidate.

The above-mentioned findings of reduced rCBF and glucose metabolism in untreated depressed patients thus appear to lend support to Mathew et al.'s [438] hypothesis of the existence of a neurone hypoactivity in depression. Some findings [109, 86, 519] seem to suggest a more precise localization of this hypoactivity at the frontal level. This hypofrontality seems to be a "status marker" [109]: a functional disorder that, according to some studies [109, 519], is corrected with the improvement in mood following pharmacological treatment.

DEPRESSION AFTER STROKE

Various studies have shown that depression is a rather common psychiatric complication in subjects affected by cerebral stroke. Folstein et al. [207] found that 45% of such patients, evaluated within 57 days of the stroke, were depressed, as opposed to 10% of patients with skeletal pathologies implying a similar level of physical disability. Similarly, Finklestein et al. [205] reported a state of clinically significant depression in 48% of stroke patients, evaluated within 111 days, as opposed to none of controls with similar physiological disability resulting from other pathologies. The prevalence rates of depressive disorders found by other investigators at variable lengths of time after the stroke (though in all cases within 3 months) range from 35% to 49% [566, 568, 617]. Robinson et al. [568], in a longitudinal study with an initial evaluation in the acute postictal phase, found initial prevalence rates of 23% for major depression (according to the diagnostic criteria of the DSM-III) and 20% for minor depression (or dysthymic disturbance in the DSM-III); by the 6-month follow-up examination, these figures had increased respectively to 34% and 26%, respectively. Six months after the stroke, 60% of the subjects presented a clinically significant depression: If not treated, the initial depression persisted in 95% of the initially depressed subjects, and 29% of the initially euthymic subjects manifested a depressive disorder by the time of the follow-up.

These findings, which confirm the results of previous studies by Robinson et al. on the duration [565] and severity [566] of depression secondary to stroke, suggest a mood disorder that is both persistent (with a duration of over 6 months in untreated subjects) and frequently severe. More than half of the cases could be diagnosed as major depression, having a clinical manifestation definable as "functional" major depression [397]. The disorder appears to be significantly associated with abnormal response to the dexamethasone suppression test [205, 396] and is accompanied by a more marked cognitive impairment (cognitive deficiency being equal, depressed patients have less extensive cerebral lesions than nondepressed patients) [564].

The clinical course of the stroke does not appear to be correlated with the duration of the depressive disorder, whether major or minor. Robinson et al. [564, 567] showed that onset of depression may occur either in the acute poststroke phase or at any later stage within a "high-risk period" estimated at 2 years [565]. Robinson et al. also analyzed the relationship between the prevalence and severity of the depression and several variables during the high-risk period. The factor most closely associated with the frequency and severity of the depression proved to be the location of the cerebral lesion [564–569], while the extent of the physical and intellectual functional impairment, validity of social support and age appeared to explain only 10–20% of the variance of the depressive symptomatology [559, 566, 562]. More specifically, approximately 70% of the patients with left cerebral infarction displayed a clinically significant depression (major depression in most cases) during their stay in the hospital, while only 15% of the patients with right hemisphere injury manifested a clinically relevant depression [567, 562]. Furthermore, it has been repeatedly demonstrated that there is a highly significant correlation between location of the cerebral lesion in the left hemisphere (as determined by CT scan) and severity of the depressive symptomatology [562, 564, 566–568]: The depression was significantly more severe in patients with left anterior lesion than in those with any other injury site ("anterior" lesion being understood as injuries having their anterior and posterior boundaries rostral to the anteroposterior axis of the hemisphere by respectively 40% and 60% of the A-P distance). In patients with left anterior lesions, the severity of the depression was significantly and directly correlated with the vicinity of the anterior boundary of the lesion to the left frontal pole. This latter correlation is extremely strong, explaining 50–70% of the variance of the depressive symptomatology [567]. Robinson et al. [562, 566, 567] also found a relationship between mood disorder and location of the lesion on the anteroposterior hemisphere axis in injuries to the right hemisphere. Patients with right posterior lesions (for example, lesions with anterior and posterior margins caudal to the axis, by respectively 40% and 60% of the A-P distance) were more depressed than patients with right anterior lesions, who manifested "apathy and inadequate gaiety."

The close relationship between the severity of the depression following stroke, the presence of left anterior hemispheric lesion, and vicinity of the latter to the frontal lobe was confirmed in other studies by Robinson et al. in left-handed patients [563] and in patients with bilateral hemispheric lesions [559]: Left anterior lesion proved to be determining in the onset of depressive symptomatology, regardless of hemispheric motor dominance and location or chronological succession of other cerebral lesions.

Further confirmation of the importance of location of the lesion in the left hemisphere for the development of a depressive disorder emerges from a comparative study by Robinson and Szetela [569] in a group of patients affected by left stroke and another group of subjects with posttraumatic left cerebral lesion and similar physical and cognitive functional impairment: The prevalence of clinically significant depression was 61% in the first group against 18% in the traumatized group; however, upon comparing the results with anteroposterior location of the lesion (more posterior in the traumatized patients), no significant difference in mood was found between the two groups of patients, the severity of the depression being closely and directly correlated to the proximity of the lesion—whether ischemic or traumatic—to the left frontal pole.

Robinson et al.'s findings on the strong correlation between location of the cerebral lesion within the left hemisphere and prevalence and severity of depression secondary to stroke are in agreement with a previous finding by Gainotti [218] of a higher frequency of "catastrophic reactions" and depressive disorders after left cerebral lesion. A single note of discord is given in Folstein et al.'s report [207] of a clear prevalence of depressive disorders after right stroke. The results of Sinyor et al. [617] are in at least partial agreement with those of Robinson et al.:

- absence of a significant relationship between the severity of depression after stroke and the extent of the functional impairment;

- absence of difference in incidence and severity of the depressive disorder between subjects with right or left hemisphere damage;

- presence of a direct, though not statistically significant, correlation between severity of the depression and proximity of the anterior margin of the lesion to the right or left frontal pole;

- presence of higher depression scores in subjects with right posterior lesion.

It is presently difficult to estimate the possible role in these partial discrepancies of factors such as the exclusion from the pools of subjects examined of patients with severe receptive aphasia or difficulties in comprehension; technical problems concerning the exact definition of the boundaries of the lesion under CT scan; or the problems of clinical evaluation that may be encountered in, for example, subjects affected by aprosodia [562, 573] as a consequence of right cerebral lesion.

However, the following data appear to be noncontroversial:

- Depression is a common complication of stroke.

- It is persistent, frequently severe (major depression), and has negative consequences on cognitive function and rehabilitation.

- There is no strong connection between the extent of the physical and cognitive impairment and the depression, which is instead strongly correlated to the location of the cerebral lesion: The closer the anterior margin of a left hemisphere injury to the frontal pole, the more severe the depression.

These findings appear to lend support to the idea that post-stroke depressive disorders are not a simple reaction to the emotional trauma of the physical and cognitive impairment [207, 617, 567], but rather—at least in most cases—a more etiopathogenetically complex event, in some way connected to the laterality and location of the cerebral lesion.

In this context, on the basis of an experimental demonstration that focal cortical lesions lead to a widespread but asymmetric (depending on the affected hemisphere) catecholamine depletion in rats, Robinson et al. [567] hypothesized that the "lateralized frontal affective syndrome" may be a behavioral manifestation of a depletion of biogenous neurotransmitter amines caused by ischemic injury to the frontal cortical nerve endings of the aminergic pathways deriving from the encephalic trunk, more anterior lesions causing greater depletion of the neurotransmitters. This biochemical lesion could itself bring about the depressive disorder—or lead to a liability to depression, on which other physical and/or psychosocial stressors later act [561]. The therapeutic efficacy of nortriptyline, which has been demonstrated in a double-blind study [395], may hence be due to the correction of the alterations of the biogenous amines induced by the stroke by means of the specific action of the drug in inhibiting the re-uptake of noradrenaline and "desensitizing" the post synaptic receptors [395].

MODIFICATIONS IN MOOD AFTER CAROTID ENDARTERECTOMY

A frequent cause of reduced cerebral blood flow is the presence of arteriosclerotic plaque creating stenosis at the level of the carotid bifurcation and/or at the root of the internal carotid. Patients with such stenoses, whether "asymptomatic" or with a history of episodes of TIA or small cerebral infarctions, commonly present varying degrees of cognitive impairment and are more depressed than control subjects without clinical signs of neurological and vascular disease [283, 270]. It is not clear how far these disorders are related to a multiinfarctual dementia in statu nascendi [283, 264] consequent on the repeated microembolic episodes caused by the plaque, or to a condition of "low-flow-endangered brain" [694, 302], namely, a cerebral blood flow deficiency caused by carotid stenosis and/or a more widespread arteriosclerotic involvement of the intracranial cerebral vessels [270].

The modification of the depressive state after removal of the ulcerated and/or stenotic arteriosclerotic plaque (the source of microembolisms) has received little research attention. Some authors [696, 242, 512] have limited themselves to noting a feeling of greater well-being reported by the patient after the endarterectomy. In an evaluation performed 6 months after the operation, King et al. [343, 344] found a significant reduction in suspicion, confusion, disorientation ". . . and other symptoms of personality generally associated with senility." Kelly et al. [334]

found a reduction in anxiety after the surgery, while other investigators [504, 183] found no modifications in mood 6–10 months after the endarterectomy.

In a series of studies on endarterectomized patients, De Leo et al. [142–144, 147–149, 153] evaluated cognitive performances, mood, and quality of life, and then compared the experimental group with subjects affected by the same pathology but not submitted to surgery. The tests were made at various time intervals: before the endarterectomy, 8 months after it, and at 2 and 3 years. While the control group, treated only with antiplatelet agents, displayed a tendency toward a progressive worsening of the parameters investigated, the experimental group showed a certain improvement in these parameters, including mood and quality of life, at the 8-month follow-up. However, results at the long-term follow-up did not confirm this tendency, and the 2-year follow-up showed a return to near the initial values [143].

It is possible, though thus far not convincingly demonstrated, that a more marked and persistent improvement may be achieved in younger subjects [144]. In subjects over the age of 70, endarterectomy gives no appreciable modifications even at the 8-month follow-up [144].

The improvement found at the first follow-up in the operated patients may be attributed to the restoration of adequate cerebral blood flow (as well as termination of the microemboli originating from the plaque). The increase in blood flow may at least partially normalize the neuronal activity of the areas of "ischemic penumbra," as defined by Astrup et al. [23]. It is equally reasonable to hypothesize that the worsening found at the long-term follow-up may be the consequence of an "arterialization" of the grafted patch, of the involvement in the arteriosclerotic process of districts distal to the operated carotid or progression of the disease in the controlateral carotid.

The development of new surgical techniques and/or other therapeutic strategies guaranteeing constant blood flow and eliminating the problem of blood clotting in the carotid may well ensure longer lasting improvements.

CHAPTER 6
Depression and Parkinson's Disease

- There are many possible organic "links" between Parkinson's disease and depression, none of which so far appear to exclude the possible role of the others in determining the affective disorder. It seems reasonable to suppose that one or more organic elements may act to predispose the individual to depression, which then manifests only in the presence of other psychogenic, genetic, or organic elements.

- The growth of our understanding of the neurophysiological connections among the extrapyramidal system, the limbic system, and the cortical structures as well as the clarification of the possible role of the extrapyramidal system in emotion should improve our insight into mood and motor disorders as well as into the relationships among them. This requires close collaboration between psychiatrists and neurologists.

The relationships between Parkinson's disease and depression are far more complex than generally believed. The link between an extrapyramidal syndrome resulting from a progressive degeneration of a central gray nucleus (locus niger) and a mood disturbance with no appreciable basis in organic damage may indeed appear artificial and irrelevant. However, the frequency with which these two pathologies are found to be associated justifies the efforts of some researchers to provide a scientific redefinition of clinical proposals. What from a clinical point of view appears as a frequent association between two different diseases may to the mind of the researcher point to the existence of a deeper connection that is as yet poorly defined. Nevertheless, today we do not yet have an answer to the fundamental question: Is the depression associated with Parkinson's disease merely a natural reaction to the disease itself, or does some "organic" explanation exist, perhaps in the alterations of cerebral amine levels found in this pathology?

In view of the interest aroused by these questions and the particular characteristics of depression associated with the— prevalently senile—manifestations of Parkinson's disease, we have dedicated a brief chapter to an exposition of the salient points of this controversial issue.

PSYCHOLOGICAL CORRELATES

In an attempt to identify a distinct premorbid personality, many studies have undertaken a retrospective analysis of the personality of Parkinsonians. Charcot [111] already believed that emotional tension, together with hereditary factors, may play an important role in the pathogenesis of Parkinson's disease. Janet [307], in his careful analysis of a series of clinical observations, also concluded that emotional stresses were important in the genesis of the disease. Besides these classical contributions, there is today unanimous agreement that a depressive type mood disturbance may precede the motor symptoms of Parkinson's disease. Moreover, it has been amply demonstrated that a considerable number of patients affected by Parkinson's disease had suffered from severe depressive episodes at the beginning of adult life, a long time before the onset of parkinsonism.

In a study by Shaw [607], for example, it emerged that 20% of 176 Parkinsonian patients had required psychiatric help for major depressive disturbances occurring prior to the onset of the motor symptomatology. The Parkinson's patients who had developed the disease in the third and fourth decades of life seemed to be the most prone to depressive episodes. Poewe et al. [524] also noted that many Parkinson's patients had shown a predisposition to depression prior to the onset of the motor symptoms.

Mouren et al. [471] studied the premorbid personality of 30 Parkinson's subjects, finding a tendency to rigidity, moralism, meticulousness, and perfectionism, against a background of an obsessive type personality. Moreover, although only two patients gave clear expression to aggressiveness, the latter was present in all patients, albeit with different manifestations. Generally, this aggression remained channelled within the subject's occupational activities and was directed to achieving promotion or social advancement. According to Mouren, the onset of the Parkinson's disease is associated with a radical transformation of personality, with the appearance of moral laxity, submission, dependence, and passivity—as if the symptoms of the disease had the power to empty the subject of aggression. The early onset of depression, which as we have seen sometimes occurs even prior to the onset of the first neurological symptoms, could perhaps be interpreted as an unconscious reaction to the profound changes that have already been initiated, and that make subjects strangers to themselves. The patients, in some sense, are like passive spectators watching the changes in their own personality and experiencing them, at least unconsciously, as a devaluation and impoverishment of their character, which thus loses its original strength and rigidity and becomes weak and submissive.

Even if there is no definitive evidence that depression is a prodromic symptom or etiological factor in Parkinson's disease (both because of the objective difficulties encountered in any enquiry into premorbid personality and because of the unlikelihood that a clear causal nexus will be found), this type of study is nevertheless important in providing systematic grounds in support of something that might be suspected from clinical observation: the considerable presence of depressive type mood disturbances in the clinical histories of future Parkinson's patients.

According to a psychosomatic perspective, the bases of the link between Parkinson's disease and depression should be sought much earlier in the patient's personal history. In this view, the occurrence of psychoaffectively significant life events in the early years of the subject's life predisposes him or her to the development of various pathologies, including depression and parkinsonism [79]. According to Todes [646], the primary traumatic event is the experience of separation from or loss of the mother occurring before the age of eleven, especially if this event is not adequately explained. However, because the interiorization of the parental model is not yet completed, the child is not in any case left unscathed by the abandonment of one of the parents—which has inevitable repercussions on the still forming ego. Defense mechanisms such as isolation and projection are brought into play to control anxiety. Normally, the child turns to fantasy and symbols to cope with absences of and separations from emotionally significant persons. In the case hypothesized, the effect of the loss of the mother during emotional development may be strong enough to determine a complete inhibition of feelings and affections in order to avoid pain. In this way the child avoids the fear of internal collapse and disintegrating abandonment. But this affective inhibition leads to the development of depression in adult life, which in turn forms the basis for the later development of a somatic complaint. Yet the mechanism underlying the cellular degeneration is unknown [646].

Mitscherlich [463] described a particular premorbid parkinsonian personality characterized by ambition, precision, industriousness, and the tendency to work even during free time. For these individuals, success at work seemed to be fundamental for their well-being. These behavioral traits seem to be established during early infancy, at the age of about two, when the motor system is deeply influenced by emotional life. Furthermore, at this age the child is learning to cope with people and things, to react, attack, and defend himself. The motor processes are given over to the control and integration of interior impulses with environmental demands, and the extrapyramidal system translates emotions and moods into behavior. Lack of self-affirmation appears to play a central role in mental disorder in Parkinsonians; individuals susceptible to development of the disease are, in this theory, continuously predisposed to motor activation, but inhibitions lead to motor block and ambivalence.

According to Brown [85], depression leads to a degeneration of the dopaminergic cells through a self-immune mechanism, which also appears to occur in certain types of cancer and in early onset diabetes preceded by depression.

CHARACTERISTICS OF DEPRESSION IN PARKINSON'S DISEASE: ORGANIC OR REACTIVE?

Although he maintained that the patients' "feelings and intellect" were not affected by the disease, Parkinson himself [506] described his patients as "unhappy," "discouraged," and "melancholy." Ball [29] found that many patients with Parkinson's disease suffered from depression with suicidal tendencies. Regis [539] maintained that depression in Parkinson's disease was a natural reaction to the disease.

These classic studies, while perceiving the importance of the problem, did not have precise clinical criteria and accurate definitions for the various psychiatric symptoms. However, notwithstanding undoubted improvements and standardization of methods of investigation, the frequency, etiology, and characteristics of depression in Parkinson's disease are still today largely an enigma.

Table 10. Depressive symptoms in Parkinson's disease.

Author	No. of pts	% depressed	Controls
Patrick & Levy [507]	100	20	None
Mjones [464] 238 40			None
Warburton [673]	140	60	Medical, surgical, gynecological disorders
Celesia & Wanamaker [108]	153	37	None
Brown & Wilson [77]	111	52	None
Marsh & Markham [435]	27	?[a]	Normals, physiotherapy patients
Horn [293]	24	?[a]	Normals, paraplegics
Robins [551]	45	?[a]	Normals, hemiplegics, spinal cord disorders, orthopedic problems
Mindham et al. [461]	89	90	Psychiatric inpatients
Lieberman et al. [385]	352	30	None
Mayeux et al. [441]	55	47	Spouses
Vogel [669]	20	?[a]	None
Mayeux et al. [443]	31	41	None

[a] no figures reported
(adapted from [245])

Table 10 summarizes the most recent studies on depressive symptoms in Parkinson's disease. As can be seen, the percentages reported by the various authors vary from 30% to 90%, and no information is provided on the nature of the dysthymia, namely, whether it is reactive or secondary to the disease, or whether it is instead a true symptom or component.

The considerable variation in the reported incidence of the disorder shown in Table 10 is due in part to the different types of populations of Parkinson's patients studied. For example, the study that reports a 90% incidence of depression related to patients admitted to the hospital with psychiatric problems. The high figure is not surprising: Depression is the most frequent reason for psychiatric admission, and the percentage of depression is thus higher in subjects admitted to the hospital than in those treated at home. Furthermore, the fact of hospital admission may itself cause a worsening of the symptoms or the onset of complications, leading to a temporary deterioration of mood.

Comparison of the various findings is also made difficult because of the different research methods employed. Nevertheless, in all studies depression is significantly higher in patients than in controls. Overall, the findings reported in Table 10 do not give a conclusive indication as to the nature of the dysthymia; however, they do show a substantial lack of correlation with elements such as the severity of the symptoms, degree of functional disability, and duration of the Parkinson's disease. The hypothesis that the depression is merely "reactive" seems unlikely [245].

Mayeux [441] outlined some of the clinical characteristics of depression in Parkinson's disease as follows:

1) mild intensity;

2) rarity of suicide;

3) lack of correlation with the severity of the disease, sex or age;

4) onset prior to or immediately following that of the Parkinson's disease in 15–25% of cases;

5) association with cognitive disturbances.

The more recent study by Gotham et al. [245] considers two groups of controls, one composed of healthy elderly volunteers and the other of patients suffering from arthritis. The group with Parkinson's disease showed much higher levels of depression, fear, and anxiety than the healthy patients, but did not differ widely from the overall affective status of the patients with arthritis. Gotham's study showed a direct relationship between severity of the disease and depression in both Parkinsonians and arthritic patients. In both groups, depression was characterized by feelings of pessimism and hopelessness, demotivation, and health worries. On the other hand, guilt feelings were absent, as were self-hatred and loss of interest in others, characteristics normally present among the cognitive elements of the more common primary depressions. Thus, for Gotham and co-workers, the depression associated with Parkinson's disease is no different from the depressive forms correlated with any other chronic disease: A good coping style and the availability of support in facing the disabilities caused by the disease will prevent the onset of depression in almost all cases [199].

Although Taylor [641] maintained that the view that depression in Parkinson's disease is a reaction to a profoundly disabling disease is both reasonable and acceptable, he nevertheless hypothesized that depression in these patients, although not purely endogenous, was not purely reactive either. He noted that depression in subjects affected by parkinsonism differed from endogenous depression—in which short-term memory is impaired—in that the patients maintained a good capacity to organize and transfer even recent information. On the other hand, Parkinsonians have some difficulty in completing correct sequences when several sentences must, for example, be repeated in an established order. This characteristic has given rise to the comparison of depressed Parkinsonians with subjects with prefrontal lobe damage [113]. It could hence be surmised that this type of memory operation depends on the frontal lobe, which, as is known [484], is also involved in control of emotional balance and the regulation of mood in functional interaction with limbic structures such as the anterior part of the cyngulus cortex and the amygdala. Dysfunctions of the nigro-striatal pathways [502] also involve the anterior and thalamic medial dorsal nuclei [297], and could interfere with the activities of the prefrontal cortex given the extensive connections of these thalamic relays with the premotor and prefrontal cortex [340]. Taylor notes that if an undamaged prefrontal region should prove to be essential for both emotional control and some short-term memory mechanisms, this would explain the observations of his study regarding the association of cognitive and affective elements.

At the current state of understanding, there is no real evidence as to the reactive or organic nature of depression in Parkinson's disease. Taylor's study probably sums up the situation in the statement that this sort of depression does not seem to be "purely" endogenous or reactive. Furthermore, it should not be forgotten that reactive elements could act to reinforce an endogenous component—especially after diagnosis of Parkinson's disease. Still within the hypothesis of an endogenous genesis of the depression, the fact that many patients with the neurological disease do not present depression remains to be explained.

PATHOGENESIS

It is known that the anatomo-pathological basis for Parkinson's disease consists in the degeneration of the compact region of the mesencephalic black substance containing the neurone cell bodies from which the nigro-striatal dopaminergic pathways derive [50]. But the disease also involves other groups of dopamine-producing cells located in the adjacent ventral tegmental area [310]. Thus, damage also appears to occur in the two main dopaminer-

gic systems originating in the mesencephalic tegment: the mesolimbic pathway, which innervates limbic structures such as the
accumbens nucleus, the hypothalamus, the amygdala, the mam-
millary corpii, the septal nuclei, etc. [84]; and the mesocortical
pathways, whose projections continue into the frontal, entorhi-
nal, and cyngulus cortical areas. A further system that should
also be taken into account is the hippocampus—fornix—mam-
milar corpi—anterior thalamic nucleus—limbic cortex (cyngulus), a pathway that is held to be essential for "recent memory
traces." The circumvention of the anterior areas of the cyngulus
(cortical areas 23, 24, 32) is the task of the prefrontal region
[676]. Damage to the mesocortical dopaminergic system could
hence also provide a partial explanation for Taylor's findings
[641].

Fibiger [202] notes that the mesolimbic and mesocortical
dopaminergic projections play an important role in certain mechanisms of reinforcement and compensation in animals, and this
could also be the case in humans. The so-called compensation
system is in fact located in a strip of tissue stretching from the
amygdaloid nuclei through the hypothalamus to the mesencephalic tegment [221]. Since an impaired ability to experience compensation or pleasure is characteristic of depression (anhedonia),
and since it has been shown that the mesolimbic and mesocortical dopaminergic pathways—which are involved in emotional behavior—degenerate in Parkinson's disease, Fibiger suggests that
damage to these systems may be directly linked to the high
incidence of depression in this pathology.

Indirect evidence for the importance of a reduced dopamine
level in certain types of depression is given by the analysis of the
action mechanism of some antidepressant drugs (nomifensine,
amineptine), which act mainly as dopaminergic agonists by
blocking the re-uptake of dopamine [584, 585].

According to one hypothesis, the tricyclic antidepressants
(TCAs) act in part by inducing a reduced sensitivity of the presynaptic dopaminergic receptors, which are responsible for the
negative feedback mechanism regulating the synthesis of dopamine. Dopamine may hence be involved in the effect of these
drugs and, indirectly, in the genesis of depression. It has also
been hypothesized that depression may be associated with an
increased sensitivity of the presynaptic receptors. In this case,
the therapeutic effect of the TCAs could be the result of an
adaptive reduction in their sensitivity to dopamine [604]. Fur-

thermore, the latency period before the TCAs become effective corresponds to the period necessary for the manifestation of the antidepressant effect, a fact lending support to the above-mentioned hypothesis [112]. Other authors reject this thesis, hypothesizing that the effectiveness of the TCAs is based on an increased sensitivity of the postsynaptic receptors. However, regardless of their mechanisms of action, chronic antidepressant treatments at least apparently alter the activity of the nigro-striatal systems in experimental animals [288]. Some investigators also report significant improvements in Parkinson's disease patients after administration of TCA [535]. Recent studies claim that repeated treatment with desipramine increases the release of dopaminergic neurones of both the mesolimbic and nigro-striatal systems [692]. In any case, the presence of motor retardation and bradyphrenia in both parkinsonism and depression suggests a common biological mechanism [647].

A shortage of dopamine cannot by itself explain depression. In this context, it is helpful to make a brief reference to the controversial role of L-dopa treatment. According to some authors [32, 709], L-dopa leads to an improvement in depression particularly in patients who are depressed and apathetic prior to treatment. Other authors do not agree [436], arguing that L-dopa actually provokes relapse or worsening of depression. Despite the absence of incontrovertible scientific evidence, our clinical experience suggests that the tendency of L-dopa is depressogenic rather than antidepressant [168].

Another possible link between Parkinson's disease and depression is suggested by evidence of an increased cholinergic activity in depression [233, 550]. Moreover, the intravenous administration of physiostygmine, an acetyl-cholinesterase inhibitor, has a depressive effect on mood [550].

Numerous antidepressants in use today have anticholinergic properties. However, many effective antidepressants have no significant anticholinergic properties [437]. It is hence unlikely that the cholinergic model provides a complete explanation of either depression or Parkinson's disease.

A further key to the understanding of the depression/parkinsonism link may be found in the serotonergic hypothesis of depression [660]. This hypothesis is based on various observations:

1) the reduced serotonin levels found in the brains of suicide victims and depressed patients who have died of natural causes [400, 56];

2) the reduction in the fluid 5-HIAA levels [18, 19] in depressed subjects;

3) the reduced ratio between blood concentrations of tryptophan and other amino acids in these subjects [467].

The depressive syndrome that is so frequent in Parkinson's disease could result from a reduction in the concentration not only of dopamine but also of serotonin. Mayeux et al. [441] found a significant reduction in fluid 5-HIAA concentration in parkinsonians. In the subgroup of patients in whom Parkinson's disease was associated with major depression, body fluid 5-HIAA levels were significantly lower than in other Parkinsonians. These authors hypothesized that alterations in not only dopamine, but also serotonin metabolism may predispose patients affected by Parkinson's disease to the development of a depressive syndrome. The reduced 5-HIAA levels found in the liquor of these patients may be due to a reduced synthesis of 5-HT in the median rafe. Hornykiewicz [294, 295] attributes the reduction in 5-HT to a process of regulation secondary to the depletion of DA. Indeed, it appears that serotonin is able to limit motor activity in animals by blocking the effect of the DA produced by the black matter. However, the role of 5-HT metabolism in motor manifestations has not yet been established: In these studies, its oral administration in depressed parkinsonians gave rise to a marked antidepressive effect. However, some Parkinsonians with low 5-HIAA levels were not depressed: 5-HT depletion probably only predisposes to depressive syndromes—and this only in patients with a severe shortage of 5-HT in the striatus, substantia nigra, and other regions such as the hypothalamus.

Lastly, a further potential connection between Parkinson's disease and depression involves the possible role of the extrapyramidal system in emotional regulation. MacLean [411] has recently stressed that while the role of the nigro-striatal system in motor function is well known, we have little insight into its relationship with behavior. The destruction of extensive portions of the striatal area in animals does not necessarily give rise to motor impairments. The role of these apparently silent zones is not known. On the other hand, it is known that intense emotions such as fear can somehow "activate" and improve the rigidity of Parkinson's patients.

CHAPTER 7
Mania in the Elderly

- In this chapter we observe that the origin of mania is more uncertain than depression, and that even the features of the disease are still being discussed. Nevertheless, despite some of the symptoms described, we can probably suspect its "secondary" nature when onset of the disease first occurs in old age. In fact, late-onset forms are less responsive to lithium, as was already mentioned in Chapter 2.

- Conversely, in the elderly, early-onset forms do not appear to possess specific features, not even with respect to symptoms, and patients generally respond well to lithium treatment. The relatively low prevalence of the disease and especially the difficult comparison of the few studies performed demonstrate that this disease must be further studied.

To date, epidemiological, etiological, clinico-diagnostic, and therapeutic studies on affective disturbances in the elderly have mainly focused on the more common depressive manifestations and not on mania. One reason certainly lies in the prevalence rate of mania, which is much lower than that of depression [529, 701, 292, 642].

The considerably disparity in the reported prevalences of opposite affective polarities was already noted by Roth [574] in his classic study undertaken more than 30 years ago. Roth found that while at least half of a study population of 464 elderly subjects with mental disturbances were suffering from an affective disturbance, only 0.6% of the patients presented clear symptoms of mania. An interesting finding of this study was that the onset of manic episodes occurred after the age of 60 years. Like Wertham [691] before him, Roth also suggested that onset of manic manifestations in old age increases the likelihood that the disorder will become chronic. He states: ". . . the fate of maniacs requires special attention, as it has been shown to be much worse . . . than that of patients suffering from other affective disturbances. Whether six months or two years after admission, most of these patients will still be in hospital or will have died" [574].

It should, of course, be remembered that these studies were undertaken prior to the introduction of treatment with neuroleptics and lithium; the course of the disease hence could not be modified by efficacious pharmacological treatment.

Over the years, some stimulating questions have been raised by studies on this disorder. One such issue that is still the object of considerable debate is whether this disorder should be classified among the bipolar or unipolar forms, and hence the need to identify specific characteristics of an etiological and psychopathological order [642, 531, 234]. Further controversial issues derive from the complex problems raised by the different approaches to the treatment of this disorder. The therapeutic indications of treatment with lithium, for example, is even today an important problem for all concerned.

EPIDEMIOLOGY

Even today little is known about the incidence of manic episodes and the relationship, if any, between incidence and age, sex, social status, and other conditions. Few studies on the elderly have tackled this problem. The prevailing opinion, however, is that though manic disturbances in the elderly are rare, their manifestations are severe [703, 328].

A large-scale in-depth study undertaken with the collaboration of investigators in many different nations [15] found that the mean age of onset of the disturbance in 393 patients diagnosed as affected by bipolar disorder was approximately 30 years, and that in 88% of the subjects the episodes first appeared before the age of 50 years. Support for a relatively early age of onset of this disorder was more recently given by Loranger and Levine [407], who, in a study using the diagnostic criteria of the DSM-III, found that the bipolar disorder most frequently manifests itself around the age of 20 years. Onset appeared never to occur before the age of 13 years and was rare after the age of 60 [407]. The same authors also affirm that that there is no significant correlation between age at onset of the bipolar symptomatology and other parameters such as sex, ethnic origin, or socioeconomic conditions. Since this study was conducted in the setting of a private psychiatric clinic, the presumably low incidence of patients of less privileged social origin may have somewhat affected the evaluation of parameters such as ethnic origin and socioeconomic status [466]. However, the findings of Loranger and Levine are in general agreement with those of other investigators [15, 703].

Yet other authors [72] suggest that the most common age of onset of the disease in the general population is between 35 and 50 years. In earlier studies, some authors reported a higher incidence of bipolar disturbances in older age groups: Silverman [614], for example, reported a maximum incidence, for both sexes, in the age range of 45 to 65 years, and authors such as Pederson et al. [508] reported the age range of maximum incidence to be as late as 50 to 70 years.

A persistently problematic area concerns the collection of precise data on the number of patients initially diagnosed as unipolar who later develop a bipolar disorder. In a study by Winokur and Morrison [704], only 4% of the patients diagnosed as affected by unipolar disorders later manifested bipolar signs. Perris [510] and Angst [14], both following the diagnostic criteria suggested by Perris for the diagnosis of unipolar depression (at least three consecutive episodes of major depression) reported respectively that 16% and 13% of unipolar patients later became bipolar.

The percentages cited are all derived from follow-up studies on hospitalized patients. Akiskal [8], who studied both in- and outpatients, reported substantially similar results: 18% of the subjects studied, whether neurotic or suffering from primary depression, later manifested bipolar symptoms. In another follow-up study conducted by Klerman in Boston [349] on a population composed exclusively of outpatients with diagnosis of neurotic depression, it was found that only 5% of these subjects became manic or hypomanic over the following 4 years.

Although this affirmation is open to more careful future evaluation, it may be considered that a percentage ranging from 5% to 18% of initially unipolar patients will later become bipolar. For further discussion, the reader is referred to the extensive review edited by Clayton [119].

With regard to the more specific question of the epidemiology of manic manifestations in the elderly, the authors who have considered this issue [119, 349, 531, 612, 642] have reported percentages of prevalence ranging from 6.5% to 18%.

In a recent retrospective study, Shulman and Post [612] identified 67 cases of bipolar disturbance with onset of the manic symptomatology at an age of over 60 years. This investigation concerned subjects admitted over a period of 10 years (1967–1976) to Bethlem Royal and Maudsley Hospital. The criteria of diagnosis adopted in this study were those proposed by Feighner et al. [198]. From the findings of this study, it appears that a depressive episode was the first pathological manifestation in 42 patients [62.7%], a manic episode was the initial sign in 15 cases [22.4%], 9 cases [13.4%] presenting with mixed symptoms, while in one case the episode was not identifiable [1.5%]. In the majority of subjects, the first manic episode appeared after the age of 40 years (mean age of onset 58.9 years), often after various depressive episodes and a considerable time after the onset of the initial pathology.

In another study conducted by Glasser and Rabins [234], only 42 elderly patients were hospitalized for manic episodes (on the basis of the criteria of the DSM-III) over a period of 5 years (1977–1982). The study of Glasser and Rabins hence also supports the conclusion that while mania in old age does exist, it cannot be considered a common problem if evaluated in the overall context of affective pathologies.

Both of the above-mentioned studies indicate that the mean age of onset of manic symptomatology is rather late: 58.9 years for Shulman and Post [612] and 51.1 years for Glasser and Rabins [234]. In a not inconsiderable percentage of subjects, manic symptoms develop only much later than the initial depressive episode: Glasser and Rabins found a mean latency of approximately 10 years—taking into account, however, the fact that for 22 subjects out of 42 this latency was about 15 years, while in 12 cases (one-fourth of the total) 25 years elapsed before emergence of the manic symptoms. Twelve patients in this same study were affected only by manic symptoms, and 6 manic patients [8%] in Shulman and Post's study were not affected later by clearly depressive episodes. It should be noted that this group of patients had manifested the first manic attack before the age of 40, while, on the contrary, those patients whose first attack was certainly depressive did not manifest manic symptoms before the age of 45 years.

The bipolar disorder is generally reported to be slightly more frequent in women than in men; Perris [510], in a review of various studies, affirms that when the disorder first appears at an early age and is identifiable as mania from the onset, the sex of the patient is more likely to be male, while if the disease first presents with depressive symptoms, the patient is more likely to be female.

A difference of sex with respect to age at onset of the disease was found in elderly subjects by Spicer et al. [628] in a study referring to the date of the first hospital admission. These authors found a maximum incidence of psychotic depression in an age range of from 60 to 65 years in men and 50 to 65 in women. These findings differ rather widely from those of Joyce [316], in another study that takes as the conventional date of onset that of the first hospital admission. The age of onset found in this study was very early (26 years) and was not different in the two sexes.

There are very few epidemiological studies specifically concerning sex-related differences in manic manifestations in the elderly. As mentioned above, an overall prevalence among women emerged in the two studies cited earlier [234, 612], the ratios cited being 4:3 in the study by Glasser and Rabins and the slightly higher 2.7:1 in that of Shulman and Post.

Further interesting data are reported in a retrospective study conducted in Scotland over the years 1969–1978 and using the criteria of the ICD-8 in the diagnosis occasioning the first admission [189]. These authors reveal a significant prevalence of women over men in depression and in affective psychoses; a prevalence of females was also found in the manic manifestations, although this was less pronounced. The female prevalence becomes even more pronounced after the onset of menopause (for all forms of dysthymia) reaching a peak between 50 and 54 years.

A large number of studies have found significant correlations between the bipolar disease and higher social class and wealth [279, 349, 514]. Moreover, this finding seems to have been confirmed in all races; only Helzer [282] found a greater representation of the association between bipolarism and high socioeconomic status among whites. As far as we are aware, there is no information in the available literature on the existence of socioeconomic differences among elderly patients affected by mania.

In conclusion, it may be said that any interpretation of the above-cited findings should take into account certain limitations, which may be summarized as follows:

1) The discrepancies between the various studies are often attributable to the different epidemiological parameters used.

2) Most of the studies, with only a few exceptions, report observations on rather small populations, particularly in the case of studies on mania.

3) There is no real uniformity in the criteria used for the diagnosis of mania. Comparative studies must hence consider populations with wide differences in terms of the subtypes of affective disorder represented.

The problems listed above are even more marked in the case of studies on bipolar and manic disorders in the elderly. It is to be hoped that future studies may take such considerations into account and hence give clearer and more definitive results.

ETIOLOGICAL CONSIDERATIONS

The most controversial of the etiological issues remains that of inheritability [4, 100, 306, 455, 531, 701]. Clearly, studies on the etiology of the senile forms treat both exogenous and psychological causes [291, 292, 529, 634]. We ourselves share the opinion of those authors [292, 278, 328] who consider this disturbance to have a mixed etiology and attribute—in general—greater importance to genetic factors in patients presenting early onset of the bipolar pathology. In this view, there is no clear hereditary predisposition in patients with late onset, in whom the cause is more probably an organic, and possibly cerebral, dysfunction.

As mentioned above, a considerable number of studies affirm the importance of hereditary factors in manic-depressive disorders. In a review published in 1969, Winokur et al. [703] attribute a determining role to these etiological factors, maintaining that the pathology is transmitted through a dominant gene bound to the X-chromosome. A similar hypothesis is held by Helzer and Winokur [282] and by Slater [621], although these authors believe that the inheritability of the disorder is linked to a dominant gene with incomplete penetration. The thesis of genetic transmission is also supported by Goetzl et al. [235] in their study of the families of 39 manic-depressive patients.

Winokur et al. [703] note that the formulation of a well-grounded etiological hypothesis would require research conducted on homogeneous groups of patients. With the present state of knowledge, they add, it is not clear whether or not manic-depressive psychoses are themselves a homogeneous category.

On the basis of these considerations, Dalen [137] studied a highly selected group of manic patients under the age of 41, establishing strict parameters for the formulation of separate subgroups for family history, electroencephalographic signs, perinatal disturbances, age at onset, and hereditary transmission. He concluded that a genetic origin of the disorder can be hypothesized only in a few cases, and that in most cases the cause should be sought rather in cerebral damage of a different sort. This being the case, the age at onset would in fact be considerably later.

A study by Hays [278] gives further support to these findings. In agreement with Dalen, Hays also distinguishes two groups, one in which hereditary factors are determinant (younger patients with family history of the manic-depressive disease) and one in which organic factors have overriding importance (patients with late onset and negative family history). Hays agrees that the two groups should be considered separately in research and recommends submitting patients to a more thorough clinical and diagnostic examination, particularly from an organic point of view [278]. Unfortunately, this study, like the others considered above in which small but significant differences are found between early-onset and late-onset subjects, the cut-off values for age at onset of the disease are rather low and close: 39 years in the group of patients with negative family history and 25 in those with positive family history. The only notable exception to this limitation is found in a study by Molinari et al. [466], in which it is affirmed that the first manic episode in the group with positive family history occurs at around the age of 48 years, while in the group with negative familiarity the mean age at onset is 62 years.

Glasser and Rabins [234], however, found no differences with regard to family history between elderly subjects affected by mania and elderly subjects affected by bipolar disorder. The presence of family history does not even distinguish between subjects aged over 60 and subjects aged under 60. Abrams and Taylor [4] are of the opinion that the group of manic patients with late onset are in fact affected by different pathological conditions of varying etiology, an important factor being early alcoholism. According to these authors, patients with late onset of the symptomatology appear to present a form that is less clinically severe than that found in patients with early onset. In view of the relative frequency of late-onset mania, these authors suggest the existence of a nosologically distinct pathology rather than simply a less severe form of bipolar disturbance.

Shulman and Post [612], who cite the study of Abrams and Taylor, feel that onset of mania in elderly subjects is a direct consequence of cerebral damage (for example, cranial traumas, vascular incidents, etc.). This might explain why the age at onset of manic symptoms may be very late, and why mania may appear much later than the depressive manifestations. It may, in fact, be the case that the bipolar disease tends to disappear with increasing age, and that any later recurrences represent a particular subgroup of patients [148]. Eagles and Whalley [189], in the study cited earlier on first hospital admissions for affective disturbances in Scotland (1969–1978), showed that biopsychosocial factors connected to aging which are thought to influence the onset of affective disorders are, in fact, more important in the determination of the onset of depression than in that of mania. This study seems to provide indirect evidence in support of the hypothesis that the etiology of mania is even less clear than that of depression. However, Eagles and Whalley suggest a comprehensive etiological model even for the genesis of mania [27], although this is less convincing than that offered for depression. In fact, loss events have been shown to be important triggering factors also in the case of mania [9, 355], and it is self-evident that mourning and loss events occur frequently in old age. From a psychodynamic point of view, it has been said that mania may represent a form of defence against loss events [348], a sort of denial of grief that is transformed into manic delusions of power.

Lastly, we should remember that increasing vulnerability to the disease with increasing age has been linked to the neurophysiological processes of senility. Many of the alterations occurring in old age affect cerebral neurophysiological function (circadian rhythms and body temperature regulations are just two examples), and the equilibrium of homeostatic regulation mechanisms is in general more precarious in the elderly. It may be hypothesized that these modifications may correlate in part with the qualitative and/or quantitative alterations of many cerebral neurotransmitters [447]. However, for the present we must limit ourselves to the presumption that these conditions have a negative, if aspecific, effect on the regulation of mood, whether in a depressive or manic direction.

SYMPTOMATOLOGICAL ASPECTS

Also in the DSM-III-R [3] there is no diagnostic category of unipolar mania, which is included in the list of bipolar disturbances.

The diagnosis of mania in the elderly subject is based on the same criteria as those used in the young patient, although, as we have seen, this view has been criticized by several authors, as some clinical manifestations of the form presenting in the elderly patient in fact appear to be dependent on age at onset. As suggested by Winokur et al [703], it might be more appropriate to use the term "symptomatic" or "secondary" mania in the case of elderly patients, as the clinical symptomatology is frequently linked to alterations of the CNS, with the result that some clinical features are peculiar to the elderly.

Apart from these considerations, the existence of secondary manic manifestations is now generally accepted. These secondary forms may be associated not only with CNS alterations, cancers, and epilepsy, but also with some medical diseases (infections, hemodialysis, vitamin B12 deficiency) and the use of certain drugs (corticosteroids and L-dopa) [356, 611].

Pitt [523] and Schatzberg et al. [591] found that symptoms such as confusion, paranoid traits, and emotional instability are often present in the elderly maniac. When patients are confused and disoriented, they may attempt to "mask" these difficulties by dissembling; here, it is advisable to perform differential diagnosis with other delirious forms and acute or chronic intoxications (e.g., alcohol abuse). There are, furthermore, many reports of mixed conditions in which the emotional instability typical of the elderly combines with attitudes of uncertainty, a consequence of the above described manifestations of space-time disorientation and loss of memory that are nearly always associated with aging. The flight of ideas typical of the manic patient are frequently slow in the elderly, and the patient's speech is often incoherent.

The mixed symptomatologies of the schizophreniform type, which have at times suggested the diagnosis of "schizomania," are generally less common in the elderly. It should be remembered that a paranoid attitude should usually be considered a reaction to the restrictions to which the patient is submitted rather than the manifestation of a primary abnormal response [529].

Lastly, it should be noted that feelings of hostility and suspicion seem to be particularly frequent in the elderly, while the typical manic symptomatology of early onset patients is characterized rather by expansive euphoria and incongruous expectations of wealth and power, with all their consequences on behavior.

PART TWO:
TREATMENT OF MOOD DISORDERS

Chapter 8

Pharmacological Treatment of Affective Disorders in the Elderly

- Drug therapy for mood disorders in the elderly is no different than that employed in younger patients. However, dosage must be carefully selected considering the pharmacodynamics and especially pharmacokinetics peculiar to the elderly: Drugs remain longer in the body, and consequently there is greater chance of toxicity and dangerous drug interaction. This last feature is very important since older persons are often affected with many diseases requiring the simultaneous use of several drugs. Nevertheless, pharmacotherapeutic results are satisfactory also in older patients, especially with the new antidepressants, which present fewer side effects, especially anticholinergic and cardiotoxic side effects.

- MAOIs could be useful in the elderly since MAOs increase constantly in the body over time. Yet the risk of dangerous hypertensive crises and relevant dietary restrictions make them only second- or third-choice drug. Conversely, electroconvulsive therapy (ECT)—apart from a few exceptions—appears to be an excellent indication for the depressed elderly, as we observe an immediate response (particularly important in those at high suicidal risk) and a lack of significant collateral effects.

- The introduction of new types of pharmacotherapy and the public disapproval have, however, considerably limited utilization of ECT. This has occurred frequently without proper scientific justification, defining electroconvulsive therapy as a means of social repression. In fact, in some countries, for example, in Italy after the Psychiatric Reform of 1978, its utilization was practically discontinued in clinics and hospitals.

Although the same drugs are used to treat depression in both young and old, prescriptions in the latter must take into account certain factors peculiar to the aging process. Besides the frequent concurrence of local pathologies that may interfere with normal pharmacokinetics, the elderly are generally more sensitive to drugs and present untoward side effects more frequently than do younger subjects [622]. However, there is no general agreement on the real extent of this phenomenon. According to Caranasos et al. [99], for example, undesirable side effects to pharmacological treatment occur twice as frequently in the elderly as in the young, while for Lippmann [393], individuals over the age of 75 are seven times more likely than the young to experience such effects. Learoyd [378] reported that 16% of 200 consecutive admissions to a psychogeriatric hospital unit were due to the side effects of psychotropic drugs.

PHARMACOKINETICS AND PHARMACODYNAMICS

The increased sensitivity to drugs and increased incidence of untoward effects are due to modifications of the pharmacokinetics and pharmacodynamics in the elderly. The physiological modifications normal to the process of aging include variations in the absorption, distribution, metabolism, and elimination of drugs. These are summarized in Table 11.

The most important changes in absorption occurring in aging are the modifications of gastric pH and blood flow. Stomach acidity generally rises, increasing the absorption of alkaline drugs and reducing that of acidic drugs. The passage of drugs absorbed through passive diffusion may be slowed by a reduction in cardiac output. The functioning of the mucous surfaces may also be reduced, hence influencing the absorption of drugs [135]. Antidepressants are generally weakly alkaline and thus rapidly absorbed under the slightly acidic [pH 6.6] conditions of the small intestine. It is held that under normal circumstances approximately one-half of the dosage of a given drug is effectively absorbed and enters into the circulation [232].

In older people, moreover, intestinal blood flow may be reduced by 40% to 50%, resulting in a further reduction of the availability of the drug [107]. The quantity of drug metabolized during the first passage may also be reduced in the elderly. Table 12, taken from Amsterdam et al. [12], shows the percentages of plasmatic bioavailability of some tricyclic antidepressants after the first liver passage. The width of the intervals reported is illustrative of the considerable variation between individuals.

Table 11. Pharmacokinetic consequences of age-related alterations.

Organ	Physiologic alteration	End-organ effect of drug	Effect on disposition
Kidney	⇓Renal blood flow;	⇓Glomerular filtration rate	⇓Drug clearance;
	⇓permeability; thickening of the basement membrane of Bowman's capsule		⇑Half-life; Altered tissue uptake
Liver	⇓Hepatic blood flow	⇓Rate and extent of delivery	⇑Bioavailability
	⇓metabolic capacity; altered hepatic tissue uptake		⇓Metabolic clearance* ⇑Half-life
Muscle	⇓Muscle mass;	⇑Absorption of lipophilic agents	Altered apparent distribution volume
	⇑Fat/lean mass ratio; Altered catabolism; ⇓Total body water		⇔Half-life
Gastro-int. tract	⇓Splanchnic blood flow	Altered drug ionization	⇓Fraction absorbed
	⇓Gastric motility; ⇓Secretory activity of gastric mucosa ⇑Gastric pH; atrophic changes in mucosal epithelium	⇓Transport efficiency	⇓Absorption rate; ⇑Peak time gastric pH
Heart & large arteries	⇓Cardiac output	⇓Ejection fraction	⇓Drug clearance;
	⇓Elastic tissue	⇓Permeability	⇑Half-life

*Depends on the extraction ratio, intrinsic clearance and whether clearance is blood flow limited for a given drug.
⇑increase; ⇓decrease; ⇔no change
Adapted from [135].

The next stage after absorption is distribution, which is also somewhat altered in the elderly subject [309]. With increasing age total body muscle mass and water content diminish, while adipose tissue increases (see Table 13) [491]. As a result, the antidepressants—which are liposoluble—are distributed in an increased volume, reducing the steady state levels.

There is a natural tendency in the elderly toward a reduction in albumin levels; the ratio between free and bound drugs is thus

Table 12. Plasmatic bioavailability of some tricyclic antidepresants after their first hepatic passage.

Drug	% of the dose orally administered available after first hepatic passage
Imipramine	29–77%
Nortriptyline	46–70%
Protriptyline	75–90%
Doxepin	13–45%

Adapted from [12]

Table 13. Age-related changes in fat/lean tissues ratio.

		At age 18	At age 55
Fat mass/body weight	Male	18%	36%
	Female	33%	48%

Adapted from [451].

generally increased. This phenomenon is thought to be responsible for the greater incidence of side effects in the elderly [393]. It is furthermore suggested that the binding affinity between drugs and plasmatic protein may be reduced [672], which may result in still higher levels of free drugs.

The elimination of drugs is also affected by aging; generally, drugs are eliminated through the kidneys after hepatic metabolism. However, it is known that renal excretion capacity is progressively reduced with increasing age. In particular, between the ages of 20 and 90 years glomerular filtration appears to undergo an approximately 35% reduction [500]. Reduced kidney function in the elderly may hence give rise to an accumulation of the drug, especially in the case of inappropriate dosage.

From the above it would appear that a pharmaceutical substance that is well tolerated in younger subjects may give much higher plasmatic levels and elimination times in elderly subjects, the result being a greater liability to side effects. Moreover, plasmatic levels may be further increased in the not uncommon eventuality that the elderly subject is taking other drugs that are able to displace the weakly bound antidepressants from the proteins.

Table 14. Substances that influence antidepressant plasmatic levels in the elderly

⇑Plasmatic levels	⇓Plasmatic Levels
Acetylsalicylic acid	Cigarette smoke
Chloropromazine	Barbiturates
Haloperidol	Steroids
Phluphenazine	
Metylphenidate	
Chloramphenico	

Adapted from [269].

Table 15. Steady-state levels of some antidepressants in young and old subjects on the assumption of identical doses (mg/kg).

Drug	Mean values in young	Mean values in elderly
Imipramine	32.3 ng/ml	83.3 ng/ml
Desipramine	21.2 ng/ml	57.2 ng/ml
Amitriptyline	81.7 ng/ml	138.7 ng/ml
Nortriptyline	122.8 ng/ml	122.8 ng/ml

Adapted from [486].

Even small dosages of common medicines such as aspirin may increase the proportion of free antidepressant and hence provoke sudden signs of toxicity. Tobacco and barbiturates, on the contrary, may cause a reduction in the plasma levels of the antidepressant by reducing the concentration of the enzymes responsible for its metabolization [269]. Table 14 shows some of the more common substances capable of interfering with the plasma levels of antidepressants in young and old subjects after administration of an identical dosage.

As can be seen in Table 15 (adapted from [486]), with the single exception of nortriptyline, most of the tricyclic antidepressants give higher blood and steady state levels in the elderly than in the young. Obviously, the plasmatic half-life of the antidepressants also normally increases with age. Table 16 shows the age-related differences in the half-life of some of these common drugs. It should be born in mind that as the time required for a given drug to reach steady state is 4 to 6 times its half-life [546], steady-state levels will be achieved proportionally later in the

Table 16. Half-life (hr) of some antidepressants in young and old subjects.

Drug	Young	Old
Imipranine	19	26
Amitriptyline	15	22
Desipramine	33	75
Maprotiline	30	32
Nortriptyline	27	40

Adapted from [581].

elderly subject. However, these are general tendencies only, and it must be remembered that blood concentrations may vary by as much as 100 times in subjects treated with identical oral doses [542].

The aging process also affects pharmacodynamics to varying extents according to the type of drug and the receptor sites involved. For example, while the cortical beta-adrenergic receptors do not appear to change with age, their function in other sites, such as the cerebellum and the corpus striatum, is reduced [76]. It has been suggested that the blood-brain barrier itself may undergo transformations in the elderly subject; such transformations have been implicated in the increased analgesic effect of morphine and pentazocine in the elderly [134].

CLASSIC TRICYCLICS AND NEW ANTIDEPRESSANTS

The first forebear of the tricyclics is imipramine, the first such drug to be used, in 1958, for its antidepressive effect. Many other derivates of the same type were later synthesized. The tetracyclics and other second-generation molecules were developed later and were introduced into clinical practice because many of them appeared to have fewer side effects than the tricyclics. The activity of the tricyclics, and of most antidepressants, seems to be linked to the fact that they are able to block the active process of re-uptake of the biogenous amines that carries these latter through the membrane and into the neurone. This mechanism of re-uptake is the principal means for the deactivation of the catecholamines and indolamines acting as neurotransmitters at the level of the CNS.

The blocking of the re-uptake process brings about an increased concentration of the amines available in the intersynaptic space for binding to the specific receptors in the post-synaptic neurone. To some extent this compensates for the monoamine deficiency considered to be the cause of the depressive disorder. Amines whose re-uptake is inhibited are prevalently noradrenaline, serotonin, and dopamine. Drugs such as imipramine inhibit re-uptake in both noradrenergic and serotonergic neurones. Other tricyclics belonging to the secondary amines (desipramine), and other drugs such as viloxazine act by blocking mainly noradrenaline re-uptake, while the tertiary amines (clomipramine, amitriptyline, doxepin, etc.) have an inhibitory effect prevalently on serotonin re-uptake. The former drugs appear mainly to determine a psychomotor activation, while the latter appear to have a prevalent effect of raising mood tone.

Hypotheses have been formulated according to which depression may be divided into the subtypes noradrenaline-dependent and serotonin-dependent depression, the former responding to drugs raising NA levels, the latter to those that raise SE levels.

The use of antidepressants that act prevalently on the re-uptake of dopamine (amineptine, nomifensine) has also provided support for the hypothesis that dopamine may also be involved in the pathogenesis of the depressive disorders. However, the therapeutic importance of the inhibition of its re-uptake still remains somewhat unclear, and may be at least partially undermined by the evidence that despite the great differences in the "power" of the various drugs to inhibit the re-uptake of the one or the other monoamines, there is no corresponding significant difference in their therapeutic efficacy [425]. Moreover, substances have now been synthesized that are active in the treatment of depression, but have no inhibitory effect on amine re-uptake.

More recently, attention has been focused on the postsynaptic receptor blocking potential of certain antidepressants, as this property may play an important role in the explanation of their action mechanism.

Postsynaptic alpha-adrenergic receptor blocking action seems to correlate with the sedative effect of the drug, while it has been hypothesized that the antidepressant effect of these drugs may result from their blocking effect on the serotonergic receptors [494]. Yet many antidepressants (e.g., nomifensine) have no blocking action on these receptors.

Although antihistaminic activity seems to be equally irrelevant from a clinical point of view, it may have a potentiating effect on the sedative action of the drug. The effect of the antidepressants as cholinergic receptor blocks seems to be linked mainly to their side effects rather than to their therapeutic effects.

The dopaminergic receptor blocking properties of, for example, clomipramine, amitriptyline, trimipramine, etc., may play an important role. Some neuroleptics that block these receptor sites, including sulpiride and thioridazine, in fact also present antidepressant properties. It may be said that, at the present state of knowledge, the primary effects of the antidepressants (i.e., their capacity to increase monoamine availability) do not appear to be linked clearly to the clinical activity of these drugs. The selective activity of the drug on a particular system (serotonergic, noradrenergic, or dopaminergic) also does not seem to be of fundamental importance.

In support of this, we should note the antidepressant effects of drugs that raise neurotransmitter concentrations (by blocking their re-uptake or inhibiting deamination), drugs that block transmission through their antagonism of postsynaptic receptors (trazodone), and other drugs that directly stimulate the postsynaptic receptor (solbutamol). In conclusion, it seems that the "primary" action of the various drugs is to stimulate long- or medium-term modifications or adjustments. In relation to this, various studies have clearly shown that at least 10–15 days of treatment must elapse before the establishment of an antidepressant action. It would thus seem that the administration of antidepressants must be subchronic in order to determine those modifications necessary for raising mood tone and improving depressive symptoms. Recent findings seem to indicate that the pathogenetic event determining a depressive state may be a "hypersensitivity" of the noradrenergic receptors [31]. According to this hypothesis, these receptors are no longer able to maintain a normal adjustment and are regulated at a higher level: A normal stimulus leads to an exaggerated response. Neurotransmitter turnover is then reduced as a physiological adjustment to the new situation. The effect of the antidepressants would hence be due to their desensitization of the noradrenergic receptors [637]. It is not yet known whether this action provides an explanation of the therapeutic effect of these drugs on the serotonergic receptors; it is only known that the modifications are adaptive and occur in subchronic treatment, several days of treatment generally being necessary prior to the manifestation of an antidepressive action. The mechanisms responsible for these effects, however, remain to be demonstrated. A further complication is given by the complex network of interactions between the various cerebral monoaminergic systems and the fact that CNS binding sites for the antidepressants have been discovered. This would seem to suggest the existence of endogenous binders such as those for the opioids. It is clear that many uncertainties remain at the present state of knowledge, and further studies will be necessary to throw more light on the problem of the pathogenesis of depression and the mechanisms underlying the therapeutic effects of the antidepressives.

SIDE EFFECTS

The side effects of the antidepressants are correlated to the blocking of specific receptor systems, as shown in Table 17. Particularly threatening adverse reactions in the elderly include orthostatic hypotension, sedation, cardiotoxicity, and anticholinergic effects.

Orthostatic Hypotension

This complication, resulting from alpha-adrenergic block, is a common side effect of many antidepressants, although its frequency and severity vary from drug to drug. Orthostatic hypoten-

Table 17. Receptorial cause of antidepressant side effects.

Anticholinergic	Anti-α1-adrenergic	Antihistamine H1	H2
Blurred Vision	Postural hypotension	Sedation	Mental confusion
Dry mouth	Dizziness	Drowsiness	
Memory disorders	Reflex tacycardia	Hypotension (?)	
Urinary retention		Weight gain (?)	
Constipation			
Attack or exacerbation			
of narrow angle glaucoma			
Speech blockage			
Decreased sweating			

From [157].

sion is a frequent cause of dizziness and falls in the elderly (with the possible consequence of serious fractures) [266]. Over 25% of geriatric patients present a difference of 20 mmHg or more on lying to standing tests [97]. Many clinical situations may explain the increased prevalence of orthostatic hypotension in the elderly, including cerebro- and cardiovascular diseases, electrolytic imbalances, diabetes, peripheral neuropathies, varicose veins, and hydropathic orthostatic hypotension. To these must be added various iatrogenic causes; besides the antidepressants and the MAO inhibitors, other drugs such as diuretics, antihypertensives, and phenotiazines may also create problems of orthostatic hypotension.

The following may be of help for an efficacious management of the possible consequences of an orthostatic hypotension resulting from the administration of antidepressants [266]:

1) the patients should be carefully evaluated for the presence of clinical conditions that may predispose them to orthostasis;

2) nonpsychotropic drugs that may induce orthostatic hypotension should be reduced prior to commencing treatment with antidepressants;

3) treatment with antidepressants should always be initiated at very low dosages, and blood pressure variations on lying and standing should be monitored, especially during the first weeks of treatment;

4) the patient should be told not to get up abruptly from bed or from a chair.

Sedation

This side effect also varies according to the antidepressant used. During the first few days of treatment, the sedative effect may be useful in counteracting the insomnia frequently associated with depression. However, it should be remembered that, given the prolonged effect of the antidepressants in elderly subjects, an unwanted drowsiness may be present on the following day. Furthermore, the sedative side effect may become much less desirable when the patient's depressive state has begun to improve. For these reasons, the less sedative drugs should generally be preferred in the elderly. When necessary, a short half-life benzodiazepine may be associated in the initial stages of treatment.

Cardiotoxicity

The influence of the antidepressants on cardiac function has aroused considerable interest; in the elderly, in particular, any cardiovascular problems, of whatever order, may be aggravated by the administration of these drugs. Although much research has been done in this area, the available data do not provide clear and detailed conclusions. Some studies have associated the tricyclic antidepressants with cardiac arrhythmias and sudden death, whilst others have failed to establish the existence of a convincing cause-effect relationship [311]. In any case, subjects under treatment with antidepressants display cardiographic evidence of lengthening of the PR, QRS, and QT intervals with aspecific alterations of the T-wave [318]. More severe alterations in conduction, including branch block and atrioventricular block, appear to occur at high plasma concentrations of the drug [581]. Because of this effect—which is similar to that of the antidepressants—the tricyclics are contraindicated in subjects with atrial or ventricular arrhythmias and under treatment with quinidine or procainamide. However, at low plasmatic concentrations, the antidepressants generally produce tachycardia and a quinidine-like stabilizing effect on any cardiac alterations. For example, imipramine has a well demonstrated antiarrhythmic effect [663] ar. may be considered a class 1 antiarrhythmic drug. The antidepressants have also been associated with acute coronary failure and acute myocardial infarction, although the relationships between the dosage of the drug, its plasmatic concentration, and cardiotoxic effects have yet to be demonstrated. In conclusion, when treating elderly patients with cardiac decompensation, arrhythmias, and stimulus conduction problems or previous myocardial infarction, antidepressants should be administered with extreme caution and the patient's cardiovascular conditions should be monitored by a specialist. Table 18 summarizes the cardiac effects of some antidepressants.

Anticholinergic Effects

To varying extents, all the antidepressants produce anticholinergic effects—the tertiary amines, especially amitriptyline and doxepin, are powerful anticholinergics, while the secondary amines have a smaller anticholinergic effect. Overall, the new antidepressants are characterized by rather weak anticholinergic ef-

Table 18. Cardiovascular effects of antidepressant compounds.

Class/agent	Effect
Trycyclics & amoxapine	Blood pressure elevation and tachycardia (early); orthostatic hypotension, possibly symtomatic; increased PR, QRS and QT intervals; antiarrhythmic effect; decreased myocardial contractility
Trazodone	Hypotension, possibly symptomatic orthostasis; possibly arrhythmogenic
Maprotiline	Hypotension, possibly symptomatic orthostasis; tachycardia; antiarrhythmic effect?
Bupropion	Tachycardia
MAO inhibitors	Hypotension, possibly symptomatic orthostasis; increase in coronary artery blood flow; hypertensive crisis in conjunction with tyramine-containing foods, sympathomimetic amines, stimulants and tricyclics
Lithium salts	Hypertensive effect due to sodium retention; possible arrhythmias

Adapted from [266].

fects. Aside from these considerations, it should be remembered that the onset of anticholinergic side effects probably depends on individual sensitivity as well as on the drug dosage and plasmatic concentration. Peripheral anticholinergic effects may frequently provide sufficient reason for suspending treatment and create considerable discomfort in the elderly patient. Even a symptom that is quite mild and generally well tolerated in a younger subject, such as dryness of the mouth and throat, may be a serious problem for the elderly subject. For example, false teeth that are normally well tolerated may be rejected during treatment with the tricyclics; xerostomia may also contribute to the development of candidiosis and parotitis [581]. In the attempt to reduce the discomfort caused by the dryness, the patient may even eat less (aggravating the state of undernutrition frequently associated with depression), or drink large quantities of water (bringing a risk of electrolytic imbalance). Constipation, a frequent problem in the elderly, may also be a common anticholinergic side effect of the antidepressants. This problem may lead to poor compliance with the treatment or refusal to take the drug. The habitual use of laxatives should always be discouraged in elderly subjects. In predisposed subjects, a paralytic ileus and megacolon may appear [269]. The anticholinergic effects of the antidepressants may also include bladder problems and urine retention, effects that are more serious in men affected by prostate hypertrophy. In severe cases, urine retention may predispose the patient to infections, possibly involving the kidneys as well as the bladder. Acute angle glaucoma is more frequently present in the elderly than in younger subjects because of concomitant cataract; this may be triggered or aggravated by the midriatic anticholinergic effects of the antidepressants. Lastly, it should be remembered that the elderly are particularly susceptible to central anticholinergic syndrome, which is normally characterized by confusion, disorientation, anxiety and restlessness. In more severe cases, frankly psychotic aspects may be present, including paranoid delusions, visual hallucination, and aggressive behavior. In extreme cases, the outcome may even be stupor and coma. If not correctly identified, the syndrome may be confused with a psychotic or demential episode and be treated with neuroleptics—the anticholinergic effects of which may aggravate the situation.

In such cases, the only measure to take in the elderly is suspension of the antidepressants and any other drugs with possible anticholinergic side effects (for example anti-Parkinsonian drugs).

Disturbances of recent memory have also been associated with pharmacological antidepressant treatment, although the presence of these disorders is commonly associated with the process of aging. However, it is possible that the anticholinergic effects of the drugs may be implicated in these recall problems.

The classic tricyclics lower the epileptogenic threshold, and this effect is not completely absent even in the new antidepressants, especially mianserin [173]. As a consequence, all subjects with history of epilepsy or focal neurological lesions should be submitted to careful neurological examination prior to the establishment of antidepressant treatment. In the case of epileptic episodes treatment should be suspended.

DOSAGE AND CHOICE OF ANTIDEPRESSANT

In view of the various considerations described above, considerable care should be taken in the pharmacological treatment of the elderly depressed patient. Heart, liver, and kidney function should be monitored, and the dosage and schedule of administration carefully checked. (Because of the particularity of pharmacokinetics in the elderly subject, the daily dose should be divided into at least two separate administrations.) The treatment should always be initiated at very low dosages and then be maintained at the lowest possible efficacious level. Clinical response should be obtained within about 3 weeks, and improvement in the sleep/wake rhythm should usually be apparent before this. The patient should always be informed about the length of time that may be expected to elapse prior to improvement. If the drug has produced neither significant improvements nor appreciable side effects after 2 weeks of treatment, the dosage can be gradually increased. If there is no clinical response after 1 month of treatment, the patient should be switched to another antidepressant.

The most frequent cause of absence of positive clinical effect—especially in the elderly—is underdosage, resulting from the doctor's reluctance to increase the dose (a problem frequently exacerbated by the patient's often undergoing treatment with several drugs) or the poor compliance typical of patients in this age range [159].

For many antidepressants, there is an approximate correlation between the plasmatic levels of the drug and its clinical efficacy. It has been observed that the antidepressants have a maximum efficacy within a certain dosage range (generally from 150 to 220 ng/ml), and that they are not more effective above this level. In this context, the most concordant results relate to nortriptyline, the therapeutic window of which appears to be located between 50 and 140 ng/ml, its clinical efficacy declining at higher or lower levels [351]. Yet the clinical usefulness of assay of plasmatic levels of the antidepressants remains controversial: Most studies have failed to establish a significant correlation between plasmatic levels, clinical response, and onset of side effects [266]. While awaiting conclusive results from further research into this important area, it should not be forgotten that the assay of plasmatic levels is in any case an excellent test of the patient's compliance. Table 19 shows the therapeutic range of some antidepressants, while Table 20 summarizes the dosages and main characteristics of some currently available antidepressants. At present, there is no reliable demonstration of the superiority of one drug over others. The choice of drug to be prescribed is hence based even today on its clinical profile and side effects as well as

Table 19. Therapeutic range of some antidepressant at steady-state conditions.

Nortriptyline	50–140 ng/ml
Amitriptyline	160–240 ng/ml
Imipramine	225 ng/ml
Desipramine	225 ng/ml
Doxepin	30–150 ng/ml
Protriptyline	70–250 ng/m

20. Mechanism of action, mean dosage, and side effects of widely used typical and .cal antidepressants.

n	Mechanism of			Dosage for adult (mg/die)	Dosage for elderly (mg/die)	Response latency	Side effects				
	NE	5-HT	DA				Sd	H	C	A	Sz
al											
riptyline	+	++	–	50–200	30–100	2–4	+++	++	+++	+++	+
iptyline	++	+	–	50–150	25– 75	2–4	+	+	+	++	+
ramine	++	++	–	50–200	30–100	2–4	+	++	++	++	+
ramine	+++	+	–	50–200	30–125	2–4	+	++	++	++	+
ipramine	+	+++	–	50–200	30–100	2–4	+	++	++	++	+
iepin	+++	+	+	75–225	75–150	2–3	++	++	+	++	+
cal											
serin	+++	–	–	60–120	30– 80	1–2	+++	+	–	+	+
azine	+++	–	–	150–600	150–300	1–2	+	–	–	+	+
otiline	+++	–	–	75–200	50–125	2–3	+++	+	+	++	+
eptine	–	–	+++	100–400	100–200	1–2	–	–	–	+	+
done	–	+++	–	100–400	75–300	1–3	++	+	–	+	–

ffects: Sd(Sedation), H(ypotension), C(ardiotoxicity), A(anticholinergic), Sz(Seizures). [159].

on the doctor's experience with each type of drug. The choice of the compound should, moreover, also be based on the personal and family history of the patient. If a subject (or family member) has been successfully treated with a given drug in the past, the chances of a favorable response to that drug are increased [206].

SECONDARY AMINES

According to Salzman [581], the secondary amines are more indicated than the tertiary in the treatment of elderly subjects, their metabolism being simpler and their side effects milder. The secondary amines include a number of substances, but here we limit ourselves to those suitable for use in the elderly: desipramine, nortriptyline, maprotiline, and amoxapine.

Desipramine

Although there are almost no controlled studies into the action of this drug in elderly depressed subjects [136], desipramine may be indicated by reason of its rather mild anticholinergic side effects and the fact that it induces only mild sedation and hypotension. However, its strong disinhibitory effect may provoke or aggravate situations of restlessness.

Nortriptyline

Like desipramine, nortriptyline is less sedative and less anticholinergic than the tertiary amines. Furthermore, its side effects in the production of hypotension are both less severe and less frequent than those of other tricyclics. Although its use in elderly subjects has been extensively studied [135], few of the studies undertaken may be considered methodologically correct [141]. It is now known that nortriptyline is the only antidepressant that has a precise "therapeutic window" that is achieved at lower doses in the elderly than in younger subjects [141].

Maprotiline

Although this drug may be classified among the new tetracyclic antidepressants, maprotiline is a secondary amine with a clinical profile similar to that of nortriptyline; its side effects are on the whole somewhat less intense. At high dosages, convulsive episodes have been observed with some frequency [581]. Although widely used, there is little information about the results of this drug in elderly populations.

Amoxapine

Amoxapine is a derivate of the neuroleptic loxapine and thus interferes with dopaminergic transmission, giving rise to extra-pyramidal symptoms. Since the elderly are particularly suscepti-ble to dopaminergic block, given the natural, age-related deterio-ration of dopaminergic neurotransmission, amoxapine is not indicated for use in elderly subjects. At high doses it is frequently associated with epilepsy [581] and equally frequently with dis-orders in the sexual sphere [161].

TERTIARY AMINES

Although this category includes several effective antidepressants such as imipramine, amitriptyline, and doxepin, the tertiary amines should be administered with extreme caution in the el-derly patient as many may give rise to severe side effects.

Amitriptyline

Although once commonly used in the elderly because its strong sedative powers, amitriptyline should no longer be prescribed in this age group given its marked anticholinergic and hypotensive side effects. It also appears that amitriptyline may be frequently associated with central anticholinergic syndromes [581]. Its use should be limited to cases that may benefit even at very low doses (with the consequent risk of an ineffective underdose!) and those in which careful monitoring of plasmatic levels is feasible.

Doxepin

Doxepin was once regarded as a suitable drug for use in elderly patients [13], but its strong anticholinergic side effects as well as its marked sedative properties seem to be contraindications. In reality, much of the published research into the use of this drug is impossible to interpret because of methodological inconsisten-cies [228]. Its clinical profile appears to be similar to that of amitriptyline.

Imipramine

The anticholinergic effects of this drug are less marked than those of amitriptyline, but its effect in inducing orthostatic hypotension appears to be equally strong. Although it has been used successfully in controlled trials in elderly patients [317], imipramine is not a readily manageable drug [228].

Trimipramine

This is a highly sedative drug with anticholinergic side effects rather similar to those of amitriptyline and doxepin [581]. Like doxepin, it is a strong H_2 histamine receptor blocker, and may hence be indicated in patients with ulcer [419]. As trimipramine has a rather weak effect on noradrenaline uptake, its action is little antagonized by antihypertensive drugs such as guanethidine [581].

NEW ANTIDEPRESSANTS

As has already been said, attempts have recently been made to produce new molecules having the therapeutic effects of the tricyclics without their adverse side effects. Moreover, many of the new substances were designed to produce a more immediate clinical response (see Table 20). At least four of the new antidepressants appear to be of interest and are adequately manageable in elderly subjects. These are viloxazine, trazodone, amineptine, and mianserin [417]. Besides these, molecules such as S-adenosylmethionine and alprazolam, which belong to other pharmacological classes, are also worthy of mention.

Viloxazine

This drug, which has a bicyclic structure, inhibits the uptake of noradrenaline and potentiates noradrenergic activity. Although various trials have been conducted against placebo and tricyclic antidepressants, the therapeutic power of this drug is not yet clear [163]. This is due, in part, to differences in the dosages and populations used, which make it difficult to compare the findings of the various research projects. Viloxazine proved more effective than placebo in at least two studies on depressed elderly subjects [152, 671]. In both cases, it was reasonably manageable, giving virtually no anticholinergic or cardiovascular side effects, but inducing headache and nausea of probable central origin in some subjects. Unlike many antidepressants, viloxazine seems to stimulate libido in a manner not attributable to the improvement in the depressive situation [158, 163].

Trazodone

The chemical structure of this substance is dissimilar from that of other antidepressants, and its action at the level of the central nervous system is also particular: It blocks serotonin re-uptake but also acts on the α-2 noradrenergic presynaptic receptor, increasing turnover and release of noradrenaline. In elderly subjects, it has been shown to have a good antidepressant action accompanied by a significant anxiolytic effect [227]. The most common side effects are drowsiness and dizziness [229], while—with the exception of dryness of the mouth—anticholinergic effects are virtually absent. In some cases trazodone has been associated with cardiac arrhythmia [581] and, in men, with priapism [156]. As it may cause gastric irritation, the patient should be advised to take it after meals.

Amineptine

This is a tricyclic molecule that differs widely from the classic tricyclics by reason of its long chain ending in an acid radical. Amineptine acts on dopamine uptake with a psychostimulant effect that is considered inferior only to that of the MAO inhibitors [404]. Blind trials against placebo and other antidepressants have proved the efficacy of this drug [149, 499] and have shown its considerable rapidity of action in the absence of significant anticholinergic side effects. Trials in elderly subjects [139, 217] have confirmed the usefulness of amineptine in this age group. Nevertheless, it does frequently provoke anxiety, especially in the first 2 weeks of treatment [149]. Cases of cholostatic hepatitis have been reported during treatment with amineptine [45].

Mianserin

A drug of tetracyclic structure, mianserin has little effect on the re-uptake of monoamines; it appears instead to increase the intrasynaptic availability of noradrenaline by blocking the α-2 presynaptic receptors that control the release of noradrenaline through a negative feedback mechanism. Mianserin has also been shown to be effective in comparative trials against classic tricyclics such as amitriptyline, imipramine, and clomipramine [73]. It has virtually no anticholinergic effects and appears to be well tolerated even in cardiopathic subjects [76]. Mianserin therapy in elderly patients has been shown to cause less orthostatic hypotension than imipramine but more than nortriptyline [469]. In some cases episodes of epilepsy and hematic dyscrasia have been reported [57], so that patients receiving mianserin must be carefully monitored. Mianserin has proved little toxic even in cases of overdose. It has a marked anxiolytic effect [73].

S-adenosylmethionine (SAM)

This molecule increases noradrenaline and serotonin turnover and increases the sensitivity of the beta-adrenergic receptors through phospholipid methylation [142]. The antidepressant effects of SAM have been demonstrated in various controlled trials against classic tricyclics [458] and placebo [143]. It has virtually no side effects, apart from a possible induction of restlessness and mania [392]. SAM has proved to be efficacious and well tolerated even in elderly patients [144]. Moreover, its use also seems to be indicated in subjects affected by minor depression [170].

Alprazolam

This drug, a member of the benzodiazepine family, seems to have given an encouraging antidepressant effect in various trials [456, 544, 577]. However, it is known that many depressed patients show signs of improvement after alleviation of anxiety. According to Bridges [76], a primary antidepressant effect of the drug has still to be convincingly demonstrated.

L-tryptophan

This natural amino acid did not prove superior to placebo in a trial in elderly patients [129]. However, it may potentiate the action of tricyclics and MAO inhibitors [76]. As it is a serotonin precursor, it is reasonable to suspect that L-tryptophan may increase the activity of this amine when the cause of the depression is identified in a reduced availability of tryptophan.

THE MONOAMINOXIDASE INHIBITORS (MAOIs)

The MAO inhibitors work through an inhibition of the mitochondrial monoamine oxidase resulting in an increase in the intraneural amine concentration and their "seepage" into the intersynaptic space. This appears to produce an increase in the quantity of transmitters for the various receptor sites. Thus, their antidepressant action appears to some extent to be similar to the re-uptake block provoked by the tricyclics. The deaminating action of the MAOIs is the main metabolic pathway for the degradation of the biogenous amines. At present, two distinct types of MAO are known, MAO-A and MAO-B. The former have a prevalent action of noradrenaline and serotonin deamination, while the latter act on benzilamine and phenylenthiamine. Tyramine and triptamine may act as substrates for both types of MAO. The hydrazinic and nonhydrazinic derivatives used in the treatment of depression seem to block both A and B types nonselectively. The MAO inhibitors bind irreversibly to the enzyme, and monoamine oxidase must be "newly" synthesized in order to "return" to normal activity.

With regard to the mechanisms underlying the therapeutic effect of these drugs, it is not known whether this is linked directly to the increase in monoamine concentration or—more probably—to a series of adaptive modifications only triggered by the primary action of increasing the concentration of the neurotransmitters, as hypothesized for the tricyclics. The primary effects of the drugs are in fact immediate, while even with the MAO inhibitors a period of 10–15 days of treatment must elapse prior to the establishment of the therapeutic effect.

For many years, the use of the MAO inhibitors in psychiatric practice has been somewhat limited, in part because various controlled studies have shown that their therapeutic action is

Table 21. Dietary restrictions for patients taking monoamine oxidase inhibitors: Foods to avoid one day before and two weeks after taking drugs.

Danger of rise in blood pressure		
*Minimal Danger	**Moderate Danger	***Very Dangerous

Foods
***	All cheese
***	All foods containing cheese, e.g., pizza, fondue, many Italian dishes, salad dressings
Safe	Fresh cottage cheese, cream cheese, yogurt in moderate amounts
**	Sour cream
**	All fermented or aged foods, especially aged meats or aged fish, e.g., aged corned beef, salami, fermented sausage (peperoni, summer sausage), pickled herring
**	Liver (chicken, beef, or pork liver)
***	Broad bean pods (English bean pods, Chinese pea pods)
**	Meat extracts or yeast extract, e.g., Bovril or Marmite
Safe	Baked products raised with yeast, e.g., bread
Safe	Yeast
**	Spoiled or dried fruit, e.g., spoiled bananas, figs, raisins
Safe	Fresh fruits, except pineapple and avocados
*	Chocolate
*	Anchovies
*	Caviar
*	Coffee
*	Cola
*	Sauerkraut
*	Mushrooms
*	Beets
*	Rhubarb
*	Curry powder
*	Junket
*	Worcestershire sauce
*	Soy sauce
*	Licorice
*	Snails

Drinks
**	Red wine, sherry, vermouth, cognac
**	Beer and ale
Safe	Other alcoholic drinks, e.g., gin, wodka, whiskey, in true moderation

Drugs
***	Cold medications
***	Nasal decogestants, sinus medicine
***	Asthma inhalants
Safe	Pure steroids asthma inhalants, e.g., beclomethasone dipropional
**	Allergy and hay fever medications

Safe Pure antihistamines
***   Meperidine
***   Amphetamines
**   Antiappetite (diet) medicine
      Sympathomimetic amines
**   Direct-acting e.g., epinephrine, isoproterenol, methoxamine, norepi-
      nephrine
***   Indirect-acting e.g., amphetamines, methylphenidate, phenylpropa-
      nolamine, ephedrine, cyclopentamine, pseudoephedrine, tyramine
***   Direct- and indirect-acting e.g., metaraminol, phenylephrine
**   Local anesthetics with epinephrine
Safe Local anasthetics without epinephrine, e.g., mepivicaine
**   Levodopa for parkinsonism
**   Dopamine
Safe Diabetics on insulin may have increased hypoglycemia requiring a
      decreased dose of insulin, but insulin is otherwise safe
Safe Patients on hypotensive agents for high blood pressure may have in-
      creased hypotension requiring a decrease in their use of hypotensive
      agent, which otherwise is safe

Adapted from [312].

equal or inferior to that of the tricyclics; and in part because they
have been shown to give rise to a series of side effects, such as a
certain anticholinergic effect, orthostatic hypotension, feelings of
mental tension, and tremor. But the side effect that arouses most
concern is the possibility of hypertensive crisis as a consequence
of interaction with substances found naturally in foods, such as
tyramine, tryptophans, and tyrosine, found in fermented cheeses,
alcohol, and other foods. Alimentary tyramine is normally deacti-
vated by gastrointestinal and hepatic monoamine oxidase; however, when this process is inhibited by the MAO inhibitors, the
result may be palpitation, intense headache, and hypertensive
crisis. Because of their fragile atherosclerotic vessel walls, the
elderly are at high risk for an infarctual episode during such
crises. Emergency treatment includes intravenous injection of
phentolamine, which is a strong alpha-adrenergic blocker, or in-
tramuscular injection of cloropromazine, which is also an alpha-
adrenergic blocker [312]. Table 21 provides a list of the substances that should be avoided or consumed with extreme caution
during treatment with the MAO inhibitors. Theoretically, the
MAO inhibitors might be considered particularly suitable for use
in elderly patients by reason of their relatively mild anticholinergic side effects and absence of cardiotoxicity, and, above all, because monoamine oxidase increases with increasing age [246].

Yet the MAO inhibitors are not generally the preferred treatment, and their use is proposed only after the failure of trials with tricyclics and new antidepressants. They have been held to be effective in the treatment of atypical depression [54], which is mainly characterized by a strong anxiety, though it is not yet clear why the other antidepressants should not be equally efficacious in such cases [76]. The MAO inhibitors may also be indicated in the treatment of depression associated with dementia [21], although the MAO inhibitors, like the tricyclics, may aggravate the loss of memory and confusion typical of dementia. While the side effects of the MAO inhibitors are slight, they should be prescribed only at very low doses and in subjects with mild dementia. Neither the MAO inhibitors nor the tricyclics should be prescribed in the case of severe dementia. As well as exacerbating the cognitive symptoms of dementia, the stimulating effect of the MAO inhibitors may give rise to restlessness, agitation, insomnia, and even paranoia [581].

In conclusion, as long as certain precautionary measures are carefully observed, the MAO inhibitors may be effectively administered to elderly patients who have shown no response to other antidepressants. The patients should be given precise instructions and a list of foods and substances to be avoided, such as that shown in Table 21. The drugs that may be used are phenelzine, isocarboxazid, and tranylcypromine. There is no evidence for the superiority of any of these over the others, although phenelzine is certainly the most commonly prescribed MAO inhibitor, tranylcypromine the most stimulating, and isocarboxazid the one with the mildest side effects.

With the MAO inhibitors—as with the other antidepressants—the dosage should be gradually adjusted upwards from a very low starting point. With phenelzine, the starting dose should be 10 mg/die, the final dose lying between 20 and 60 mg/die. Isocarboxazid and tranylcypromine require smaller doses, their therapeutic range being from 10 to 30 mg/die. To reduce the possibility of insomnia, the last dose of the drug should be taken before 4 p.m.. Blood pressure must be monitored carefully for at least 1 month after beginning the treatment, as pressure variations tend to appear rather late [312].

THE STIMULANTS

Stimulants such as methylphenidate and dextroamphetamine are not generally used in the treatment of depression because the brief duration of the stimulating effect, their cardiotoxic side effects, the possibility of depressive "rebound," and the frequency of the side effects of anorexia and insomnia. Furthermore, they may rapidly induce tolerance and sometimes dependence [306]. They have recently been suggested for use in association with tricyclic treatments [347] and as a predictive test for response to antidepressants [408]. Methylphenidate, in particular, has been used successfully in the short-term treatment of elderly subjects displaying intolerance to more traditional treatments [324, 545]. In general, treatment with methylphenidate may be indicated in subjects characterized by extreme apathy, withdrawal, refusal to collaborate in rehabilitation and clear resignation to death. However, it is important to note that the stimulants have no appreciable effect in melancholic major depression [581]. Methylphenidate commonly provokes tachycardia and a slight increase in blood pressure.

LITHIUM

Much research has been done into the mechanisms underlying the therapeutic activity of lithium, which still remains a mystery. It is presumed that lithium has a stabilizing or regulating effect on neurotransmission and on the receptor systems [175]. A large number of studies have shown the therapeutic efficacy of lithium and its superiority over placebo in the treatment of mania, in which it is the preferred drug. Other elective indications of lithium are in the treatment of hypomania and prevention of bipolar disorders. However, while the clinical efficacy of lithium in the depressive stages of a bipolar disorder has been clinically demonstrated [266], the results of studies concerning its action in relapse of unipolar depression are less satisfactory. Various investigators [599] have suggested that lithium may be used in the treatment of depression, either alone or in association with a tricyclic: Lithium appears to sensitize the postsynaptic adrenergic receptor and hence increase the antidepressant effect of the tricyclics. In any case, the antidepressant effect of lithium is still controversial, and its use on its own in the treatment of unipolar depression is not advisable.

Certain modifications of the pharmacokinetics of lithium in the elderly should be borne in mind. While its rapid absorption remains unchanged, its distribution is significantly altered. Lithium is water-soluble, and since the total water content of the body diminishes with increasing age (especially in women), the volume of distribution of lithium is proportionally reduced in the elderly. As a consequence, concentrations are higher at a given dose than in younger subjects. Lithium does not bind to the plasmatic proteins or undergo hepatic metabolism; it competes with sodium in the proximal renal tubule, so that any interference with the elimination of sodium inevitably compromises the excretion of lithium. It is known that renal function diminishes in advanced age, and that physical diseases, dehydration, and drug consumption may lead to further deterioration. The result is generally a reduced clearance of lithium, with a doubling of its half-life to about 40 hours as against the 18–20 hours generally found in young subjects.

Lithium, usually used in a carbonate form, should be administered with great care as the therapeutic dose is very close to the toxic level. Careful monitoring of blood concentration is essential. In general, the therapeutic range is considered to be from 0.5 to 1.2 mEq/l, especially if the treatment is prescribed for mania, while a safer range of 0.4 to 0.8 mEq/l is considered more appropriate in preventive treatment [76]. Since the commercially available preparation is generally of 300 mg doses, it may be a good idea to start the treatment with a halved tablet and increase the dosage gradually (every 4 to 5 days). At each increase, lithium blood levels should be assayed about 12 hours after the last dose. Obviously, the optimum dosage should be established on the basis of blood concentrations.

As has been mentioned elsewhere in this volume, many elderly subjects experience a maniacal episode for the first time; some of these subjects may even be over the age of 80. However, most patients are continuing a treatment with lithium that was begun before the age of 65 [266]. In all cases, the cure must be begun or continued with careful monitoring of the patient's physical and mental conditions and frequent blood tests (hemochrome, glycemia, uremia, creatinine-emia, electrolytic, and thyroid hormone levels [T3, T4, and TSH], urine analysis, creatinine clearance tests and electrocardiogram). In elderly subjects, lithium-related

Table 22. Side effects of lithium.

	Serum Levels (mEq/L)	Manifestations
Early	Rising rapidly	Gastrointestinal symptoms
Maintenance	Stable at 0.6–1.2	Tremor, polyuria (from nephrogenic diabetes insipidus), hypotyroidism
Toxicity	>1.5	Disorders of consciousness, neuromuscolar irritability

From [175].

side effects may appear at lower plasmatic levels than in younger subjects. However, the adverse effects are similar in both age groups. In most cases, treatment with lithium is well tolerated in the elderly, and serious toxicity problems normally arise only in very old subjects or patients with severe physical disease. Table 22 summarizes the main side effects of lithium.

At the beginning of treatment, there may be onset of nausea, abdominal pains, diarrhea, and feelings of tiredness. These disturbances generally disappear spontaneously. Tremor of the hands, if present, may be longer lasting and is a particular problem if the patient's occupation requires manual dexterity. The tremor may be treated by reducing the dosage of lithium.

In prolonged treatment, there may be onset of problems connected to thyroid function; the volume of the gland may increase and its function be impaired with the onset of mixedema (especially in women). If the lithium treatment cannot be suspended, the permanent association of thyroxine becomes necessary. In any case, thyroid function should be tested every 6–12 months.

Even at therapeutic doses, lithium may also affect the cardiovascular apparatus, though these effects are generally negligible. The electrocardiogram may display an inversion or flattening of the T-wave of little clinical relevance; these alterations disappear when the treatment is stopped. It has been reported that lithium may exacerbate persistent ventricular arrhythmias and cause serious conduction disorders [266], but such cases are rare. Careful monitoring of cardiac function is in any case essential.

Lithium generally causes a reduction in urine concentration with elimination of large quantities of very dilute urine, so that the patient consequently drinks a large amount of fluids (diabetes insipidus). In the elderly, urine concentration is generally reduced. The administration of lithium may hence give rise to possibly severe electrolytic imbalance, manifesting with lethargy, confusion, or even coma. Diabetes insipidus, however, is rapidly reversible on suspension of the treatment. In some subjects, chronic treatment with lithium has been associated with irreversible alterations to the glomerules and tubules, but recent research has drastically reduced the estimated frequency of these consequences [667], and it is now held that the effect of lithium on glomerule filtration is slight [175].

Confusion, memory disorders, disorientation, and altered states of consciousness may be considered the first and most common signs of lithium toxicity in the elderly. The association of other drugs, such as diuretics, antiinflammatory agents, and neuroleptics, may result in an increase in these confusional episodes. It has been observed that the phenothiazines increase the intracellular concentration of lithium, toxic effects appearing even at doses within the therapeutic range [266]. Yet findings suggesting the danger of the association haloperidol-lithium have not been confirmed in later studies [175]. If the intensity of the confusional state increases, there may be onset of neuromuscular irritability, atonia, speech disorders, nystagmus, sphincter incontinence, and convulsions—which can rapidly lead to coma and, in the absence of immediate emergency intervention, death. As there is no specific antidote to lithium, treatment essentially entails an attempt to restore the patient's hydroelectrolytic balance. To accelerate the diuresis and hence elimination of the lithium, the subjects must be catheterized; in some cases dialysis may become necessary.

Concurrent diseases, viral infections, fever, dehydration, vomiting, diarrhea, and profuse sweating may all lead to increased blood concentration and electrolytic imbalance, bringing the possibility that the lithium concentration may rise to toxic levels.

CARBAMAZEPINE

Used primarily in the treatment of epilepsy, carbamazepine has proved to be an effective drug in the treatment and prevention of mania. Taken as a monotherapy, however, carbamazepine is not as efficacious as lithium [581], and its use is practically restricted to association with lithium in those patients who are resistant to treatment with lithium alone.

Carbamazepine is structurally similar to the tricyclic antidepressants, and like the latter, it may give rise to anticholinergic and cardiovascular side effects. It may, furthermore, produce confusion and ataxia. Its most serious side effect is leucopenia. Like most of the tricyclics, carbamazepine should be administered with particular care in the elderly. As well as in subjects resistant to lithium, it may also be indicated in cases of so-called "rapid cyclizers" or subjects with serious kidney problems in whom the use of lithium might be dangerous [530].

INTERACTIONS BETWEEN DRUGS

The problem of the contemporaneous use of several drugs is particularly present in the elderly [196]. The pharmacological substances described above may interact with each other or with other drugs to produce possibly serious adverse effects. It is known that interactions between drugs are the result of a combination of many different variables. At the risk of oversimplification, it may be said that the interactive mechanisms derive from pharmacokinetic and pharmacodynamic factors.

Tricyclic and Atypical Antidepressants

An argument that has recently aroused interest in many investigators is the interaction between the MAO inhibitors and tricyclics. The combined use of these two groups of drugs is traditionally considered contraindicated in view of the risk of possibly fatal hypertensive crisis. Recently, however, it has been shown that the use of these drugs in association may be very efficacious in subjects who have shown no response to separate trials with tricyclics and MAO inhibitors [629]. However, this question is still controversial [331], and in our opinion the tricyclic-MAOI association should not be prescribed in the elderly until it is settled.

Since the pharmacological action of the tricyclics is based on blockage of the re-uptake of the catecholamines, the cardiovascular effects of adrenaline and noradrenaline may be potentiated in subjects under treatment with this drug. In this context, it has been reported that even an ordinary dental anesthesia may cause dangerous hypertensive crises, although reports of this are rare [331]. In any case, the catecholamines should be administered with care in patients being treated with tricyclics.

The barbiturates generally increase the sedation induced by the tricyclics, increasing their metabolism and lowering plasmatic levels. When insomnia must be treated it is hence advisable to use a benzodiazepine, which does not significantly interfere with the metabolism of the antidepressants.

The interaction of alcohol with the tricyclics is not yet entirely clear; what is known is that it gives rise to a CNS depression with marked slowing of reaction times, which may be very dangerous in drivers. Furthermore, the tricyclics also interact with antihypertensive agents such as clonidine, guanethidine, betanidine (blocking the antihypertensive effect); the anticholinergics (potentiating their action); methylphenidate (which increases the plasmatic levels of the tricyclics); amphetamine (with possibly fatal consequences); phenylbutazone (delaying its absorption); and oral contraceptives (which reduce the plasma tricyclic levels) [256].

MAO Inhibitors

The interaction of these drugs with the tricyclics was examined above. With regard to their interactions with tyramine (the "cheese effect") and other amines, we refer the reader to the specific section and to Table 21. The MAO inhibitors dangerously potentiate the effects of alcohol, ether, barbiturates, insulin, morphine, and cocaine.

Lithium

The principal interactions of lithium were also described in the specific section above. The most dangerous interactions occur with the diuretics, which bring about an increase in the lithium blood concentration. For a summary of the various interactions between drugs, see Table 23.

Table 23. Drug interactions.

Interacting Drugs	Severity of Interaction	Effect of Interaction
Tricyclics & antidepressants		
Barbiturates	Moderate	These drugs lower tricyclic plasma levels because of enzyme induction
Antipsychotic & MAOIs	Serious	Both increase levels of circulating amines
Antihypertensive agents	Serious	Decrease antihypertensive effect
Sympathomimetic amines	Serious	Potentiation of pressor response
Local anesthetics	Serious	Potentiation of pressor response
Alcohol	Serious	Alcohol interferes with tricyclic metabolism, affects psychomotor skills
Anticholinergic agents	Mild	Potentiates anticholinergic effects
IMAOs		
Adrenaline, amphetamines, simpathomimetic amines	Serious	Potentiation of pressor response
L-dopa	Moderate	Increase in circulating dopamine
Alcoholic beverages	Moderate	Tyramine in beverages causes a "cheese effect"
Phenylpropanolamine	Serious	Increases noradrenaline levels causing hypertension, headaches, etc
LITHIUM		
Sodium ion	Moderate	Increases renal clearance of lithium
Phenotiazines	Unknown	Lithium alters phenotiazine kinetics by delaying gastric emtying rate
Diuretics	Serious	Increase in lithium concentration

ELECTROCONVULSIVE THERAPY

Electroconvulsive therapy (ECT) is an efficacious treatment with no significant side effects in depressed elderly subjects. Its clinical action is at least as valid as that of the antidepressants [211]. This form of therapy is an appropriate choice in subjects who do not respond to pharmacological treatments and who have developed severe side effects [581].

Response to electroconvulsive therapy is more rapid than that obtained with drugs [3]. This characteristic may be particularly useful in those patients in whom there is a high risk of

suicide, and who are suffering from severe dehydration and mal-
nutrition [575]. Generally, electroconvulsive therapy has no contraindications; however, since it provokes a temporary increase
in endocranial pressure, an absolute contraindication is a preex-
isting endocranial hypertension, which could be exacerbated by
the treatment leading to dangerous and possibly lethal hernia-
tion of the cerebral tissue through the tentorium. Severe and
diffuse osteoporosis also requires extreme caution, since the
clonic convulsive movements could cause fractures [210].

Electroconvulsive therapy is generally well tolerated, especially if performed unilaterally from the nondominant part of the
hemisphere. This procedure minimizes the temporary loss of recent memory—the most typical side effect [210]. Electroconvulsive therapy generally requires a hospital stay and exposure to
the risks of a brief general anesthesia.

CHAPTER 9
Benzodiazepine Treatment of Minor Depressions in the Elderly

- In the pharmacological treatment of minor affective disorders benzodiazepines should be prescribed to help patients to get over the acute phase of the crisis, especially when this is characterized by strong anxiety possibly associated with insomnia. They should be prescribed at full dose for a period not exceeding 3 weeks and should then be gradually reduced. For patients in whom this treatment does not give a satisfactory response, a possible alternative may be antidepressives, preferably of the new generation.

- Both clinical experience and the literature [313] suggest that a certain percentage of subjects does not respond to any form of pharmacological treatment, with symptoms persisting for at least 6 months; the advisable treatment in such cases is not yet known [105]. In any case, the validity of structured psychotherapy is well confirmed, and it appears to be the ideal treatment in the case of subjects with dysthymia [144]. For patients who refuse drug treatment and present adjustment disorders correlated with physical diseases, bereavement, and other untoward events, techniques such as "crisis intervention" [633], based on empathic understanding of the patient's situation, may prove useful.

- Only after reestablishment of equilibrium—after a complete expression of the subject's emotional response—can possible alternatives be examined together [516]. In such cases, group therapy may also be a valid alternative strategy in the elderly subject in crisis [547].

As we have seen in other sections of this volume, whereas there are a few clinical-epidemiological studies concerning the percentage prevalences of the various forms of depression in the general population, virtually nothing is available on this area in geriatric populations. Old age has been correctly defined as "the age of losses," and it is self-evident that the elderly are at high risk of encountering affective manifestations that were once called "reactive depressions" [145, 164] and are now categorized in the DSM-III-3 [11] as "Adjustment Disorders." Given the weakened psychophysical resources of the elderly and their "natural" tendency toward chronicity, it is clear that an initial depressive reaction may easily evolve into a major depression or, more frequently still, a dysthymia (DSM-III-R).

There is a common tendency among authors to classify clinical conditions such as dysthymia (or depressive neuroses), depressive disorders NOS, and adjustment disorders with the "Minor Mood Disorders" (a diagnostic category that is formally absent in the DSM-III and is a carryover from the so-called "Feighner's criteria," [198]).

This chapter discusses the available pharmacotherapeutic approaches to minor mood disorders in the elderly, with particular focus on the adjustment disorders.

PHARMACOLOGICAL TREATMENT OF MINOR MOOD DISORDERS

The real effectiveness of the tricyclics as well as antidepressants in general in the treatment of dysthymic disorders and adjustment disorders is still controversial [157, 313]. While there is general consensus that these drugs are effective in the treatment of major affective disorders, they are of questionable value in minor disorders, in which their effect has been shown to be similar to, though not greater than, that of placebo [105, 145].

A trial carried out by ourselves [145] on a population of 85 adult subjects with adjustment disorders randomly assigned to treatment with placebo, lormetazepam, viloxazine, S-adenosylmethionine, or support psychotherapy did not find any significant differences between the clinical effects of the five types of treatment, appreciable improvement being observed in all groups. A similar evaluation conducted on elderly subjects [144] revealed very similar tendencies. These findings suggest that the question of the best treatment of adjustment disorders remains open—and is indeed possibly nonexistent in the absence of convincing proof of the superiority of the one or the other of the treatments considered.

The most frequent forms of adjustment disorders are generally characterized by depression, anxiety, and insomnia. In both old and young, these disturbances may be associated with a single life event (for example, retirement) or a complex of life events (retirement and marital problems, etc.); the disturbances may, moreover, be recurrent or continuous. Theoretically, adjustment disorders persist until the cause is removed, or until a new level of adjustment is reached [11]. It is generally believed that spontaneous remission may be achieved in 6 months to a year [427]. It has also been noted that subjects with this disorder rarely use psychiatric clinics and are more likely to consult their general practitioners [238]. It is also known that the latter prescribe benzodiazepines much more frequently than antidepressants for these disorders. Because the minor affective disorders are a very widespread problem in the general population [238], the prescription and consumption of benzodiazepines have progressively assumed the proportions of a minor epidemic, a cause of concern for many investigators [127]. The rising medical prescriptions for benzodiazepines (the most frequently prescribed psychotropic drugs in both younger adults [418] and the elderly [16, 423]) are accompanied by an uncontrollable percentage of self-prescription [16], the overwhelming majority of which relates to this class of drug.

EFFECTS OF BENZODIAZEPINE TREATMENT

Although the benzodiazepines appear safely manageable and effective in the reduction of anxiety, especially when severe, [138] and in sleep induction (at least for limited periods of time [498]), their use is not entirely risk-free. The development of physical dependence, although uncommon, is not unheard of even at standard doses [651]; withdrawal symptoms have also been observed [22]. The latter phenomenon is, of course, also present in elderly subjects [135], a fact that also feeds the considerable discussion in meetings and the literature on the choice of the most suitable benzodiazepine. The benzodiazepine selected should have either be a short half-life drug (which can give withdrawal effects but does not give rise to appreciable accumulation); this includes oxazepam, lorazepam, and the more recent triazolam and alprazolam. Or it should be one of the long half-life drugs (e.g., diazepam), which permit better compliance and less frequently associated with withdrawal symptoms, although they may induce drowsiness, especially on awakening [255]. It seems reasonable to maintain that the choice of the most appropriate

Table 24. Benzodiazepines commonly prescribed for elderly patients.

Drug name	Active metabolite in blood	Primary route of biotrans-formation	Overall rate of elimination	Accumula-tion propensity
Diazepam	Diazepam, Demoxepam, Desmethyl-diazepam	Oxidation	Slow	High
Flurazepam	Desalkyl-, Hydroxyethyl-, flurazepam, Flurazepam aldehyde	Oxidation	Slow	High
Chlordiaze-poxide	Desmetilchor-diazepoxide	Oxidation	Slow	High
Lorazepam	Lorazepam	Conjugation	Intermediate	Medium
Temazepam	Temazepam	Conjugation	Intermediate	Medium
Alprazolam	Alprazolam, Hydroxytriazolam	Oxidation	Fast	Low
Oxazepam	Oxazepam	Conjugation	Fast	Low

Adapted from [135].

Table 25. Benzodiazepines: Indications and kinetic variables for dosage modification in elderly patients.

Drug Name	Major clinical indication	Elimination half-life range (hours)	Time to reach steady-state (days)	Time to peak (hours)
Diazepam	Anxiety, muscle spasm	21–46	5–9*	0.5–1.5
Flurazepam**	Insomnia	50–120	10–30	0.5–1
Chlordiazepoxide	Anxiety	8–15	2–3*	0.5–2
Lorazepam	Anxiety	10–8	2–4	2–6
Temazepam	Anxiety	6–8	1–2	1.4–4
Alprazolam	Anxiety	12–15	2–4	1–2
Triazolam	Insomnia	3–5	1–1.5	0.5–2
Oxazepam	Anxiety	4–13	1–3	2–4

* Time to reach steady-state for all active moieties may be significantly longer.
** Data refer to the active metabolite desalkyltlurazepam.
Adapted from [135].

Table 26. Influence of age on benzodiazepine pharmacokinetics.

Drug name	Elimination half-life	Systemic clearance
Diazepam	Prolonged	Reduced
Flurazepam	Prolonged	Reduced
Chlordiazepoxide	Prolonged	Reduced
Lorazepam	Prolonged	Reduced
Temazepam	Prolonged	Reduced
Alprazolam	Prolonged	Reduced
Triazolam	Unchanged	Reduced
Oxazepam	Unchanged	Unchanged

From [135].

benzodiazepine should be based on other elements besides these, such as an evaluation of the individual characteristics of the subject, the setting in which the treatment is implemented (home or hospital), and concurrence with other treatments (a frequent problem in the elderly). In general, products undergoing oxidative biotransformation with slow elimination and accumulation are preferable in patients with chronic anxiety, while those subject to conjugation, with rapid elimination and short duration of action, are more appropriate in patients with insomnia [135]. Tables 24–26 indicate the main characteristics of some of the benzodiazepines most commonly prescribed in the elderly.

Side effects frequently associated with the benzodiazepines, such as sleepiness (found in 39% of the elderly treated during the Boston Collaborative Surveillance Drug Program [68]), reduction of cognitive capacities, and ataxia, assume particular importance in the elderly. The use of diazepam, for example, has been associated with a significant increase in bone fractures from accidental falls among residents of North American homes for the elderly [354], a tendency paralleled by increased car accident rates among other age groups [619]. The benzodiazepines are also implicated in outbreaks of aggression in persons with a tendency toward aggressive behavior [184], a paradoxical finding that has received support from research on volunteers [582]. The possibility of this sort of reaction should be born in mind, especially in the case of those patients (especially in a hospital setting) who display restlessness with aggressive undertones after the establishment of treatment. Such subjects may frequently be sub-

mitted to considerably increased doses, with the possible consequence of iatrogenic persistence of the symptom.

A further insidious side effect of benzodiazepine treatment is
depression, which arises especially in very old patients with severe physical disorders [254]. This possibility should receive careful attention in the treatment of subjects with minor mood disorders, in whom the depressive component—which is often in
itself severe—may be *increased* by the administration of benzodiazepine.

In view of the clinical side effects, and also because of the
"social" consequences of the consumption of benzodiazepines (it
has been reported that these drugs reduce the subject's ability to
use their own resources to cope with life events [650] and hence
constitute a sort of new "opium for the masses," dulling the
emotional content of intra- and interpersonal conflicts [367]),
some authors have attempted to verify the real consequences of
the failure to administer benzodiazepines in clinical circumstances in which they would normally be used. The first observations were reported in the early 1970s: Kaufman et al. [325] were
able to detect a marked decrease in recourse to anxiolytics in a
North American clinic that distributed illustrative literature
about anxiety and tranquilizers and gave explanatory talks.
Their research found no evidence of clinical manifestations attributable to the failure to administrate the drugs.

Similar conclusions were reached by Keeler and McCurdy
[333] in their evaluation of the consequences of withdrawal of the
drug from the market in an entire North American state. But the
most indicative study so far in this context was the recent investigation by Catalan et al. [105, 106] into the consequences of the
abolition of benzodiazepines by two general practitioners in Oxford. Ninety subjects with minor mood disorders were randomly
assigned to treatment with anxiolytics or a brief consultation
involving an explanation of the symptoms, analysis of the underlying problems and ways of overcoming them, as well as an
explanation of the reasons why no drugs were being prescribed.
Clinical conditions, social adjustment, and cure motivation were
completely comparable in the two groups of subjects before treatment. The study, which lasted 7 months, lead to the surprising
conclusion that improvement in the subjects of the two groups
was similar according to all the various measurements employed.
None of the subjects showed an increased consumption of alcohol,
tobacco, or nonprescribed drugs. Furthermore, the consultation

did not give rise to an increase in the time spent on the patients during their visits to the surgery, and the subjects treated with consultation seemed more satisfied with their relationship with the doctor than those who had received benzodiazepines. In short, brief consultation with the general practitioner was just as effective as the prescription of anxiolytics in the treatment of minor affective disorders, especially of recent onset. Catalan et al.'s study did not relate particularly to the elderly, but it would seem reasonable to believe that the same situation would also pertain in this age group, in which the "attention effect" is very important [157] and the consequences of the nonprescription of benzodiazepines might be even clearer. It may be hoped that specific trials will soon confirm this logical prediction.

CHAPTER 10

The Psychotherapy of Mood Disorders in the Elderly

- The strategies adopted in the treatment of psychological disorders in the elderly differ in certain respects from those used with younger patients, as certain difficulties, problems and limitations connected with old age must be taken into account.

- While bearing in mind all the limitations posed by the patient's general conditions, it is imperative to seek the best possible results, and this will in all cases require understanding and acceptance of these limits by both patient and therapist.

- The treatment of mood disorders in geriatric patients is hence a complicated, delicate and complex task that provides a challenge not only to the therapists' professional abilities, but also to their human resources.

Relatively few controlled studies have investigated the efficacy of the various therapeutic strategies employed in the treatment of affective pathologies in the elderly. However, it is generally accepted that drug therapy is the most manageable, if not the most effective, approach to the treatment of depression in such subjects [424]. Nevertheless, great caution is required in the administration of drugs to elderly subjects, both because of the presence of age-related biological modifications that may interfere with the normal kinetics of the preparation, and because of the possibility of concomitant physical diseases.

For this reason, among others, it is extremely important to evaluate whether and to what extent the elderly subject may benefit from psychotherapy. The use of psychotherapeutic treatment by doctors for mood disorders in the elderly has frequently encountered considerable resistance, partly because of negative cultural attitudes toward old age, and partly because of the objective limitations of the use of a psychotherapeutic strategy in the elderly. On the one hand, there are the stereotyped views of old age as being characterized by rigidity, the deterioration of intellectual powers, and the impossibility of establishing a worthwhile therapeutic relationship; on the other hand, there is the tendency to see the symptoms referred to by the elderly patients as signs of an irreversible deterioration inherent in aging. Attention has recently been drawn to a marked tendency in the United States to overrate the organic significance of clinical states that might otherwise be identified as depressive disorders [96].

A further obstacle to a psychotherapeutic approach lies in the natural reluctance of the elderly to speak about their disorders and hence to place themselves at risk for possible hospitalization and a consequent loss of independence.

Despite the general agreement among authors that the presence of a certain psychoaffective rigidity in the elderly creates serious difficulties for the overcoming of defences [326], most maintain that appropriate psychotherapy, whether family, couple, or group therapy, may achieve satisfactory results in these subjects [96, 241, 286].

The therapist working with the elderly must often show particular sensitivity in entering into contact with the patient, as most of these subjects have not directly requested treatment but have been urged on by relatives and friends [58].

PSYCHOANALYTIC THERAPY IN THE ELDERLY

There is much controversy about the efficacy of psychoanalysis with elderly patients. Freud wrote that age is important in the selection of patients to be submitted to psychoanalytic treatment because persons near or over the age of 50 lack the plasticity of the psychic processes upon which the therapy depends—elderly people are no longer educable—and, on the other hand, the material that has to be elaborated and the duration of the treatment is immensely increased.

Fenichel, in his *Textbook of Psychoanalysis* [200] sets the upper age limit for psychoanalysis at 40 years, but a few pages further on he states that generalization on this question is impossible:

> It is certainly true that advanced age limits the plasticity of the personality; however, this occurs to different extents and at different ages, so that no general rule may be assumed . . . For analysis in advanced age, the patient's overall situation is decisive. If he has had the opportunity for libidinal and narcissistic satisfactions, analysis is more likely to be successful than if it serves only to show the failure of a whole life without

offering any chance of compensation. Analysis may be attempted even with elderly people in order to remove the specific symptom; however, if a profound change in character should prove necessary to effect the cure, it should be remembered that the possibility of change is very limited in the elderly.

A different position is taken by Abraham [1], who, citing cases from his clinical practice, cautiously upholds the possibility of treating elderly subjects psychoanalytically. Abraham considers that it is "wrong to deny a priori the possibility of a therapeutic (psychoanalytical) undertaking in the neuroses of the involutive period."

Recently, after a long period of silence on the argument, various authors have affirmed the possibility of using the psychoanalytic technique with the elderly [120, 344, 402, 526]. These analysts maintain that although the interpretative work involved is undoubtedly difficult or at any rate partial—rigidity of thought favoring the refusal of interpretations that are too new or unexpected—the treatment may benefit from a transference that, in their experience, frequently evolves and develops with greater ease than in the young.

The vitality of the psychoanalytic process, designed to harmonize as far as possible the contradictions between interior and external life, is in itself a meaning and an aim, and this is the major objection raised by these authors against those who are opposed to the application of this therapeutic technique with the elderly on the basis of modifications in the structure of their psyche. At present, the main point at issue seems to be not so much the feasibility as the *advisability* of analyzing elderly patients. The most frequent underlying problem in much of the psychopathology arising in this age group (and especially in affective problems relates to narcissistic wounds that are reopened by the progressive loss of objects important for the individual's narcissistic balance [433]. It is hence clear that personalities with strong narcissistic traits are most vulnerable to the inevitable injuries accompanying the process of aging, and that they experience the greatest difficulty in coping with the typical critical situations of advanced age. King [344] summarizes these situations in the following five descriptive categories:

1) fear of losing sexual potency and the consequences of this for relations with the opposite sex;

2) the fear that one's role will be usurped by younger people, and awareness of a diminishing professional efficiency, which is

often accompanied by a fear of being unable to face retirement adequately;

3) tensions and instability in the marital relationship once the children have left home and can no longer be "used" to mask the reciprocal problems of the parents;

4) awareness of aging and fear of illness and dependence on others;

5) awareness of the inevitable approach of death and disappointment about unfulfilled objectives.

When the subject has good powers of insight, self-observation, and development and elaboration of transference, the analysis may permit the adaptive reorganization of libidinal investments, permitting the elderly to cope better with the various traumas and loss events that are an inevitable part of old age [433].

Rechtschaffen [536], in a review of the literature concerning psychoanalytically oriented psychotherapeutic techniques, beginning from the work of Fenichel and Alexander, finds a surprising disparity in results, which are substantially positive in some, such as Wayne [677] and Meerloo [452], but lead to pessimistic conclusions in others, such as Hollender [290]. Rechtschaffen stresses the importance of the contribution of Goldfan (cited in [536]), who proposes an approach especially designed for work with the elderly rather than an old technique applied to a new psychoanalytic population. Goldfan's work brings into focus the problems most frequently encountered in work with elderly patients and identifies the practical problems that the therapist may experience in the treatment of psychological disorders in this age group. Since the publication of Rechtschaffen's work in 1959, other contributions on this subject have appeared, although none have matched its depth. As Sparacino remarks: "To date, a systematic rereading of Rechtschaffen on psychotherapy in the elderly is the only project of this sort worth undertaking" [627].

After a wide-ranging examination of the issue, Bellak and Small [46] maintain, with Sparacino, the utility of analytically oriented psychotherapy with the elderly.

It is the opinion of most authors that a useful preliminary to therapy may be trial interpretations designed to test the willingness and capacity of the elderly subject for phantasmatic elaboration and interpretative receptiveness [46, 290]. If the therapeutic work proceeds too slowly, both patient and doctor may become increasingly frustrated, at worst culminating in the therapist's declaration that "the elderly patient is not a suitable subject for therapy" [713].

Therapist who dedicate themselves to the cure of affective disturbances in the elderly must be able to use the method that seems most appropriate at the time, after giving individual attention to a series of characteristics ranging from the diagnostic evaluation to the type of support available to the patient. We feel it may be helpful here to report the selective criteria used by Goodstein for the application of short- or long-term psychotherapy [243]. The points examined by this author relate to diagnosis, assessment of the subject's socio-familiar environment, and the duration of symptomatology. Short-term psychotherapy suffices if the symptoms were triggered by real and contingent events, if the elderly subjects have a valid family and social support network, and if they has the intrinsic quality of good and rapid adjustment. Long-term therapy, on the other hand, is indicated when the elderly subject cannot rely on a supportive and reassuring external environment and when the symptomatology is compounded by neurotic conflicts and is hence more difficult to dismantle [243].

SHORT-TERM PSYCHOTHERAPIES

Even today, little literature is available on short-term psychoanalytic psychotherapy with the elderly. Marmor [432] advises the use of short-term psychoanalytic psychotherapy in the elderly so long as the following conditions are satisfied:

1) that the patient sits face to face with the therapist;

2) that preestablished time limits are set to the duration of the therapy;

3) that the session is selectively oriented toward a focal conflict;

4) that the therapist is "active."

In general, it may be sustained that psychotherapeutic work with the elderly requires a more guided, directive, and protective style of approach than with younger subjects [2, 176], while the interpretative work and deepening of insight should be rather restrained [231]. Even touching the patient, which is not generally considered advisable in the young, may be reassuring and alleviate the anxiety of the elderly subject [547].

At present, especially in the United States, attention is increasingly focusing on nonpsychoanalytic short-term psychotherapy, and controlled studies have been performed to evaluate the efficacy of the various techniques proposed. Gallagher and Thompson, in a study published in 1982 [220], examine the efficacy of a form of psychodynamic psychotherapy, "relational insight," versus two other forms of nonpsychoanalytic therapy in the treatment of depression in the elderly. To this aim, two recent forms of structured therapy were selected: behavioral and cognitive. The efficacy of these two forms has been verified in several trials with young subjects [142]. Later, we address the use of this form of psychotherapy in elderly depressed subjects. Here, let it suffice to say that the behavioral model, as developed by Lewinsohn [382], places great importance on social input and negative reinforcement in the onset and maintenance of depression, problems that are particularly important in the elderly and derive from the numerous deficiencies typically associated with the aging process. Beck's cognitive model [40], on the contrary, emphasizes the role of negative thought processes in the development of depression. Since cognitive processes change with age [69], elderly subjects may be more vulnerable to this type of "distortion" of thought. The third model is mainly based on the use of the therapeutic relationship to help subjects to gain insight into their own problems and formulate plans for the modification thereof. Here, the therapeutic relationship itself is the main means for acting on mood.

As well as assessing the efficacy of these forms of therapy, Gallagher and Thompson's research raised the problem of their comparative worth. The authors postulated that the two latter forms of therapy would prove to be the most useful since the problems experienced by the elderly may easily trigger and maintain a depressive episode.

Patients were selected according to the following criteria:

- age over 55 years;
- presence of an episode of major depression;
- exclusion of subjects at risk for suicide;
- score of more than 17 on Beck's *Depression Inventory* and of more than 14 on Hamilton's *Depression Scale*;
- absence or little evidence of other psychopathologies (alcoholism, bipolar disorders, etc.).

Ten patients were assigned to each form of therapy; the treatment included 16 individual sessions, lasting 90 minutes each, distributed at regular intervals over a period of 12 weeks. Follow-up was performed 1 year after the end of psychotherapy.

The differences in results did not emerge immediately, but at the 1-year follow-up the patients treated with behavioral and cognitive psychotherapy had maintained the progress achieved longer than those treated with the psychodynamically oriented therapy.

According to the authors, these differences may be accounted for by the fact that the first two forms of therapy have more specific objectives. In fact, in the follow-up interview, the patients were asked which of the experiences developed during psychotherapy later proved to be usefully applicable in their daily lives. Approximately two-thirds of the patients submitted to cognitive and behavioral therapy declared that during therapy they had acquired certain specific abilities that they had then applied regularly, against only one-third in the psychodynamic therapy group.

Gallagher and Thompson's data provide support for the hypothesis of Bandura [30], according to which an increased awareness of one's own abilities may lead to a reduction in psychological distress. This author maintains that treatment directed at specific target areas of practical behavior render the patients more able to recognize and use their own resources. These considerations appear to be the basis of the efficacy in the elderly of techniques based on the acquisition of specific behaviors that can then be repeated at the end of therapy.

In a later study, Gallagher and Thompson [219] suggest the use of the psychotherapeutic techniques described above especially with subjects affected by nonendogenous depression. In this second study, carried out with an identical methodological approach, 80% of the patients fell within the "normal" range at the end of therapy, and none presented relapse 1 year after the end of treatment.

Gallagher and Thompson's studies also sustain the effectiveness of directive therapies within definite and preestablished time limits. In fact, perception of time is altered in the elderly with respect to the young, and the older subject's need for concrete results would be frustrated by an infinite or indefinite extension of treatment [383].

Despite its widespread use, there are few examples of the application of behavioral therapy in elderly depressed subjects [547]. As correctly noted by Cooper and Murphy [126], behavioral—or, as they are sometimes known, "cognitive behavioral"—therapies are today easily confused with the "cognitive" therapies according to Beck's school. This is not the place for a theoretical discussion of the two models, for which the reader is referred elsewhere (e.g., [181, 191]). Here, it will suffice to recall that while cognitive therapy is addressed particularly to thought and elaboration (and may thus properly be called "psychotherapy"), behavioral, or "cognitive-behavioral," therapy is designed to modify behavior through a learning process and is not strictly speaking "psychotherapeutic." The elderly person is offered experiences oriented toward increasing sense of control over self and the surrounding environment. Corby [130] has given assertion training as an example of this sort of therapy, and Rodin, in a review of this field, also emphasized that the quest for control at any cost may sometimes be counterproductive. In the elderly, behavioral therapy may be directed toward an improvement in control and self-management, but also toward teaching people to attract the attention of the staff or those caring for them [268, 700].

There are very few studies on the use of cognitive therapy in the elderly depressed subject [547]. Because these are "short-term," problem-oriented therapies, they have been considered particularly suitable for the elderly [635, 698]. The therapist must be able to create a strong therapeutic alliance with the patient in which together they eliminate the particular and habitual modes of thought that lead to maladjustment and psychologically disturbance of the patient's reality. Behavioral techniques may be used to achieve this aim. Church [114] has also expressed himself in favor of the use of cognitive therapy in the elderly, although he underlines the greater difficulties involved in their treatment.

Another form of short-term, nonanalytically oriented therapy indicated for the elderly is interpersonal psychotherapy (IPT) as proposed by Sholomskas et al. [610]. IPT is aimed at the reduction of the symptom and improvement of current interpersonal relationships. Unlike psychodynamic therapies, IPT focuses on problems contingent to the patient's experience of social relationships. This form of psychotherapy does not attempt to restructure the patients' personality, but is rather designed to help them develop more constructive strategies to resolve the problems affecting the course of the depression. It appears to be specifically adapted to the elderly subject, as it may be focused on any one of the following points:

* reactions to mourning;
* disputes arising in interpersonal relationships;
* problems concerning changes in role;
* absence or inadequacy of social relationships.

The elderly patient experiences great difficulties in coping with changes in life, such as retirement or the move into an old person's residential home, often perceiving them as losses. In any case, patients feels themselves unable to enact these changes, which are perceived as a threat to identity. In this case, the aim of the therapy is to help the patient to understand that the depression is connected not so much to the change in role as to the psychological significance of a diminished self-respect resulting from it, and to point out the advantages and possibilities of the new situation.

IPT is also, clearly, a directive therapy, based on the presupposition that depression is linked to a specific psychosocial context, and that the patient's recovery and the prevention of future relapses depend on an understanding and restructuring of this context. These characteristics seem to make it a valid therapeutic instrument with elderly subjects.

In a 1983 study, Sholomskas et al. [610] reported significant improvements in 61% of cases treated with a form of interpersonal therapy they had modified for use with the elderly. The sessions were made more flexible in relation to the patients' specific needs, and the therapist was expected to take a particularly active role, including intervention in the daily problems of the patient such as financial worries or physical ill health.

Another form of treatment for affective disorders in the elderly is reminiscence and life-review therapy as proposed by Lewis and Butler [384]. This form of therapy involves the mental or verbal activity of recalling past events, experiences, places, and people. Life-review therapy is not just a recollection of the past, but requires the patient to analyze, restructure, and reconstruct past events and their significance in order to achieve a better understanding of the his or her life. The therapy is thus an active process of personality reorganization. The reminiscences may give rise to pleasure, nostalgia, and idealization of the past, but also to anxiety, guilt, and desperation. For this reason, Hanley and Baikie [271] recently cautioned against the use of reminiscence in depressed subjects, in whom the therapy could prove counterproductive as they typically tend to recall negative events. These authors advise guidance of recollections toward pleasant and morale-raising memories. Yet other authors hold that life review cannot have a negative influence on the psychological equilibrium of the elderly patient, and advise the stimulation of precisely those reminiscences linked to stressful events[216, 679].

GROUP PSYCHOTHERAPY

Group psychotherapy with elderly subjects has been the object of systematic study for some years. Here, we may cite the studies by Silver [613], Linden [387], Wolff [707], and the more recent studies by Lewis and Butler [384], as well as Lopez' affirmation that even disabled elderly subjects may benefit from group strategies in psychotherapy [405].

However, there is considerable disagreement among the various authors with regard to theories and techniques. Yalom suggests that the optimum number of participants in the group is 5 to 8 subjects [710]; Linden proposes up to 40 persons [387]. Butler advises mixed-age groups [96], while Grotjahn suggests that all participants should be of a similar age [259]. There is a general agreement about the mechanisms of the therapeutic group thought, which should comprise mutual support and cohesion. Lazarus and Weinberg [374] provide a list of reasons why group therapy is particularly appropriate with elderly subjects: socialization is encouraged, motivation to take up old interests and relationships is increased, and suggestions for solutions to practical problems are drawn. For Bednar and Kaul [44], group therapy is particularly advisable with elderly subjects, as in the group the members learn to develop their own new social microcosm and experience its resources. Furthermore, they may also learn through a feedback process of give and take, in which they have a chance to be both givers and receivers at the same time. The work of the leader is clearly extremely important, as the leader must facilitate the orderly and productive development of these mechanisms, whatever problem has been identified as the group target.

Variations on the standard technique have been suggested to adapt it more specifically to the exigencies of work with older patients. Lesser et al. [380], for example, described psychotherapeutic experiences with groups of hospitalized patients based on the use of "focused recall." At every session, the patients were stimulated to recall a particular moment of their lives—the earliest memory, the first day at school, etc. Reminiscence proves to be a useful instrument for the stimulation of discussion and interaction between the members of the group. This study in fact showed an increase in the percentage of dischargeable subjects among these patients, who were mostly affected by dementia or schizophrenia, as compared to patients not submitted to therapy.

Positive results were also obtained by Mintz et al. [462], who describe their experiences of group therapy with elderly depressed subjects, many of whom presented significant improvements after regular and committed participation in group therapy. The results of all the studies cited (and others as well, see [518] for a more exhaustive review) provide the stimulation to continue this line of research, especially in view of the growing need for valid therapeutic instruments for adoption in the various institutions and communities for the elderly.

TRANSFERENCE AND COUNTERTRANSFERENCE

Before concluding this chapter on the psychotherapy of affective disorders in the elderly, it is worth mentioning some of the particular features that may appear in the mechanisms of transference and countertransference in such patients [243].

In general, transference in the elderly appears more rapidly, is clearer, and is resolved spontaneously by the patient. However, as the therapist is often younger than the patients, and may be perceived by the elderly subjectd as very different from themselves, problems may occur in the establishment of a correct transference.

However, despite the age difference, the therapist may sometimes be unconsciously assimilated as an important figure already integrated by the patient.

Various types of transfer relationships may develop in elderly subjects, ranging from the classic relationship in which the patient is regressed and childlike, experiencing the therapist as a parental and protective figure, to the strongly erotic transference, in which the unconscious dynamics of the patient include a reevaluation of self-image in an attempt to resurrect lost roles.

At times, an equal relationship may be established in which the elderly subjects feels free to ask for advice without feeling dependent and weak. At other times, the patient may assume an attitude of teacher in relation to the therapist, or become the therapist's parent, as in the case of the so-called "reverse transference" of Grotjahn [258], a classic example of defense projection [231].

The countertransference responses of the therapist may be equally varied. Faced with an elderly patient in poor health condition, the normal defenses against the fear of death may be seriously compromised, and therapists may activate mechanisms designed to defend themselves from anxiety and preserve their narcissistic integrity. Therapists may feel narcissistic pleasure in their omnipotent role, or, on the contrary, they may reject a patient as unable to produce a valid therapeutic relationship.

The hostile attitude of therapists is frequently founded in their own roots of infantile aggression toward their parents and in a contemporaneous fear for their death. While denial of the disease means that the help offered is not realistic, it nevertheless permits therapists to neutralize their guilt feelings about their own youth and good health.

In their relationship with the elderly patient the therapists must put into play both their role as parent and their role as child. It is hence important that they have understood and resolved their conflicts with their own parents, and that they remember that the elderly subject may represent parental figures with regard to whom oedipal conflicts may be reactivated.

According to Giberti,

> . . . without a certain conscious control of "gerontophilia" it is often difficult or impossible to give psychotherapeutic treatment to the elderly; the negative attitudes arising in this context are exemplified by the "reluctant" and impotent therapist; the failure to overcome attitudes of "gerontophobic reluctance" is an index of problems concerning his own parents and his own aging [231].

OTHER TREATMENTS

Here it is worth noting that other strategies that are not technically structured in any particular form of therapy or psychotherapy, but that nevertheless may prove to be useful instruments of support therapy, may also be used with the elderly. The medical practitioner, for example, may play an extremely important role in supporting the family and in developing, together with the family and the patient, a strategy for improving the patient's ability to adjust and preventing moments of crisis, maintaining relations with welfare services, suggesting necessary changes in the patient's living environment, and so on.

Home visits are a useful means of getting to know the patient's surroundings with regard to shops, chemists, hospitals, churches, etc. It also allows one to learn more about the social microcosm within which the elderly subject lives, namely, the spouse, family members, neighbors. On the occasion of these visits, the themes of the conversation may be more general than in the case of a more formal situation such as the hospital or outpatient unit. Talk about politics, sex, economy, religion, etc., lets patients form their own opinions, with positive repercussion for self-respect.

In some circumstances, doctors may present themselves as points of reference for self-care, attempting, whenever possible, to alter the behavior of those who repeatedly request help for problems they could safely and efficaciously resolve on their own.

It is very important to know how to stimulate subjects' relational and social sphere, encouraging them, for example, to take brief vacations, so long as these are to appropriate places adequate for the needs of the elderly, and not necessarily in the so-called "off season."

Sometimes it may be sufficient to have the walls of a house or room painted in bright colors to influence mood positively. It is, in any case, useful to give elderly subjects some points of reference to help them orient themselves within reality, such as a calendar indicating the day, month, and year, a watch with a luminous dial that can be easily read during both night and day, a radio, daily newspapers, etc. [620].

In short, any strategy that tends to reduce the feelings of isolation experienced by the elderly may be considered therapeutic.

FINAL COMMENTS

Therapy must act at various levels: identifying and alleviating the various sources of stress; slackening tensions resulting from difficulties in the patient's interpersonal relations; where necessary giving all-round support to patients who are not self-sufficient, and, when appropriate, making use of psychotherapeutic treatments designed at least to improve coping style if not actually to bring about structural changes in the subject's character.

Psychological distress in the elderly subject, which appears as the underlying cause of a variety of symptoms and illnesses, should be seen in the context of the patient's relations with his or her environment; relations that may often be difficult, but that are nevertheless fundamental. Therapeutic work must clearly be oriented firmly within reality, in a constant confrontation with the external world: The possible sources of support for the patient must in fact be sought in the social and family setting.

The superiority of one technique over another cannot be affirmed a priori: Therapist must make the best possible use of the instruments available to them at a given time for a given patient.

In the case of elderly subjects who are not self-sufficient or who have severe physical handicaps, the starting point for treatment must be the resolution of the patient's practical problems of everyday survival. The elderly subject must often be brought to accept the inevitable rather than encouraged to harbor hopes that are unrealistic in view of the changes naturally consequent on the process of aging and of one's own particular situation.

In the case of severe impairment of intellectual activities, treatment should be based almost exclusively on directive and didactic techniques.

The patient's interior world may become the focus of attention only when material needs are adequately satisfied and cognitive functions are intact. In this case, appeal may be made to the intact parts of the ego, and the patient's collaboration in the achievement of a feasible therapeutic goal may be sought. It is advisable here to bear in mind some of the psychological traits and behavior patterns common to elderly subjects.

First of all, the elderly person has a greater need for gratification than the younger subject, and the therapist must be able to balance the satisfaction of this need against the risk of triggering an overly dependent attitude. The power of resurrecting recollections of the past is very important; it may even almost be considered a need. However, this ability is often denied the old person—or at least is not well tolerated by younger people. Memories and reminiscences of life stimulate the rejuvenation of those systems of adjustment that functioned in the past, and therapist must hence do their best to encourage the patient to talk about the past, especially about events of importance for the affective sphere [243].

The more therapists are able to establish themselves as a benevolent superego coming to the aid of the patient in the initial intense guilt feelings and self-hatred that are normal reactions to the process of aging, the more successful this strategy is. The elderly subjects are spared the experience of anxiety and depression and are more able to recollect life experiences. On the other hand, an overly condescending and protective attitude may add to the patient's feelings of insecurity and inadequacy. Therapist must thus fit their strategy to the case in hand, without excluding a priori the possibility of tackling old unresolved conflicts that may emerge during therapy and hence the possibility of structural changes representing a more complete development of personality and an improved integration of the ego and superego [120].

The therapist should, in any case, be aware that a certain level of self-knowledge in the elderly subject may become a source of conflicts and guilt feelings, causing serious emotional upset. It has been noticed, for example, that when elderly depressed subjects becomes aware of their own aggressiveness, the depression worsens [96].

APPENDIX: Learned Helplessness

The learned helplessness model or theory of depression holds that a major cause of depression in humans as well as in animals is the expectation of future noncontingency between responding and outcomes after uncontrollable events have occurred to them. This generalized expectation that future response is futile causes two cognitive-behavioral deficits:

1) It produces deficits in responding by dismantling the motivation to respond.
2) It produces later difficulty in seeing that outcomes are indeed contingent upon response.

When human beings experience problems as unsolvable and their response as ineffective, they proceed to the important question of what is causing present helplessness. Individuals with a generalized helplessness expectation tend to make so-called internal attributions, that is, to attribute the cause of failure to solve the problem to personal characteristics and not to situational characteristics. They also tend to consider those personal characteristics as stable rather than as transient, meaning that they have a generalized view of themselves as inefficient, powerless, or inferior. The symptoms, cause, cure, prevention, and predisposition between learned helplessness in the laboratory and depression as it occurs in real life are shown in the following.

Symptoms

The failure to escape noise and to solve problems after experiences with uncontrollable events is the basic passivity deficit of learned helplessness. This passivity seems similar to the motivational deficits of depression. Failure to initiate responses by depressed individuals has been systematically demonstrated in the laboratory, where depressed students and patients fail to escape noise and fail to solve anagrams. The more depressed they are, the more severe is this deficit.

Nondepressed individuals given inescapable noise or unsolvable problems show the cognitive deficit of learned helplessness: They have difficulty learning that responding is successful, even when it is. Depressed individuals show exactly the same deficit. Nondepressed humans made helpless fail to see patterns in anagrams and fail to change their expectancy of future success when they succeed and fail in skill tasks. Depressed students and patients show these same deficits in the laboratory.

These results suggest that the cognitive deficit both in learned helplessness and depression may be produced by the expectation that future response will be ineffective, and this expectation seems to support the negative beliefs about oneself, ongoing experience, and about the future, which cognitive therapists like Beck postulate as the central cause of depression.

When individuals are made helpless by inescapable noise and attribute their failure to their own shortcomings as opposed to external causes, we observe not only the motivational and cognitive deficits of helplessness and depression, but drops in self-esteem as well. In contrast, when helpless subjects are led to make external attribution and blame the task difficulty for their failure, we observe motivational and cognitive deficits but not self-esteem deficits. This parallels the low self-esteem that occurs in depressives, particularly among individuals who blame themselves for their troubles. Parallel mood changes occur both in learned helplessness and depression.

When nondepressed subjects are made helpless by inescapable noise or unsolvable problems, they become sadder, more hostile, and more anxious. These reports parallel the emotional changes in depression of increased sadness, anxiety, and perhaps hostility.

In the laboratory, rats receiving inescapable shock eat less food, lose more weight, are less aggressive against other rats, and lose out in the competition for food with rats who had received either escapable shock or no shock. This loss of appetite and loss of aggression produced by helplessness parallels the somatic symptoms of depressives, who lose weight, eat less, decrease their social desires and status, and become less aggressive.

Finally, learned helplessness in the rat is accompanied by norepinephrine depletion. In an exciting series of studies over the last decade, Jay Weiss at Rockefeller University has demonstrated that the brains of rats receiving inescapable shock have less norepinephrine available than the brains of animals who receive no shock or escapable shock. Weiss argues that the norepinephrine depletion and not the expectation of response-outcome independence causes learned helplessness. While proof is not yet available whether norepinephrine depletion, the expectancies of response-outcome independence—or both—are the fundamental agents in learned helplessness, it is important that norepinephrine depletion is probably a correlate of depression in humans [182].

In summary, several parallel symptoms have been discovered in laboratory-created learned helplessness and natural depression. And in both conditions, the four basic symptoms of depression are displayed: motivational deficits, thought deficits, mood changes, and physical deficits.

Because these four deficits can be created in the laboratory through a known factor—by imposing the expectation that future responses and important outcomes do not correlate—this leads us to an important question: When we observe the same four symptoms in nature and call this condition depression, is the same cause—a belief in the futility of responding—at work?

Cause

The learned helplessness hypothesis says that the depressive deficits that parallel the learned helplessness deficits are produced when an individual expects that negative events may occur, and that they will be independent of one's response. When this is attributed to internal factors, self-esteem drops; when attributed to stable factors, the depression will be long-term; and when attributed to global factors, the depression will be general. Recent evidence confirms this. This attributional style has been found in depressed students, children, and patients. Depressed patients, moreover, believe that the important goals in their life are less under their control than do other psychiatric patients. Most important, however, is that individuals who have this attributional style but are not depressed become depressed when they later encounter bad events.

Therapy

Since the cause of learned helplessness and depression is hypothesized to be the expectation that response will be ineffective in controlling future events, the basic therapeutic approach should be to change this belief into one whereby the individual believes that response will indeed be effective and participated bad events can be avoided. The attributional theory of learned helplessness suggests some basic strategies for doing this. For example, learned helplessness theory suggests that therapies such as teaching social skills and assertiveness training should be antidepressive because they teach the individual that one can control affection and the esteem of other people by one's own actions. Further tactics such as criticizing automatic thoughts ("It's not that I'm an unfit mother, I'm just grouchy at 7 in the morning") help alleviate depression because they change attributions for failure from internal, stable, and global ("unfit mother") to external, unstable, and specific ("7 in the morning").

Evidently, these strategies are very similar to the techniques employed in cognitive and behavioral therapies.

But in addition to these parallels, there are parallels to somatic therapy as well. Four kinds of somatic therapy appear to resolve learned helplessness in animals: electroconvulsive shock, MAO inhibitors, tricyclics, and dream deprivation—which are the four somatic therapies that also can resolve unipolar depression.

In summary, there is reason to believe that the somatic, the cognitive, and the behavioral therapies that reverse learned helplessness also reverse depression.

Prevention and Predisposition

Learned helplessness in animals is prevented by prior experience with mastery and immunization. If an animal first controls important events, such as shock and food, later helplessness never occurs. In effect, it is prevented. Such immunization seems to be lifelong: Rats who learn to escape shock as weanlings do not become helpless when as adults they are given inescapable shock. Conversely, lifelong vulnerability to helplessness is produced by early experience with inescapable shock: Rats who receive inescapable shock as weanlings become helpless adults. This parallels the data on the prevention of and vulnerability to depression. Individuals who have lost their mother before the age of 11 are more vulnerable to depression than those whose mother is still alive. There are, however, "invulnerability factors" that prevent depression from occurring in such individuals: a job, an intimate relationship with spouse or lover, not having life burdened with child care, and religious belief. These factors may increase the expectation of future control and reduce the expectations of future helplessness.

The final parallel in the predisposition to helplessness and depression is that depressed individuals have an insidious attributional style. When they fail, they tend to attribute their failure to internal, global, and stable factors, but when they succeed, they attribute their success to external, unstable, and specific factors. This is a style that maximizes the expectation that responding will be ineffective in the future. The helplessness model suggest that this attributional style predisposes an individual to depression, and recent evidence confirms this.

Two groups of equally nondepressed students with opposite attributional styles for failure—one internal, stable, and global, the other external, unstable, and specific—were investigated during one semester. Those students with the insidious attributional style became more depressed when confronted with later failure (i.e., disappointing mid-term grades) than those students with the opposite attributional style. This suggests that a catastrophizing attributional style is common in depression: "It's going to last forever, and it's going to affect everything I do," predisposing an individual to depression, and that the opposite attributional style may prevent depression when negative events occur [182].

Table. Similarity of learned helplessness and depression.

	Learned Helplessness	Depression
Symptoms	Passivity	Passivity
	Cognitive deficits	Negative cognitive triad
	Self-esteem deficits	Low self-esteem
	Sadness, hostility, anxiety	Sadness, hostility, anxiety
	Loss of appetite	Loss of appetite
	Loss of aggression	Loss of aggression
	Norepinephrine depletion	Norepinephrine depletion
Cause	Learned belief that response is independent of important outcomes (plus attributions to internal, global, and stable factors)	Generalized belief that response will be ineffective
Therapy	Change belief in response futility to belief in response effectiveness ECT, MAOI, tricyclics, REM deprivation Time	Cognitive and behavioral antidepressant therapy ECT, MAOI, tricyclics REM deprivation Time
Prevention	Immunization	Invulnerability factors
Predisposition	Insidious attributional style	Insidious attributional style

From [182].

CHAPTER 11
The Prognosis of Depression in the Elderly

- Because of their frequency and the still poor prognosis, mood disturbances in the elderly represent a problem requiring further research. Available studies are both limited in number and can be hardly compared because of the various criteria used in selecting samples, defining diagnosis, and prescribing treatments. Thus, although the results of single studies are coherent and reliable, it is not possible to draw any general conclusions regarding prognosis evaluation or depressive problems in the elderly.

- This chapter presents an overview of the various studies and stresses the factors potentially responsible for the difficult comparison and generalization of their results.

One of the main variables to consider is the type of treatment offered to patients in the various studies. Christie [113] and Blessed and Wilson [62] recently published two studies conducted in Great Britain in which the prognosis of affective disorders in the 1970s was compared to the results of a study by Roth [574] on hospital patients admitted for similar disturbances in the late 1940s, hence prior to the introduction of the modern antidepressants in pharmacological antidepressive therapy. Both studies employed the diagnostic criteria proposed by Roth for psychiatric diseases in the elderly, namely, senile dementia, atherosclerotic dementia, acute states of confusion, paraphrenia, and affective disorders.

Prognosis was evaluated at 6 and 24 months on the basis of the number of patients discharged, admitted and deceased [62, 113]. The two studies show a clear improvement, as compared to Roth's results of the prognosis at 6 months, with discharge percentages as high as 80%, Roth's figures showing a discharge rate of less than 60%. However, the situation had changed by the 24-month prognosis, the discharge percentages reported by Blessed and Wilson being equal to those of Roth, whereas the

Table 27. Prognosis of depression in old age.

Author	Sample	Follow-up (months)	Well	Outcome relapsed	Ill	Death
Kay [327a]	Consecutive inpatients	9–27	40	20	30	10
Gordon [244a]	Consecutive inpatients	12	48	14	26	12
Murphy [475]	First consecutive consultations	12	35	19	29	14
Cole [122]	Consecutive inpatients	7–31	41	25	22	12
Post [528[	Consecutive inpatients	72	31	52	17	—
Post [529]	Consecutive inpatients	36	26	52	12	10
Cole [134]	Consecutive outpatients	24–63	18	52	30	—

Adapted from Cole [124].

admission rates were higher, while Christie's study [113] reported an overall improvement on Roth's figures.

Murphy [475] confirmed the "negative" findings of Blessed and Wilson in a study conducted on 124 patients in an age range of 65 to 89 years. The author found only one-third of the patients were well 12 months after the initial evaluation—despite drug treatment, ECT, and the availability of a day hospital. In Murphy's research, unfavorable prognosis was associated with the initial severity of the disorder, poor physical health, and low social class.

Even these factors are difficult to compare since they are rarely found in other studies. This is particularly important when evaluating the severity of the initial clinical symptomatology, which was indicated by other authors as important elements in determining prognosis. For instance, in this study, subjects with depressive delusions were more seriously affected. Recently, Baldwin [28] refuted these data in research aimed at verifying the importance of depressive delusions in affective disturbances of the elderly and the possibility of identifying two separate clinical entities. In this retrospective study, two groups of 24 older persons each were followed up for 104 months. It showed certain characteristics in patients with depressive delusions that had already been observed in younger subjects, namely, a poorer response to antidepressive treatment and need to resort to a treatment combination, especially major tranquilizers and ECT, with longer hospitalizations and more frequent relapses.

Nevertheless, the author believes it is unlikely that the presence of depressive delusions can determine a worse prognosis. Instead, he thinks these clinical patterns, which already initially present themselves as more severe, can be related to a general predisposition of the elderly for affective disorders depending on neurobiologic changes of the central nervous system [664]. This supports the necessity for conducting a careful initial diagnosis considering the possible presence of clinical signs related to organic lesions or biochemical alterations referable to the age of subjects studied.

Post [528] conducted a follow-up study on 92 elderly patients admitted to Maudsley Hospital for depression in 1966–1967 and found that 3 years later only 26% were completely cured, 37% had been readmitted to hospital following relapse, 25% presented recurrent episodes in a chronic depressive condition, and 12% had been continuously ill throughout the entire follow-up period.

A study by Jolley and Arie [314] revealed patterns similar to the above with regard to hospital admissions in patients over 65 years of age. The same author also stressed that most psychiatric services for the elderly are dedicated to the care of patients who are chronically ill or undergo frequent relapses.

Better results were reported by Cole [122] on a group of physically healthy patients admitted to hospital for primary depression (Feighner's criteria) [198]. In a 7–31-month follow-up (mean 18 months), only 22% were still depressed, while 67% were in a good or reasonably good condition. In the absence of organic involvement or severe physical diseases, the age of onset (the first depressive episode after the age of 60 years) was significantly correlated with prognosis, though age on evaluation was not. The subjects with late onset were more often completely well during the follow-up than those with early onset and were less prone to relapse.

Later, Cole [124] published a study on 55 elderly depressed patients attending the psychogeriatric outpatient unit of a general hospital during the follow-up period (from 24 to 63 months, mean 48 months): 38 patients were well for more than 60% of the period, and 17 remained chronically ill. In most cases, a favorable prognosis was associated with absence of disabling physical disease, with long-term follow-up, and with compliance with the pharmacological antidepressant therapy. There was a trend toward better prognosis in cases with late onset of the first depressive episode. The following factors had no influence on prognosis: age, sex, marital status, number of previous depressive episodes, presence of triggering factors for depressive episodes, and presence of slight signs of organic involvement of the CNS.

In these two studies performed by Cole, the similarity in results between in- and outpatients appears to refute the hypothesis of a different clinical involvement in these two groups, which is often referred to in various studies.

Recently, Baldwin and Jolley [27] reported the findings of evaluations in 100 elderly subjects suffering from severe nonneurotic depression. In observation periods ranging from 42 to 104 months, they found that 60% of the subjects experienced complete remission, despite some cases of relapse followed once by remission. The disorder persisted in only 7% of the subjects. In this study, poor outcome was associated with factors such as male sex and poor physical health. It should be noted that roughly half (48%) of the patients participating in this study had been treated with bilateral ECT; in the authors' opinion this may have been a factor in the better outcome of these patients as compared, for example, with those of Murphy's study [475], in which only 16% of the patients were treated with ECT.

Kiloh et al. [342] followed up patients with depressive illness for a period of 15 years; 133 completed the entire follow-up. During this period, 7% of patients committed suicide, 12% continued to be affected by disturbances, and only 20% were "well" on a long-term basis. Only regarding the possibility of new admission, endogenous depression, and previous hospitalizations resulted in determinants with respect to neurotic depression. But considering all other parameters, the two diagnoses overlapped, showing a clear morbidity in both especially in long-term evaluations.

Recently, Murphy et al. [478] studied how the high mortality rate in depressed elderly patients correlated with their general psychophysical condition over a period of 4 years. The reported mortality rate for depressed subjects was 34.2% compared to 14% for control groups with a level of significance of 0.1% in males and 5% in females. Detailed analysis of the results suggested to the authors that the physical situation may not represent the primary cause, but only one of the many factors involved in increasing the mortality in elderly depressed subjects, and that possible correlations (especially neurobiologic ones) between depression and mortality must be further studied.

In this regard, recent works have reported the possibility of unidentified cerebral organic pathology as the common cause both of the poor prognosis and the high mortality of some subgroups of depressed elderly patients [284]. Jacoby and Bird [303] used computer tomography to show a positive correlation between the widening of cerebral ventricles and increased mortality rate in the two subsequent years in depressed patients compared to subjects with similar general characteristic and found instead a negative correlation with respect to CT scan findings. Bird [55] also demonstrated a correlation between death of the spouse, depression, and widening of cerebral ventricles as observed with CT scans. Also known is the relationship between depression and abnormalities of the immunologic system, and how this can affect the morbidity and mortality and also the prognosis of depression itself in these patients [596].

We conducted a study [424] designed to evaluate the evolution of depressive disorders in a group of elderly depressed outpatients and to examine the role played in prognosis by various sociodemographic and clinical factors. Our population was made up of subjects over the age of 60 years attending the outpatient clinics of the Mental Health Centre of the University of Padua during their first visits. The patients presented clinical disorders identified by two different evaluators as "affective disorders" according to the criteria of the Diagnostic and Statistical Manual of Mental Disorders (DSM-III) [11]. Out of the 94 initial patients, 64 were included in the study, follow-up being from 6 to 24 months (mean 15 months). The most frequent diagnosis was dysthymic disorder followed by major and typical depression. Treatment principally consisted of tricyclic and second-generation antidepressive drugs often combined with anxiolytic drugs, and in 19% of cases also psychotherapy. During follow-up, 31% of patients were well or sufficiently well, 69% being still ill, though no one died.

In more detail, the results were as follows:

* In agreement with Cole's [122] and Kay's [330] findings, onset age rather than the actual age was correlated with the prognosis, the latter being better in the group with a late onset.

- CNS diseases negatively affected the prognosis in agreement
  with previously reported data [125, 291, 528, 529], whereas
  contrary to what others have reported [125, 291, 475, 528,
  529], organic diseases did not appear to have a significant
  influence.

- Diagnosis was observed to be relevant, prognosis being clearly more favorable for adjustment disorders with depressed
  mood than in all other diagnoses. The prognosis of the dysthymic disorders was better than that of the major depressions.

- Social support and loneliness were less important than previously reports had claimed [77, 420, 427, 476, 638].

Thus, in our report, the poor prognosis of depression in the
elderly is confirmed, especially in certain diagnostic groups with
chronic and disabling consequences. This could be partly linked
to an accumulation of early onset cases in the elderly with a
chronic pattern and frequent presence of concomitant diseases of
CNS.

DISCUSSION AND CONCLUSION

From the above one can see that only a few studies exist regarding prognosis depression in the elderly. And considering the
methodological difficulties and controversies still existing, they
cannot represent scientifically definite conclusions. In fact, these
reports present many nonstandardized variables with respect to
both selection of samples and especially diagnostic-therapeutic
approaches. Thus, even if they are reliable in the specific case,
their prognostic evaluation cannot be properly compared with
other experiences. This leads to the impossibility of establishing
generalized prognoses and detecting possible factors involved to
date in obtaining the few satisfactory results.

For instance, many studies were performed on sample groups
of hospitalized or psychiatric patients, which might have led to
overly negative results [92]. Often, even diagnostic criteria are
not comparable, and although data exist on the importance of the
"severity" of the clinical manifestations as a prognostic index,
most studies focused their attention on the specific type of depression without identifying any parameter related to the intensity of the disorder itself. Moreover, even in this context, there

are different interpretations related to the classification of depressive disturbances. Some favor the distinction between "neurotic" and "endogenous," whereas others support the continuum. Nevertheless, it is possible that more importance is given to the distinction of depression into primary and secondary when we consider the high frequency of concomitant organic diseases, psychosocial problems, and loss events. All these aspects must be further clarified in order to detect possible direct or indirect interferences, especially at the level of neurobiologic or neurochemical mediators. Specifically, in the light of modern biological theories on the genesis of affective disturbances and aging, it is necessary to concentrate our efforts on the relationships among various physical and psychic endogenous and exogenous factors that can lead to specific characteristics of depression among the elderly. In this regard, we detected another scarcely comparable factor in previous studies: the qualitative and quantitative entity of therapy, especially pharmacologic therapy.

The coexistence in these patients of many factors affecting the general situation makes it difficult to analyze which are prognostically speaking essential and how we can interact with them. Nevertheless, it is exactly this form of detailed analysis that can demonstrate whether it is proper to believe the depressed elderly have a worse prognosis than do younger patients. This obviously does not mean we ought not also to adequately evaluate the quality and quantity of treatment and assistance offered and how these can be improved to make these subjects become more adequate to their specific need. Only though studies that overcome methodological difficulties and possibly represent references making comparisons can we analyze the factors involved in the development of prognosis of depression in old age and detect which tools and modalities can be used to obtain positive results.

PART THREE:
SUICIDE IN THE ELDERLY

CHAPTER 12
Suicide in the Elderly

- Despite its positive relationship with age, suicide is a quite rare phenomenon, representing in this age group "only" the 9th or 10th cause of death in Western countries compared to the 2nd or 3rd among young adults. Thus, one could argue that many other problems of old age are more prevalent (and thus important) than suicide and should require more attention. However, both in relative and absolute terms, suicide in the elderly constitutes a problem far bigger than in other ages groups. In this chapter we consider the practically ubiquitous seriousness of this problem worldwide, taking into account differences between various societies.

- Generally speaking, suicide and attempted suicide in old age have specific characteristics. First of all, it appears evident that the elderly are more determined to actually die. It is quite striking how attempted suicide resembles completed suicide, so that one could often consider a suicide attempt in an elderly subject as a "failed suicide." Confirming the general impression of greater determination to die, the elderly also use "harder" methods and seem less prone to communicate their intention.

- Despite our knowledge on demographic and psychosocial characteristics of suicide in the elderly, many problems remain unanswered. For instance, physical illness—so prevalent in later life—plays an important, but in some way confounding, role, especially if a link exists with depression, the most common denominator of suicidal behaviors. Physical diseases create the aura of "rationality" so frequently tied to suicide in old age and so misleading to a proper explanation of suicidal behaviors.

It has been known for a long time that the elderly are more likely to take their own lives than individuals of any other age group. Nevertheless, much less interest has been shown in suicidal behavior among the elderly than in suicide and attempted suicide in adolescents, youths, and younger adults.

In fact, the suicide of an elderly person is generally seen—in a somewhat nihilistic way—as the death of a person who is no longer socially and economically productive, and who, furthermore, has already lived out his or her days: An event, thus, that is much less tragic than the death of young persons who "still have their whole life ahead of them."

One reason that may underlie the apparent disinterest of scientists and the public health sector may be found in the fact that in most nations suicide is a more important cause of death in persons under 65 than over 65 years [695]. In 1983, in Anglo-Saxon countries, 11% of total mortality in the 20–25-year age group resulted from suicide, while the corresponding percentage in the elderly was only 0.2% [391]. Hence, the comparison between situations in which suicide is the second or third greatest cause of death [126] and others—as in the case of the elderly—in which suicide as a cause of death is far overshadowed by, for example, cardiovascular and respiratory problems probably explains the lack of interest—even by the World Health Organization—in suicide in senescence. But it should be noted that despite its low frequency as cause of death in the elderly, the suicide rate remains virtually constant, against a general reduction reported for other causes of death in the elderly [429].

To this must be added the rather widespread idea according to which suicide may be a "rational" choice in certain circumstances of old age, for example, in the presence of a severe chronic disease or a serious limitation of personal independence.

As maintained by Lindesay [391], there are, however, many valid reasons for increased attention to the problem of suicide in the elderly. Suicide is always a traumatic event for the victim's family. Its epidemiological relevance—as we shall see further on—constitutes a valid index of the distress and discontent of elderly subjects. Finally, the suicide of an elderly person should always be considered a potentially preventable cause of death.

DEFINITION AND EPIDEMIOLOGY OF SUICIDAL BEHAVIOR

At present there are no internationally standardized and accepted definitions of the main types of suicidal behavior. Although most authors agree on the existence of two main types, usually distinguished by their (fatal or nonfatal) outcome, the terms to designate them may differ as well as the criteria for inclusion or exclusion of behaviors under a specific type. Suicidal acts with a nonfatal outcome are labeled either suicide attempts, attempted suicides, parasuicides or acts of deliberate self-harm, depending upon the country of origin of the author(s) or the "school" he or she adheres to. While those terms are often used as synonyms, several authors also distinguish between attempted suicide and parasuicide, the former implying an intention (however vague and ambiguous) to do away with oneself, while the latter encompasses also so-called "contraintentioned" acts, meaning that the individual uses the semantic blanket of "suicide" with a conscious absence of any lethal intention.

In a recent WHO copublication [182a], the following set of definitions is proposed:

- *Suicide:*
1) An act with a fatal outcome;
2) that is deliberately initiated and performed by the deceased him- or herself;
3) in the knowledge or expectation of its fatal outcome;
4) the outcome being considered by the actor as instrumental in bringing about desired changes in consciousness and/or social conditions.

- *Attempted suicide:*
1) A nonhabitual act with nonfatal outcome;
2) that is deliberately initiated and performed by the individual involved;
3) that causes self-harm or without intervention from others will do so or consists of ingesting a substance in excess of its generally recognized therapeutic dosage.

- *Parasuicide:*
1) A nonhabitual act with nonfatal outcome;
2) that is deliberately initiated and performed by the individual involved *in expectation of such an outcome*;
3) that causes self-harm of without intervention from others will do so or consists of ingesting a substance in excess of its generally recognized therapeutic dosage;
4) the outcome being considered by the actor as instrumental in bringing about desired changes in expectancies and/or social condition.

Like every general definition, these definitions have to be used with certain legends or inclusion/exclusion criteria. For example, a person who lies on a railway track in order to be killed by the next passing train but who is rescued in time, or a person who jumps off a bridge in order to drown him- of herself but is then quickly pulled out of the water by others, might not have yet injured him-/herself. However, such an act should certainly be considered a case of attempted suicide according to the definition given above.

Furthermore, when a nonhabitual drinker of alcohol or user of tranquilizers deliberately takes an overdose and at the same time fulfills criterion (c) of the attempted suicide definition (assuming the act is not simply undertaken to find out how alcohol or tranquilizers feel), he or she has to be considered a case of attempted suicide. However, if that same person had taken clear precautions to prevent his or her act from resulting in death, for example, by taking a substance that provokes later vomiting of the substance taken such as alcohol of tranquilizers, he/she should be considered as a case of parasuicide.

The definitions are based on the following assumptions:

1) Attempted suicides are not simply failed or bungled suicides, for there are important epidemiological, etiological, and motivational differences between attempted and completed suicides.

2) The prefix "para" in parasuicide should be taken to refer to acts that are intended by the actor to resemble suicidal acts while both in terms of outcome and motivation they do not.

As to the first point, available research evidence suggests characteristic differences between suicide and attempted suicide in relation to the methods of self-harm used, clinical aspects (such as psychiatric diagnosis and treatment), psychological features and personality patterns. Also, there are differences in terms of age and sex of the persons involved and in relation to the emotional precipitants of the behavior. As to social antecedents, such as unemployment or loss of work, suicide and parasuicide populations seem to overlap considerably.

As to the second point, to date most studies tend to adopt somewhat idiosyncratic nominal definitions of suicide/attempted suicide/parasuicide, and it is not unusual to find studies in which attempted suicide and parasuicide are brought together under the same heading, thereby making comparisons between different investigations more or less problematic. It is with these precautions in mind that the reader should approach the following description of the nature and magnitude of suicidal behavior in the elderly.

EPIDEMIOLOGY OF SUICIDAL BEHAVIOR IN THE ELDERLY

One of the most basic facts about suicide is that this risk increases as a function of age in practically all countries in the world. Completed suicide is very rare in children under the age of 12; but it becomes more common after puberty, with incidence increasing in each of the adolescent years. In most countries the increase continues throughout adulthood, although in certain countries young adults have higher rates than the middle aged.

However, the highest rates of suicide are generally found among the elderly, those age 60 and over, particularly among elderly men.

Figures from 22 European countries confirm that the percentage of suicides in persons aged 60 and over is considerably higher than that found among adolescents and adults, both in absolute terms and in deaths per 100,000 of the population [695]

Over the period 1955–1979, the European suicide percentages varied considerably from country to country. For the age group 10–64 years, the figures of most countries show an upward tendency. This is particularly the case in the countries of Northern Europe such as Ireland, Norway, Belgium, and The Netherlands. Mediterranean countries such as Spain, Italy, and Greece diverge from the general tendency, showing a reduction in suicide percentages. The percentage increase in suicides in women, both in terms of the number of nations involved and in percentage changes, is notably higher than in men. This latter tendency is rather difficult to interpret, although it may be a repercussion of the changing role of women in contemporary society [95].

The trend is similar in subjects aged 65 and over (see Table 28), with fewer countries showing an increase, especially among males.

From our own analyses, using data from the World Health Organization data bank in Geneva for 19 countries over the period 1970–1985/86, the following picture of trends in different age categories emerge (see Figure 2):

Table 28. Suicide in 22 European countries 1955–1959 and 1975–1979 for persons aged 65–84. Standard mortality rates based on average rates.

MALES			FEMALES		
	Time period			Time period	
Country	55–59	75–79	Country	55–59	75–79
1. Hungary	91.17	139.19	1. Hungary	31.75	65.99
2. Czechoslovakia	80.61	70.56	2. Czechoslovakia	30.40	28.20
3. France	70.99	58.76	3. Denmark	26.76	30.84
4. Switzerland	69.70	56.58	4. Austria	25.37	27.99
5. Belgium	63.97	64.33	5. FRG	21.51	27.20
6. Portugal	60.68	49.25	6. France	21.11	20.17
7. Austria	59.84	74.69	7. Bulgaria	20.72	24.93
8. Finland	59.09	62.93	8. England &Wales	19.39	11.42
9. Bulgaria	57.55	71.94	9. Belgium	18.76	26.38
10. Sweden	56.83	43.53	10. Switzerland	17.93	23.31
11. Denmark	55.27	51.07	11. Netherlands	17.77	14.99
12. FRG	48.58	53.47	12. Sweden	12.49	16.13
13. England & Wales	42.50	18.44	13. Finland	10.71	14.20
14. Netherlands	32.33	27.60	14. Portugal	9.26	10.46
15. Spain	27.05	21.01	15. Scotland	9.26	7.27
16. Italy	26.64	26.52	16. Italy	7.34	8.04
17. Scotland	24.84	15.29	17. Spain	6.77	5.66
18. Norway	21.41	24.67	18. Norway	6.25	6.85
19. Poland	17.90	26.16	19. Northern Ireland	5.33	4.27
20. Greece	13.78	10.28	20. Poland	4.04	5.98
21. Northern Ireland	9.60	8.09	21. Greece	3.17	3.69
22. Ireland	8.53	9.13	22. Ireland	1.28	4.17

Source: Who/EURO, Copenhagen

Upward trends are most frequent and sizeable in the 15–29-year-olds, followed by the 60+ group, while in both age categories the majority of countries show a rise in rates. This picture, however, is considerably more pronounced among males than among females.

The 30–59-year-old age group deviates from the other two categories in that

1) fewer countries show an increase,

2) where an increase is observed, it is comparatively small and

3) among 30–59-year-old females the majority of countries show a considerable decrease.

It seems therefore warranted to conclude that, from an international perspective, the recent general rise in suicide rates has particularly affected the two ends of the age spectrum.

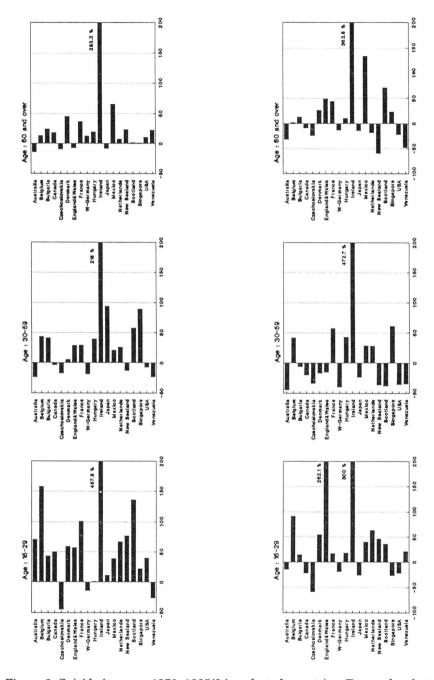

Figure 2. Suicide increase 1970–1985/6 in selected countries. Top: males; bottom: females. Source: WHO data bank.

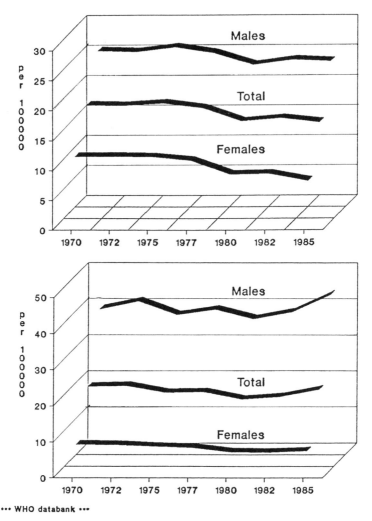

Figure 3. Suicide in the United States. Top: 30–59 years; bottom: 60+ years.

Figure 3 shows the comparative trends for the age groups 30–59 and 60+ for one particular country, the United States. While for females the trend is slightly downwards in both groups, the older men show a slightly upward trend.

Table 29 presents data on the relative importance of suicide as a cause of death in different age groups. It appears that compared to adolescents and young adults, suicide as a cause of death among the elderly is of relatively minor importance. This

Table 29. Suicide as a percentage of all death causes in that age group. Above: males, below: females. Source: WHO data bank.

Country	Age group 15–24	25–34	65–74	All ages
Australia	17.7	20.3	0.5	2.2
Bulgaria	10.8	9.6	1.1	1.7
Czechoslovakia	13.0	20.0	1.0	2.3
Canada	20.7	20.6	0.8	2.6
Denmark	18.6	28.2	1.4	2.9
England & Wales	10.9	18.1	0.4	1.0
France	13.9	21.7	1.8	3.1
Hungary	18.8	27.8	2.0	4.4
Ireland	9.0	14.3	0.4	0.9
Japan	19.5	29.6	1.6	4.1
Netherlands	15.2	21.5	0.7	1.6
New Zealand	12.8	14.4	0.9	1.8
Scotland	16.6	17.4	0.5	1.3
Singapore	12.6	13.6	1.2	2.6
USA	14.5	14.3	0.9	2.1

Country	Age group 15–24	25–34	65–74	All ages
Australia	10.3	8.5	0.1	0.7
Bulgaria	9.9	7.9	0.8	0.9
Czechoslovakia	10.4	13.5	0.7	0.8
Canada	9.6	12.5	0.4	0.9
Denmark	23.3	25.0	1.5	1.9
England & Wales	6.2	9.5	0.5	0.5
France	10.1	16.2	1.7	1.4
Hungary	18.8	18.6	1.6	2.0
Ireland	8.5	7.0	0.2	0.5
Japan	28.0	24.9	2.3	2.7
Netherlands	11.2	10.5	0.9	1.0
New Zealand	9.0	7.3	0.4	0.6
Scotland	9.4	11.1	0.5	0.5
Singapore	15.0	17.6	0.6	2.5
USA	8.6	8.9	0.3	0.7

picture is, however, misleading, since for example in the United States, the NCHS (National Center for Health Statistics) figures for 1985 showed that 25% of all suicides occurred in the over-65 age group, which accounted for only 12% of the population as a whole [346]. The decline in mortality for other causes was paralleled by an increase in that for suicide, especially in persons over

Table 30. Deaths from suicide in the elderly. Comparison between years 1960 and 1985 (rate per 100,000 population). Source: WHO data bank.

Country		Age	65–69	70–74	75–79	80–84	85+
CANADA	1960	M	25.3	26.5	36.1	11.0	16.7
		F	6.3	7.6	3.6	6.9	–
	1985	M	25.9	31.7	25.6	34.8	26.4
		F	8.0	7.6	72.6	5.1	–
USA	1960	M	26.4	43.9	49.7	58.0	57.4
		F	8.1	8.9	9.3	8.0	6.0
	1985	M	29.0	38.9	48.4	61.9	55.4
		F	6.7	7.2	7.4	6.0	4.6
URUGUAY	1960	M	47.0	29.7	78.9	40.0	51.3
		F	15.0	6.8	–	–	36.1
	1985	M	3.4	13.2	5.6	10.2	–
		F	3.4	13.2	5.6	10.2	–
HONG KONG	1960	M	76.9	53.3	176.5	142.9	–
		F	22.0	33.1	62.5	50.0	–
	1985	M	42.6	57.6	53.6	42.0	93.8
		F	19.0	38.5	32.5	63.0	46.2
JAPAN	1960	M	60.3	72.7	86.3	97.6	85.0
		F	42.8	51.0	62.8	74.3	70.7
	1985	M	38.5	47.5	65.5	79.5	102.1
		F	26.4	33.6	47.9	59.9	62.1
AUSTRIA	1960	M	66.4	53.2	84.1	77.4	63.0
		F	24.7	31.6	23.4	21.6	16.9
	1985	M	59.7	82.0	88.4	110.2	90.0
		F	29.0	32.6	32.8	33.1	28.8
CZECHO-SLOVAKIA	1960	M	66.9	77.1	90.2	119.4	107.0
		F	30.2	35.0	29.2	43.1	51.7
	1985	M	53.1	68.1	91.1	110.3	112.0
		F	21.2	25.1	29.2	39.3	33.3
DENMARK	1960	M	46.5	42.6	67.4	42.9	38.1
		F	31.4	13.5	31.6	18.5	30.3
	1985	M	57.9	57.5	79.7	76.9	105.8
		F	36.5	31.4	30.1	24.8	13.0
FINLAND	1960	M	53.8	62.1	39.6	75.3	27.0
		F	18.2	13.3	5.2	10.5	–
	1985	M	45.4	53.4	56.3	71.4	85.1
		F	13.9	4.5	10.1	11.7	10.2
FRANCE	1960	M	52.5	64.4	87.7	107.0	131.2
		F	17.6	19.4	21.7	22.2	21.0
	1985	M	50.3	72.1	101.9	132.0	158.9
		F	24.7	28.5	27.6	26.6	28.5
FRG	1960	M	43.2	49.9	50.8	55.6	76.3
		F	21.0	19.2	20.5	18.0	19.2
	1985	M	41.8	57.6	67.2	90.7	103.6
		F	23.3	25.9	23.5	24.3	27.9
HUNGARY	1960	M	63.2	70.5	105.1	118.9	152.0
		F	28.7	35.9	36.0	72.5	52.1

	1985	M	95.6	145.7	173.5	236.1	302.1
		F	34.6	49.1	62.9	84.4	82.0
IRELAND	1960	M	15.4	4.5	3.3	–	13.2
		F	1.9	8.3	6.0	–	–
	1985	M	17.7	23.7	12.5	–	–
		F	5.8	10.1	2.4	–	–
NETHER-	1960	M	24.1	21.0	29.5	40.2	58.8
LANDS		F	13.7	18.7	12.4	10.3	21.4
	1985	M	24.4	28.2	30.4	47.9	60.2
		F	15.7	15.4	10.8	10.1	11.5
NORWAY	1960	M	18.1	6.3	12.8	15.5	–
		F	2.6	3.4	2.4	–	–
	1985	M	17.8	19.5	36.0	13.3	33.1
		F	8.1	8.2	7.7	1.9	–
POLAND	1960	M	19.4	21.0	27.2	19.0	20.2
		F	3.8	3.8	4.4	4.5	2.1
	1985	M	28.3	27.2	29.3	29.5	36.0
		F	6.0	5.0	6.6	7.7	7.4
PORTUGAL	1960	M	44.8	44.2	80.3	58.1	70.8
		F	7.2	8.2	8.7	4.4	14.8
	1985	M	30.7	45.9	45.2	49.7	103.6
		F	9.6	18.4	14.1	10.8	14.6
SWEDEN	1960	M	42.1	56.7	47.1	51.8	62.8
		F	16.4	12.5	10.9	7.6	7.7
	1985	M	35.5	43.9	44.4	43.1	68.9
		F	11.8	13.6	9.4	8.2	8.1
SWITZER-	1960	M	60.9	51.3	53.2	64.2	103.4
LAND		F	12.9	18.0	25.7	5.7	12.5
	1985	M	56.9	68.4	55.6	87.6	114.2
		F	29.3	27.2	16.2	14.3	21.6
ENGLAND	1960	M	31.5	35.0	37.2	42.9	34.6
		F	20.0	16.9	13.2	12.4	6.3
	1985	M	16.9	17.0	21.5	25.0	20.3
		F	11.8	12.0	10.9	11.2	7.0
NORTHERN	1960	M	9.1	18.8	27.0	24.1	–
IRELAND		F	14.4	18.1	–	9.9	–
	1985	M	11.3	27.5	13.3	83.3	–
		F	17.7	9.8	12.0	–	–
SCOTLAND	1960	M	15.6	28.1	19.7	13.6	22.5
		F	13.3	10.8	4.7	–	–
	1985	M	22.7	15.2	26.2	17.7	8.2
		F	12.7	10.5	8.0	9.2	7.0
AUSTRALIA	1960	M	43.5	31.3	33.1	28.2	32.7
		F	10.9	11.1	8.7	11.8	3.7
	1985	M	21.5	28.8	21.7	27.0	51.1
		F	7.1	8.1	11.4	8.8	7.0
NEW	1960	M	19.0	41.7	37.4	29.7	21.7
ZEALAND		F	15.7	15.2	4.2	7.5	–
	1985	M	39.1	33.1	40.7	37.3	30.8
		F	8.2	11.3	7.7	4.0	–

85, with a relative and absolute increase during the years 1968–1981.

Three-fourths of all suicides in the United States among the elderly are committed by men, the rate increasing progressively with age: from 31/100,000 in the age range 65 to 74 years, to 45/100,000 in the age range 74 to 84 years, to 50/100,000 in persons over 85 [346].

Table 30 shows suicide rates of elderly populations in 24 nations. Although the figures differ markedly from country to country, a general trend toward an increase in suicides with increasing age can nevertheless be noted, especially among males. The suicide rate in most countries in fact peaks among persons over 80.

Table 30 shows that there is no general trend over time with regard to suicidal behavior in the countries studied: 25 years after the first survey (1960), some countries showed a substantial increase in suicide rate, others a significant reduction, while still others experienced a steady rate or marked differences in trends between the sexes. There was a sharp rise in elderly suicides in Hungary, and to a lesser degree in countries such as France, Denmark, Austria, and Poland. With exception of Sweden and England/Wales, significant reductions in suicides among elderly subjects were only found in the non-European nations, such as Japan, Hong Kong, and Australia.

From an international perspective then, it would appear that suicide among the elderly constitutes a serious problem even though there are wide divergences between nations in rates as well as in trends.

In contrast to suicides, nonfatal suicide attempts, or "para-suicides," are both relatively and absolutely more common in the younger age groups than in the elderly, attempted suicides being three times more common than completed suicides in the elderly, as against 40 times in subjects between 15 and 30 years of age [180, 525]. In a 10-year study in the Mannheim area (West Germany), Welz [689] found a 100% increase in attempted suicides that was negatively correlated with age: While the rate for the population over the age of 65 years remained constant, the 15–19 age group presented an increase of 300%. This marked increase appears to be linked to high rates of alcohol and drug abuse located in areas considered to have a high index of social disintegration [690].

Although the total number of suicidal acts—including suicide attempts without a fatal outcome—is both absolutely and relatively lower in the elderly than in the young, the probability of fatal outcome is much higher in the elderly. The comparatively greater seriousness of suicidal intent among the elderly who attempt suicide may be deduced from their increased risk of fatal outcome in a subsequent attempt as compared to the total population of attempts. Gardner [225] reports that risk of death in (later) attempts compared to the general population is 9 times higher in persons under the age of 55 as against 19 times higher in those 55 years and over. In 1976, Kreitman found that 8% of elderly persons with a history of suicide attempts killed themselves within 3 years of the first attempt [357].

CHARACTERISTICS OF SUICIDAL BEHAVIOR IN THE ELDERLY

In general, suicide attempts in the elderly are very serious, in both medical and psychological terms, and "failure" of a suicidal act is often due to unforeseeable circumstances or factors (e.g., the unexpected intervention of others). Attempted suicides in the elderly should thus frequently be considered "failed suicides" [94]. This means that, when compared to attempted suicides among the younger age groups, the elderly are generally far more determined to die. This may be deduced, on the one hand, from the content of suicide notes, as shown in various studies [460], and on the other hand, from the different methods and circumstances in which the suicidal behaviors occur.

The elderly frequently use "harder" methods, such as hanging, drowning, throwing themselves in front of moving vehicles, jumping from heights, seriously wounding themselves with a knife or sharp instrument or firearm [197]. Miller [459] has shown in Arizona that 85% of elderly suicides used a firearm, and that one-fourth of these (versus none of the control group of subjects who died of natural causes) had bought a gun during the month preceding the suicide. In most Western countries, however, it appears that over 85% of the total suicides among the elderly occur by hanging (especially in men), poisoning (especially in women), and drowning [391]. At present, there also appears to be an appreciable increase in suicides by inhaling car exhaust fumes.

The correlation in England and Wales between a decline in the suicide rate and the switchover to nontoxic domestic gas after 1960 may be interesting in this context. Before this date, poisoning by domestic gas was the most common suicidal method among both younger adults and the elderly [391]. After 1960, there was a notable decline in suicide rates for the elderly, but not for other age groups. This might be the result of a quicker adjustment or greater knowledge of alternative methods among the younger population. 85% of suicides in the elderly in England and Wales are now by defenestration, hanging, and poisoning [391].

Men of all ages use more violent methods than do women, and they are less likely to survive a suicide attempt [289]. This finding is confirmed in black populations, in whom lethal outcome, moreover, is higher in all age groups [451].

Compared to other age groups, elderly subjects may rather frequently allow themselves to die by means of "slow" methods, the intrinsic characteristics of which make it difficult to assess whether there was an effective desire for death. Classic cases of this type are, for example, elderly persons who intentionally neglect themselves, refusing food, refusing to take medical prescriptions, not complying with treatments, etc. These slow and gradual suicides, which are grouped under the term "suicidal erosion," and which are virtually absent among younger subjects, do not appear in official statistics. This has been stressed by many authors [179], as it has been found to be one of the most important causes of the underestimation of suicide among the elderly [274].

Furthermore, a number of studies have shown that the elderly subject is less disposed than young persons to communicate suicidal intentions to others [197, 431]. According to Robins et al. [553], such communications are generally addressed to family members rather than to the general health care workers. This appears to underline the importance of the fact that, compared to younger subjects, suicidal behavior in the elderly is much less motivated by the desire to mobilize others and draw their attention to themselves and their plight, or, more simply, to cry for help.

Moreover, the elderly subject more frequently attempts suicide in conditions in which interference by others is normally impossible or highly unlikely.

PSYCHOSOCIAL CHARACTERISTICS CORRELATED WITH
SUICIDE IN THE ELDERLY

Apart from gender-related factors, other conditions have also
been shown to increase predisposition to suicide. For example,
with regard to marital status, it has been found that divorce
(especially in the age group 75–79 years) entails a high risk,
followed by widowhood and single status [94]. This increased risk
may derive not only from the loss of the partner per se, but from
a feeling of guilt and "failure" [525]. Bojanowsky [66] has also
revealed that the risk of death is markedly higher for males in
the first 6 months after the loss of the partner. The risk for
women is only slightly increased, but the period of risk is more
prolonged and increases with increasing age. Marriage appears
to have the greatest "immunizing" effect, especially when associated with involvement in social activities or membership of
associations, clubs, etc., as demonstrated by Bock's study [65]
conducted in Florida.

Unlike in the younger age groups, the rate of suicide in the
60+ age group tends to decrease with age in the higher socioeconomic categories (executives, professionals) and to increase in the
lower ones [578], probably because the former benefit from a
financially more favorable situation and have a greater chance of
finding positive and creative interests. This trend is confirmed in
the study by Robins et al. [551], in which it was found that there
was no increase in suicidal behaviors among blue-collar workers
before retirement, but after this event the increase was appreciable. It is clear that education in life planning after retirement
could have a positive influence on this trend in suicide rates.

Retirement has frequently been associated with risk of suicide, especially in the first few years after the end of active
employment [624]. In fact, there is a high risk of suicide not only
among individuals who face retirement without the support of
alternative activities or interests, but also in those whose plans
are unexpectedly upset [289]. A reduction in income resulting
from retirement from productive life has also been associated
with suicide, although Sainsbury [579] has shown that the introduction of the Old Age Pension in Great Britain did not lead to
significant changes in suicide rates.

We have already discussed the different distributions of suicide rates in different nations; however, differences in ethnic
origin within a single nation may also be substantial. The most

significant example relates to the United States, where whites commit suicide 2–3 times more frequently than blacks [391]. Robins et al. [553] have suggested that the intensity of religious faith and different attitudes toward suicide among black people may explain their smaller propensity to suicide. Similar reasons have also been invoked to explain the very low suicide rates found among the Amish communities [94], among whom—it should be noted—the elderly enjoy particular respect. A similar finding, though in a completely different cultural context, may explain the relatively low suicide rates among elderly subjects in prerevolutionary China [391].

Generally speaking, urban areas are more strongly associated with risk of suicide than are rural zones. An exception to this is provided by The Netherlands (at least up to 1965)—a country in which many persons living in the cities for reasons of work return to their towns and villages of origin on retirement [578]. Gardner et al. [225] showed that the persons most at risk for suicide are male urban dwellers who live alone or in conditions of social isolation in the poorer socioeconomic areas of the city. The utilization of the psychiatric services by such subjects seems to be very low, and diagnoses of personality disorders seem to occur more frequently than affective disorders in these individuals.

Depression is certainly the most frequent factor in the association between mental disorders and suicide. Barraclough [34] found that 27 out of every 30 elderly suicides [85%] were diagnosed as affected by mental disorder, and all were depressed. Yet only a few had received psychiatric attention. Harkey [274] found that mortality from suicide among elderly psychiatric patients is very high, possibly higher than in any other group. Although the timely identification of these high-risk patients is difficult, previous diagnosis of depression and the manifestation of suicidal thoughts appear to be indicative.

Chynoweth [115] has reported that among suicidal elderly mental disorders were present for less than 1 year before suicide in two-thirds of the women and one-fourth of the men. Case histories revealed that 33% had presented psychiatric diseases, 29% had previously attempted suicide, and 13% had similar cases in their family histories.

In an Arizona study on 301 suicides, Miller [459] found that 76% of the subjects had contacted a doctor in the month prior to committing suicide, one-third of the subjects in the last week.

From a psychiatric point of view, however, elderly suicides appear to be a diagnostically heterogeneous group [289]. Key symptoms indicating a high risk for suicide among elderly depressed subjects include persistent insomnia, marked feelings of guilt and inadequacy, hypochondriac delirium, and agitation [65]. Alcoholism appears to be correlated to suicide in more than one-third of cases in the United States and in many European countries [182c], and there has been a clear increase in this phenomenon over the last 10 years. However, while it has been shown that the percentages of deaths by suicide are 10 times higher among alcoholics of all ages [244], this figure drops by more than half in alcoholics over the age of 65 [551]. Among the elderly, widow/ers seem to be most at risk for both alcoholism and, as we have seen, suicide. Clearly, alcoholism itself tends to erode the family and social relations and activities that function as a support for the elderly person [497].

Beck et al. [41] administered the *Beck Depression Inventory* and the *Hopelessness Scale* to 105 alcoholics who had attempted suicide. Stepwise multiple regression analysis of the results revealed that "hopelessness" was the major predictive factor for suicide. The authors concluded that the sense of hopelessness accompanying alcoholism is a major factor in suicide [41].

In the elderly, organic mental disturbances may also contribute significantly to the high numbers of deaths by suicide, as suggested by Sainsbury [578]. However, it has been objected [603] that such organic conditions, especially if characterized by states of confusion (for example, from excessive drug doses or physical diseases) could actually increase the numbers of so called "failed suicides," by interfering with an adequate planning of the act.

DEPRESSION, BIOLOGICAL FACTORS, AND SUICIDE

Although depression is a very common disorder in old age, and although the connections between depression—especially in its delusional forms—and suicide is well established [572], "only" 0.5% of elderly depressed subjects actually commit suicide [391]. Hence various studies have been directed toward broadening our understanding of this problem, in order to identify other factors connected with depression that might play a determining role in the dynamics of suicide. According to Beck et al. [39], for example, the intensity of feelings of hopelessness may be a more sen-

ple, the intensity of feelings of hopelessness may be a more sensitive indicator than the severity of the depression. Wolff [706], instead, concentrated his attention on those personality profiles characterized by marked adjustment difficulties. More precisely, according to Wolff the elderly subjects most at risk for suicide are those who—as well as being unable to to adjust to changes—are marked by their great rigidity, compulsion, fear of aging, and fear of expressing their hostility.

On the other hand, as long ago as 1956 Moss and Hamilton [468] showed that the death of a close relative was at least twice as frequently associated with subjects who had attempted to commit suicide as with controls. It has been known for some time that mourning and the anniversaries of the death of a loved one are occasions of increased risk of suicide [90].

Over the last 20 years the attention of an ever-increasing number of researchers has been focused on the "biology" of suicide, and certain important phenomena have been identified that are now an essential part of modern suicidology. Although not generally arising from studies on elderly populations, these elements—more or less directly connected with depression—are worthy of a brief discussion here.

A disorder of the amine neurotransmitter function may be associated with an increased risk for suicide. A reduced monoamine oxidase (MAO) activity has been found in the brains of suicide victims [246], and low platelet MAO activity has been found in depressed subjects who had made serious suicide attempts [249]. MAO platelet activity is, at least in part, under genetic control [487], and a high incidence of suicide has been found in families of subjects with low MAO platelet activity [87]. It is known that an alteration of monoamine function is still the most accredited interpretative hypothesis of the physiopathology of the major depressions. This is especially true in the case of serotonin, whose cerebral metabolite—5-hydroxyindolacetic acid—proves to be constantly reduced in severely depressed subjects [17]. However, because low levels of 5-HIAA acid may also be found in the relatives of depressed subjects [661] and in healthy controls [602], it would today seem more plausible to maintain that these low levels actually represent a marker of susceptibility rather than an index of pathology in course. On the other hand, it has been shown that subjects with low levels of 5-HIAA have a much higher frequency of depressive episodes than other subjects. This is the theory underlying the prescription of 5-hydroxytriptophan as a prophylactic against depressive relapse [661].

The nature of the relationship between serotonin turnover and depression is not yet known, but there is some evidence that depressions with low levels of 5-HIAA are associated with clinical profiles different from those associated with other forms of depression. Numerous studies have shown, for example, that there is a marked proneness to suicidal behavior in depressed subjects with low levels of the serotonin metabolite [17]. Particularly patients who use the most violent methods of suicide are also those that are most concentrated among the depressed with low levels of 5-HIAA. Furthermore, for those subjects who have attempted suicide and have presented low levels of 5-HIAA, the risk of suicide appears to be very high. Traskman [649] in fact found a mortality rate of 22% per year for this group of subjects.

The existence of a link between aggressiveness/hostility and suicide has also recently been empirically demonstrated [683], and it is well known that serotonin is one of the neurotransmitters that is certainly involved in the regulation of aggressive animal behaviors [657]. At the moment, the biological bases of aggressive human behaviors are largely unknown, but it is of interest to note that in two studies on soldiers [81, 82] Brown et al. found a significant association between number of violent acts committed and low concentrations of 5-HIAA.

Unfortunately, the clinical applicability of these results still appears to be limited. The need for hospital admission, the high frequency of false positives, and the dreadful procedure of lumbar puncture are some of the features that make the 5-HIAA assay currently feasible only in patients held to be at very high risk for suicide. A more general marker of serotonergic function may be an evaluation of serotonin platelet receptor sites, as these seem to provide a satisfactory parallel with cerebral sites [540], and because a reduced number of imipramine binding sites has been found in the frontal cortex of suicide victims [631].

It has been suggested that the predictive value of low levels of 5-HIAA may be increased by using this test in conjunction with other biological markers, such as the dexamethasone suppression test (DST). In fact, abnormal results at the DST have been associated with an increased risk of suicide [104], though Asberg et al. [17] showed the substantial independence of the two parameters, low levels of 5-HIAA being found among both responders and nonresponders to DST. In a previous study by ourselves

[164], furthermore, DST—according to several rating scales—showed a good sensitivity but low specificity in a heterogeneous group of subjects who had attempted suicide but were not diagnosed as major depressives. It is, however, true that low levels of the serotonin metabolite have been found in subjects who had attempted suicide but were not identified as affected by major depression. It may be hypothesized, though not proven, that the link between suicidal behavior and low levels of 5-HIAA is not correlated to any specific clinical syndrome, but rather to some forms of personality disorder [17].

High percentages of physical disease have been found among elderly suicide victims [187]. Faced by a painful and debilitating disease, suicide may represent a rational choice to avoid severe distress and dependence [391]. As physical disease is frequently associated with psychiatric disorders—especially depression—in the elderly, and as these circumstances clearly worsen the prognosis for both types of pathology [391], the importance of the high percentage of physical disease is clear. For example, Dorpat et al. [187] showed that a serious physical disease is associated with 70% of the cases of deaths by suicide observed, as against 50% in subjects aged between 40 and 59 years and 13% in younger subjects. The estimates of Sainsbury [578], dating from 13 years before, reported considerably lower figures of 35%, 27%, and 10%.

Clearly, in some cases, the depression leading to suicide may be a reaction to physical disease. Examples of this are given, amongst others, in Ullman's study on the consequences of stroke on mood [653], or the perspective of undergoing major surgery for cancer [187]. It is also possible that the organic disease may directly induce the depression. Tumors of the pancreas, brain, ovaries, and lungs are known to be associated with severe depression sometimes preceding the clinical manifestation of the cancer [391]. A common denominator may originate in viral factors connected to immunity [80].

A hypothesis that is gaining growing consensus is that depression is accompanied by a hypofunction of the T-lymphocytes, hence rendering the organism more vulnerable to those diseases correlated with a compromised immune regulation [594]. However, as Forman [209] points out, only a small percentage of cancer patients commit suicide. In the author's opinion, this act appears as the expression of a personal denial of the disease.

It is clear that much remains to be done to achieve a better understanding of the links between suicide, depression and physical disease. It is also clear that depression is the most important correlate of suicide in the elderly. Since "depression-based suicide is perhaps the most preventable through treatment" [95], this fact should alert the physician to the urgency of attentive consideration of depressive states in the elderly.

CHAPTER 13
Treatment of Suicidal Elderly Persons and Preventive Strategies

- Suicide and attempted suicide can be prevented, but the development and evaluation of effective large-scale programs is still in its very initial stages. The organizational structures required for well-coordinated programs of research and practice in the area of suicide prevention are yet to be established. Training of health workers and other relevant groups in the assessment and management of suicide risk is still rather deficient.

- This is the diagnosis of the status quo on which national task forces on suicide prevention in the United States, Canada, and The Netherlands have founded comprehensive national strategies for the prevention of suicide. The main components of these national strategies are (a) the design and implementation of national research programs; (b) the improvement of services; (c) the provision of information and/or training on suicide prevention to relevant professional groups, organizations and the general public; (d) the formulation of strategies and techniques to deal with special risk groups.

Given the magnitude of the suicide problem, one should expect that the development, implementation, and evaluation of programs for intervention and prevention have become an important public health priority. In the United States, Canada and several European countries efforts have recently been made to establish such programs on the national, provincial, and local community level involving health professionals, volunteer organizations, and human services personnel (teachers, police), either separately or in a variety of combinations. Some of those programs and the organizations responsible for them date back from the beginning of this century when social concern for the "victims of the industrial society" was growing, especially in the big cities. Yet it took some 60 years before national and local governments hesitantly came to take an interest in the suicide problem—and in some cases started to provide funds for preventive activities. But to the present day it has remained rather the exception than the rule for governments and health-care policymakers both in the developed world and, for obvious reasons, in the developing world to support suicide prevention activities.

Consequently, although there is a rich and scholarly literature on sociological, psychological, and biological aspects of suicide, there is a relative scarcity of studies on the development and evaluation of well-structured programs and schemes for treatment and prevention. As will become clear from the remainder of this chapter, there is hardly any exaggeration in the statement that, from a scientific point of view, the prevention of suicidal behavior is still in its infancy. Preceding the discussion of the nature and efficacy of preventive measures and schemes, a description is given of recent insights into the nature and characteristics of different types of suicidal behavior and their relevance to our understanding of self-destructive behavior in the elderly.

TYPOLOGY OF SUICIDAL BEHAVIOR

The differences between suicidal behavior in the young and old, which are of course only relative differences, can be understood in terms of the suicidal behavior model developed by Diekstra [177, 179].

An important assumption in this model is that behavior, including suicidal behavior, generally has two types of possible outcomes: *direct* (as a matter of course) and *indirect* (possible but not a matter of course). For example, if someone takes a loaded pistol and holds it up to his temple and pull the trigger, then the direct results are a wound, loss of consciousness, and probably death. Indirect results might be an attempt to stop the person, an attempt to save the person's life, grief reactions by others (in case of death), and the like.

In general, a certain pattern of behavior is followed by an individual because he or she expects to achieve certain ends, like solving a problem, be it as a direct result, an indirect result, or a combination thereof. The extent to which the direct and indirect results of suicidal behavior are expected to be effective in goal attainment have a close relationship to the degree of lethality. If expectations of the effectivity of the direct results are high, inasmuch as a solution to the problem situation is concerned, and if expectations of the goal attainment value of the indirect results (for example, other people's reactions) are at the same time very low, then the likelihood of the behavior having a lethal outcome is very high ("real" suicide). When, however, on the other hand, the expectations of the direct results (Ed) are very low and the expectation of the indirect results (Ei) are very high, the likelihood of the behavior having a nonlethal outcome is very high ("manipulative" suicide attempts/parasuicide).

If one gives the sum of both expectancies the maximal value of 1.0, then the relationship between them can be mapped on a continuum on which three nuclear positions can be shown, namely

1) Ed:Ei = 1:0

2) Ed:Ei = .5:.5

3) Ed:Ei = 0:1

- With (1) there is no goal attainment value attached at all to any indirect consequences of suicidal behavior (reactions of other people), while the expectations of the direct results (destruction of consciousness) are maximal. Under such conditions, suicidal behavior is normally lethal, and one can speak of "real" suicides.

- With (2) the expectations of the effectivity of both types of results is equal. In other words, we could say that the person is ambivalent, or has a number of competitive motives: "I want to die, save my life." This type is most numerous in the so-called suicide attempts, and the method used is sometimes fatal, though not as a general rule, either because other people interfere or because of the nonlethalness of the method used.

- With (3) the expectations are all geared toward other people's reactions, and the lethality of the suicidal act is more or less nil. These are often referred to as manipulative suicide attempts, parasuicides, or suicidal gestures.

Generally speaking, types 1 and 3 occur the least often, type 2 incorporating the bulk of suicidal behaviors.

One of the most important factors governing the Ed/Ei relationship is the changeability or reversibility of the dilemma, problem, or disruption the suicidal person is confronted with.

For example, an incurably ill person cannot escape his or her condition through any indirect outcome of a suicidal act; only direct consequences will suffice. Thus, the chances of suicide attempts being fatal under such circumstances are very high. On the other hand, failing an exam is often not a irreversible situation, and consequently a suicide attempt as a reaction to such a situation rarely ends in death.

Generally speaking, the reversibility of the dilemma or dilemmas leading to suicidal behavior is greater in the young than in the elderly, and this is the reason why the elderly more often terminate their lives in the attempt.

It is, by the way, worth mentioning that we are concerned here with what is known as "objective" reversibility. This does not have to correspond with the degree to which the suicidal person feels the dilemma concerned is one that can be resolved or not, that is, "subjective" reversibility.

The degree to which both categories of reversibility overlap is extremely important when assessing how much chance there is of preventing suicidal behavior in individual cases.

MOTIVES FOR SUICIDAL BEHAVIOR

The basic motivation for most suicidal behavior by both young and old is, broadly speaking, a desire to bring to an end a situation that is felt to be unbearable. The subjectively unbearable experience might originate from a physical, psychological, and/or social disruption, which objectively speaking may be insoluble or unchangeable. It is, however, just as likely that the disruption concerned is reversible, but that the suicidal person concerned is not in a position to arrange for its solution or management, or expects that the required ways and means will not be available or will not work in the particular case. It is also possible that the person is not motivated enough to make use of the resources available. Both categories, nonreversible and seemingly nonreversible, can be found among the young and the old; but as was mentioned earlier, suicidal behavior among the old is more often to be relegated to the first category and among the young more often to the second. This becomes clear when we look at the main motives that play a role in suicidal behavior among the elderly:

1) chronic physical illness,

2) the death of a partner,

3) the threat of extreme dependency or institutionalization,

4) leaving an active position in society or retirement,

5) severe psychiatric or psychological distress,

6) alcohol or drug addiction,

7) severely disturbed or pathological dyadic/social relations.

Obviously the above-mentioned conditions are not mutually exclusive. Indeed, often more than one of these motives are present at the same time, but their relative importance can vary quite considerably in individual cases.

CHRONIC SUICIDAL TENDENCIES

The last three motives mentioned refer to states that, on the whole, are neither of a recent nature nor acute, but rather of a chronic character. The people concerned usually have a long record of problems in which periods of psychiatric hospitalization or treatment as well as episodes of other forms of medico-social assistance are recurring themes. Earlier attempts are not unusual, either.

This group, or at least a major part of it, is often defined as "lifestyle suicides" [179], that is, the pattern of suicidal behavior is a characteristic and often dominant aspect of a person's personality structure. It is quite amazing how some people in this group, often after numerous suicide attempts, nevertheless manage to reach old age. But generally speaking, both in the case of young people and old people who belong to this category, given clinical experience (systematic large-scale research is not available) there is not much reason for therapeutic optimism.

The type of people we are concerned with here often have, because of their difficult and conflictuous behavior, become estranged from their next of kin, their partners and children, and have become extremely isolated. The result is, on the one hand, a strong or intensified need for social relations, particularly if the person concerned lives alone; and on the other hand, an extremely demanding or often suicidally manipulative behavior toward those who do not meet their needs in the expected fashion, including professional helpers.

On the long term, relationships continually waver or break down altogether. Changing this pattern, if at all possible, is an extremely difficult and time-consuming task, demanding from the professional worker concerned above all clear insight and great skill in handling interaction processes [179].

Nevertheless, it is worth mentioning though that this group constitutes a significant minority compared to the total population of suicidal elderly.

ACUTE SUICIDAL TENDENCIES

In most cases the four motives first outlined, which might be described as "attacks" of old age, are most prominent. The process leading up to suicide in these cases can generally be described as follows: Sudden disruption or disruptions occur in what was up to a certain point a normal and more or less peaceful life, followed by a fairly short period of depression, sometimes accompanied by excessive drinking, and finally flowing over into a self-destructive pattern of behavior. Usually, there has been no previous psychiatric treatment, previous suicidal behavior (suicide attempts) being fairly rare. Other indications of serious mental breakdowns are usually not present. More often than not, the disruption concerned is so serious that it leads to a breakdown of the social network in which the old person had been nested up that moment. This means that an important risk factor for suicidal behavior is created, namely, social isolation. From numerous studies one may conclude that, particularly among older people, social isolation increases the chance of suicide [179]. Social isolation is frequently the reason for, or a component of, an underlying depressive disturbance, of which one of the most important symptoms is the inclination to isolate oneself socially.

For the prevention of suicidal behavior in this group, it is essential to make the following distinctions. On the one hand, there may be a disruption or disruptions penetrating all aspects of life and seen on the whole as intolerable or unbearable, so that it is impossible to carry on as before. The most obvious example of this is suicide in case of an extremely painful and completely invalidating physical illness. On the other hand, suicide may be a way of terminating a period of mourning, great sorrow, or suffering at the loss of an aspect of one's personality or lifestyle. The difference with the first form is that here the loss of a certain identifiable element is what determines how unbearable life is. In such cases, the question is not so much "Why suicide?" but more often "Why has this particular aspect assumed such a central position in the individual's life?" Along with the disruptions already cited that may bring about this type of effect, such as the loss of a partner, work, social position, or independence, we may add the threatened or actual loss of physical and intellectual functions, which are often a necessary accompaniment of old age, and which, even when not pathological in degree, are frequently felt by some older people to be so unbearable that they choose death instead of living on.

The distinction between the two groups may have important consequences for management and treatment, as outlined in later in this chapter.

While in the case of the first group, one might wonder whether such a suicide could not be considered a "good death" or a type of euthanasia, this is usually not the case with the second group because the chance of diminishing the risk of suicide by improving the quality of the lives of persons in this group are often quite good.

In the following, we first review the present state of knowledge with regard to the efficacy of clinical and community-based programs for suicide prevention. Then, we briefly describe a number of guidelines for the assessment of suicide risk and for intervention.

PREVENTION, INTERVENTION AND TREATMENT OF SUICIDAL BEHAVIOR

Although there has been substantial criticism on the tripartite definition of prevention, in this context we will, for the sake of simplicity, use this scheme, distinguishing between *primary, secondary,* and *tertiary* prevention. As applied to suicide, the terms "prevention" (primary prevention), "intervention" (secondary prevention) and "postvention" (tertiary prevention) are more commonly used.

Prevention of suicide at the primary level implies measures adopted by or practiced on persons who are currently not feeling or manifesting any sign or symptom of suicidal tendency; they are intended to decrease the risk that such a tendency will afflict them in the future. This could be accomplished by eliminating or alleviating circumstances or societal practices that may promote distress and suicidal behavior, such as mental disorder, unemployment, prejudice, or isolation. Prevention at this level is the most pervasive, but it is also the slowest to take effect because it often demands societal changes, or changes in behavior of large social groups—a notoriously gradual occurrence at best. As a result, most preventive efforts have been at the secondary or intervention level, after suicidal tendencies or conditions that carry a high risk for such tendencies, such as depression, have become apparent. In fact, there is not a single study in the present literature that describes and evaluates a primary prevention program dealing specifically with suicidal behavior, both fatal and nonfatal suicide attempts.

Intervention strategies dealing with suicidal tendencies or crises can take one of several forms. One often employed method is the crisis intervention center or suicide prevention center telephone service, 24-hour "lifelines" or "hotlines" for those who are suicidal or in despair. Once suicidal tendencies have become manifest as expressed ideation, depressive symptomatology or a nonfatal suicide attempt, medical and psychological/social interventions and management techniques may be employed, often followed by some form of therapy to alleviate the circumstances and problems leading to the distress and suicidal crisis. Over the last 30 years, a considerable number of studies have been published in which such interventions and their effects on subsequent suicidal behaviors are described.

Postvention or "after-the-fact" prevention refers to efforts to aid those who remain following a suicide of a family member, partner, or friend, and who are very often deeply affected by the death. Preventive measures at this level have only recently received attention, and no systematic studies evaluating such measures are already available.

Given the lack of information on the effect of primary prevention or postvention programs, this chapter reviews only studies dealing with the evaluation or programs at the secondary level. Within this group, two categories can be identified, i.e., on the one hand a category of studies evaluating the effect of (community-based) suicide prevention centers, and on the other hand studies of the efficacy of clinical programs for suicidal in- or outpatients.

EFFECTIVENESS OF SUICIDE PREVENTION CENTERS

Virtually all metropolitan areas as well as many smaller urban areas in the United States and Great Britain now have at least one suicide prevention center, which typically provide a 24-hour hotline plus referrals to other mental health or social work agencies as well as (in some cases) a walk-in center and trained volunteers who can act as "befrienders" or confidants to persons in a suicidal crisis or in despair. Although suicide prevention centers may employ mental health consultants, such as trained psychiatrists, psychologists, and psychotherapists as external consultants or as staff members, the actual work is usually carried by lay persons with varying degrees of training and expertise. Traditionally, the clergy has played an important role in the foundation and operation of crisis centers, and to a considerable extent this is still the case in many centers.

Today, telephone hotlines are also available in many cities and towns in continental Europe and Japan as well as in many developing countries, though there they usually form a part of telephone emergency services dealing with problems of living in general and not predominantly or specifically with suicidal or depressed individuals.

Although crisis or suicide hotlines were already present in several large European and Northern American cities before World War II, the spread of such services across the United States, Great Britain, and elsewhere really started in the beginning of the 1960s, stimulated by the establishment of the Samaritans in London and the first Suicide Prevention Center in Los Angeles.

Suicide prevention centers are essentially equipped for secondary prevention, that is to say, for early intervention with persons who already carry an elevated risk for suicidal behavior. Generally such centers do not have an active outreach, that is, they do not systematically seek out and try to establish contact with groups in the community who can be considered high risk. It is essentially the suicidal person who has to contact the center.

For that reason studies on the efficacy of such centers have addressed two major facets of their functioning:

1) whether centers attract persons with an elevated risk for suicidal behavior,

2) whether they prevent these individuals' suicide or suicide attempt [175a].

These facets are closely intertwined, for if centers do not attract high-risk individuals, it goes without saying that they will not exert any major influence on reducing suicide rates.

In the most recent review of studies addressing these two questions—and the only one thus far using metaanalysis as method of reviewing—Dew and her colleagues [175a] draw the following general conclusions:

- First, centers indeed seem to attract a high-risk population: Center clients were more likely to commit suicide then were members of the general population (7 studies analyzed). The average client-suicide rate ranges from 2 times higher to almost 109 times higher than the general population rate. Individuals who committed suicide were more likely to have been clients of a suicide prevention than were members of the general population (6 studies analyzed). The average annual client rate among suicides ranges from 2.5 times higher to almost 10 times higher than the client rate in the general population.

- Next, whether the suicide rate declines more in communities that have such a center than in communities that do not is not yet certain. Of the five studies analyzed, three show an effect in favor of center effectiveness, whereas the other two do not. Combined, however, there was virtually no effect, suggesting that the center establishment has neither an overall positive nor a negative effect on community suicide rates.

Given the fact that centers are at least somewhat successful in attracting the population they are designed to help, the question arises as to whether center effectiveness should be established within specific cohorts rather than simply across the entire population of a community. Miller et al. [460a] are the only investigators who have reported data on specific cohorts. They compared 28 center communities with 48 control communities over the period 1968–1973, and found no significant difference in overall suicide rate change between those two groups of communities. However, the suicide rate for white women and girls under the age of 25 showed a large and significant decrease in communities with a center as compared to control communities. This finding is especially important because in the United States as well as in many other countries, young (white) women are the most frequent users of prevention centers and telephone emergency centers.

Since this group is also characterized by a relatively high rate of attempted suicide, the question arises whether prevention center evaluations should focus on outcomes other than suicide, such as attempted suicide. Unfortunately, there are no studies available yet that have examined other kinds of outcome in a scientifically sound way.

There are still other reasons to look for outcome measures other than suicide rate change. The population suicide rate is effectively an *under*estimate of the true incidence of suicide. There is convincing evidence that this underestimation is systematically greater in certain parts of the population than in others. For example, suicide is particularly underreported among the elderly. Even if centers have a positive effect among those aged 60 years and over, this effect would presumably not show up as a reduction of the suicide rate in that group, let alone in the overall suicide rate.

In addition, suicide rates are influenced by a multitude of factors and their interactions (such as unemployment rate, divorce rate, drug/alcohol (ab)use, prevalence of mental disorders, changes in age and sex composition of populations, which can easily obscure a true effect of a suicide prevention center in a community (see Diekstra [182d] for an overview of the most important social factors related to changes in suicide rates). None of the studies carried out thus far on the effectiveness of centers has been able to control adequately for the possible influence of those factors, one of the reasons being that it is often extremely difficult, if not impossible, to obtain the necessary data on them.

In sum, it is extremely difficult to conclude that centers do not prevent suicide, while at the same time it is not difficult to conclude that centers deal with persons who are at greater risk for suicidal behavior (not just suicide) compared with the general population. Even though the actual percentage of clients who commit suicide annually remains a small percentage of all clients seen (an average approximately 0.03–2% of all clients [175a]), the corresponding average annual suicide rate of approximately 34 to 1775 individuals per 100,000 clients indicates that the potential for prevention of suicidal deaths by centers is great. It is still largely unknown in what ways that potential can be most effectively realized. Suicide prevention and crisis intervention centers are quite diverse, not only in services offered but also in the background and training of counselors, volunteers, and the like. Such variables may be important moderators of centers effects, but the existing body of literature does not allow for any systematic evaluation of their potential moderating effects.

Finally, the available literature on client characteristics and effect of prevention centers is almost exclusively Anglo-Saxon in origin and nature. It therefore remains to be seen whether the potential role with regard to suicide prevention of centers as it emerges from that literature does apply to other parts of the world as well.

AFTERCARE PROGRAMS FOR HOSPITAL-TREATED SUICIDE ATTEMPTERS

In the past 30 years, both the absolute and the relative number of people that are treated and/or admitted to hospitals following a suicide attempt or parasuicidal act has increased dramatically in most countries in Western Europe, North America, and presumably also in many other parts of the world [182d]. A considerable percentage of those treated in hospital after a suicidal act are "repeaters," i.e., they have received hospital treatment before for the same reason. Estimates of the percentage of attempters that have made earlier attempts vary between 20% and 40%. Follow-up studies show that the risk for repetition is particularly high in the first few months after discharge from treatment or hospital: Approximately 10% make another attempt within the first 3 months. This percentage rises to 15% after 1 year, and to 30–40% after 10–15 years.

As to the outcome of subsequent attempts, there is a remarkable difference between studies published before and after 1982. From the first group of studies, it emerges that approximately 1% of suicide attempters dies from the consequences of a subsequent attempt within a year after discharge. After 2 years this percentage rises to 2%, after 3 years to 3% and so forth, until it reaches approximately 10% after 10 years. Thereafter, the percentage remains stable at this level.

Since 1982, a growing number of studies is being published indicating that the percentage of repeaters dying from a suicide attempt can be as high as 8% to 10% within 12 months after a previous attempt followed by treatment or admission in hospital. It remains to be seen whether this is an "acceleration" phenomenon or a reflection of true increase in risk for suicide among suicide attempters.

In any case, suicide attempters constitute a group with a very high risk for suicide—a rate 50 to 100 times the overall population rate—and therefore a pool from which many future suicides are drawn. This raises the issue as to the possibilities for prevention of suicide by interventions specifically geared toward reducing the risk of subsequent attempts among suicide attempters in contact with medical services. Such interventions can be divided into three categories:

1) psychosocial/psychotherapeutic interventions,

2) somatic interventions, such as drug therapy and electroconvulsive therapy (ECT),

3) combinations of 1) and 2).

In the following we first review the literature on the efficacy of special aftercare programs for suicide attempters using mainly of psychosocial/psychotherapeutic intervention or treatment modalities. Next, we present the available information on the suicide preventive effects of psychotherapeutic and somatic treatment methods among patients suffering from affective disorders. Information on the preventive effects of combinations of 1) and 2) is virtually nonexistent. The same holds true for information on the differential effects of 1) versus 2) in reducing and preventing suicidal behavior.

THE EFFICACY OF SPECIAL AFTERCARE PROGRAMS

After a careful screening of the literature, we identified 12 publications reporting a systematic evaluation of the effects of special nonsomatic psychiatric/psychosocial aftercare programs for suicide attempters [182e]. In terms of design these studies can be divided into two categories: those using a retrospective and those using a prospective design. Studies in the first category retrospectively collected data on treatment history of suicide attempters after an index attempt and related those data to incidence of further attempts, either with a fatal or nonfatal outcome.

While retrospective studies usually report a relationship between more specialized psychiatric or psychosocial treatment on the one hand, and incidence of suicidal acts on the other, suggesting an reducing effect of such treatments [182e], such results have to be taken with great caution because of poor matching of comparison groups especially with regard to factors like motivation for treatment, reasons for offering treatment by agencies, and the like.

The design used in most prospective studies can generally be described as follows: When a patient has been admitted or treated in a hospital for the physical consequences of a suicide attempt, he or she is seen by a psychiatrist, a psychologist, or another member of the treatment/research team as soon as possible in order to assess the social and mental health status as well as the suicide risk. Consequently, the patient is assigned to one of several treatment conditions or a control (= no treatment) group. Treatment conditions in most studies are either

1) "the usual minimum procedure" of one or a few interviews with a psychiatrist, psychologist, or social worker during admission and referral to family physician or other health care professional after discharge;

2) a treatment program specially designed for suicide attempters including regular individual or group sessions (usually on a once-a-week basis) during a period of 3–6 months. The individual or group sessions with one or two members of the treatment/research team focus mainly on helping the patients in alleviating or solving social and practical problems in their everyday lives.

After termination of the treatment there are one or several follow-up meetings in which changes in social conditions, psychological well-being and behaviour problems are assessed, among them subsequent suicidal acts.

Almost all of the studies presently published [182e] report on projects that were in operation for a limited number of years, on the average 2 to 5 years, after which they were terminated often because of lack of further funding. Unfortunately, most of the prospective studies have not used a properly controlled design in which patients have been randomly assigned to either a treatment or nontreatment group. This is often because of ethical and practical considerations.

Not surprisingly, the overall picture with regard to the efficacy of special aftercare programs that emerges from the available studies contains a number of contradictions. First of all, seven (of the 12) studies report a reduction in suicide attempts in the special aftercare condition compared to three studies in which no difference was found. The total number of patients involved in each of these two sets of studies is practically the same. The picture, however, changes somewhat if one looks at fatal and nonfatal subsequent attempts separately. In two of the three studies that include suicide as an outcome measure, no differences in favor of the special treatment condition is found. When we limit outcome to nonfatal suicide attempts, we find seven studies with positive effects of the special treatment conditions against two studies in which no difference between treatment-as-usual and special treatment was found. The number of patients involved in the first set of studies, however, is several times bigger than in the second set.

There are two studies in which a distinction is made between suicide attempters with a low and suicide attempters with a high risk for repetition and where outcomes are assessed for these two groups separately. In one of the studies, there is a large and impressive difference between the control group, the treatment-as-usual group and the special treatment condition with low-risk attempters. In the other study such differences are not found, but the high-risk special treatment group did fare much worse than each of the other groups.

In one study [182e] that focused exclusively on chronic suicidal persons with a high risk for repetition, no effect was found of a special aftercare program with regard to incidence of suicide and suicide attempt in comparison with a control condition.

In sum, the identification of effective psychosocial/psychotherapeutic methods for the prevention of further episodes of suicidal behavior continues to be a problem. It is noteworthy, however, that in most of the studies reviewed the special or intensive forms of treatment have had a positive effect on the psychological and social functioning of patients. This seemingly contradictory finding has yet to be explained.

In the opinion of the present authors, the following possible explanations are worth considering:

1) Most of the special treatment programs focus on the alleviation of the immediate emotional and social problems of the patient. Consequently, it is not at all certain whether the patient indeed learns different ways of coping with identical or similar problems whenever they recur.

2) In the majority of the available studies, no data have been assembled on the relationship between psychiatric diagnosis (presence or absence of psychiatric illness) on the one hand, and risk of repetition on the other hand. It might well be that (new) episodes of acute psychiatric disturbance are an impor-

tant factor of suicidal recidivism, especially because of the fact that judging from their description most special aftercare programs do not seem to be particularly tailored to deal with such conditions.

3) No studies control for the effect of treatment history on subsequent suicide attempts. Many suicidal patients, including first-evers, have previously been in contact with helping agencies and health-care professionals, and their experiences in this respect may be rather negative than positive (since they proceed to attempt suicide in the first place), and may give rise to negative expectations (after the index attempt) of further help and therewith to rather low compliance. The latter phenomenon has indeed been reported in the majority of studies reviewed.

4) Selecting patients for a specific treatment method on the basis of the fact that they have attempted suicide might well be a questionable procedure. Suicidal behavior can be reached by very different roads, and it might be more appropriate to select treatment modalities on the base of "how the patient got there," i.e., using the underlying social and psychological problems as criteria, instead of on the base of a particular symptomatic behavior. The available literature indeed testifies to the fact that selecting a specific treatment for a specific subgroup of suicidal persons, such as suicidal persons suffering from a depressive disorder, might be preferable.

THERAPIES FOR AFFECTIVE DISORDERS AND THE PREVENTION OF SUICIDE BEHAVIOR

The evidence for a close association between mental illness and the prevalence of fatal or nonfatal suicidal behavior is convincing. Although the estimated absolute percentages may differ from study to study, most studies on the topic concur in the conclusion that the majority of persons dying through their own hand suffer from an ascertainable mental disorder at the time of their death. Of the suicides suffering from a mental illness, most are diagnosed as patients of depressive disorders. In a recent review of the literature [182f], the present state of knowledge with regard to the relationship between depression and suicidal behavior was summarized as follows:

- between 15–20% of patients suffering from major depression finally die by their own hand;

- 50–60% of persons committing or attempting suicide suffer from depressive disturbances.

Given these data, it seems safe to assume that there is a positive association between changes in the prevalence and incidence of depressive disturbances in a population and (possibly but not certainly lagged) changes in the suicide and suicide attempt rate of that population. To date, no aggregate longitudinal studies are available that have validly tested this hypothesis on the population level, with the exception of a recent study carried out in The Netherlands [182f], where over a period of about 10 years rates of suicide, attempted suicide, and depressive disturbance were found to be closely associated. It therefore seems safe to assume that effective methods for the treatment and/or prevention of depressive disorders also have an effect on the incidence of suicidal acts.

Within contemporary psychiatry, the three main modalities for the treatment of depressive disorders are psychotherapy (ranging from classical psychoanalysis via interpersonal approaches to behavior therapy), antidepressant drug therapy, and electroconvulsive therapy (ECT). Available literature reviews [191, 640a] indicate that all three modalities are effective in diminishing, reducing, and preventing depressive disorders, and that the differences in efficacy between them are relatively small for unipolar depressive disturbances, while drug treatment and ECT seem to be considerably more effective in bipolar depression.

If all three modalities are effective in depressive disorders where suicidal behavior is a recognized complication, the question arises within the present context as to the available evidence for their efficacy in diminishing, reducing, and preventing suicidal behavior.

With regard to psychotherapeutic treatment modalities, the overall conclusion emerging from the literature is that psychotherapy deserves its place among the therapies for depression and has a symptom-reducing effect, including reduction of suicidal ideation, though it is not possible to state anything definite with regard to its effect on the incidence of suicidal behavior. The reason for this is that among the many controlled studies in this area, studies using subsequent suicidal behavior as an outcome criterion are virtually nonexistent.

With regard to antidepressant drug therapy, the situation is slightly different: Several studies (182e) indicate that, if prescribed and used appropriately, antidepressant medication may have an effect on suicidal ideation and possibly also on suicidal behavior, but at the same time such medication might also be a risk factor since many suicidal patients overdose with their antidepressant medication.

Remarkably, we know most about the effectiveness of ECT in preventing suicidal behavior. In his review of the literature on this topic, Tanney [160a] used several methods to evaluate the impact of ECT on the frequency of suicidal behaviors in affective disorders. On the one hand, one can compare the number of suicidal deaths in different treatment eras (pre-ECT versus ECT). Although Tanney suggests that the available studies warrant the conclusion that introduction of ECT had a reducing effect, careful examination of their designs indicate that

1) they are all retrospective,

2) they contain many methodological flaws,

3) they do not accurately specify the distribution of the patients included in the studies over the diagnostic categories.

Therefore, in the opinion of the present authors, any definite conclusion with regard to the effects of ECT on suicidal behavior on the base of this set of studies would be premature.

However, when we look at the set of published controlled studies on the role of ECT in reducing suicidal behavior in depressed patients, the picture that emerges is somewhat clearer: Five of the six available studies [640a] show a preventive effect of ECT. The one exception is the most recent study [25a] that found no advantage to ECT in preventing suicide within 5 years of the first psychiatric hospitalization for depression. Since the number of patients in this study is larger than the total sum of patients included in the other five studies, a metaanalytic review would probably conclude that the verdict on the preventive effect of ECT is still undetermined, even though the control group used in the study presumably included many patients that received antidepressant and other psychotropic drug therapy as well as continuation and maintenance therapies.

This raises the question as to the differential effects of ECT versus drug therapy and other treatment modalities in reducing suicidal behavior in patients suffering from affective disorders. Again, there is a scarcity of information. The only controlled study that reported on the differential outcome of ECT versus antidepressant drug therapy [25] suggests that ECT has the advantage when suicide attempt, and not suicide, is used as outcome criterion. Several other studies using retrospective designs failed to show such a difference between ECT and antidepressant drug therapy [640a].

While Tanney [640a] concludes that ECT has demonstrated its effectiveness in preventing suicide and can be appropriately described as a "life-saving" measure, our conclusion is a more cautious one: The available evidence for a preventive effect of ECT is at most suggestive, but certainly not convincing.

STATE OF THE ART: STILL "CLINICAL WISDOM"

The overall conclusion that can be drawn from our review of the literature on suicide prevention programs and methods is that at present it is not possible to indicate what is "the best, state-of-the-art" treatment or prevention scenario as determined by scientific research. The present state of science-based knowledge does not allow for any definite or even intermediate recommendations in this respect. This is not to say that no suicides and suicide attempts are being prevented by the approaches and methods for prevention and intervention that are currently in place. What it does mean is that no data, sufficiently hard and replicated, are available that *testify* to such an effect.

On the one hand, this may be a consequence of the fact that the majority of the studies on this topic suffer from severe methodological flaws and shortcomings. There is ample room for improvement here, but it seems unlikely that much progress will be made unless governments, health-care policymakers, and academia take a more profound and continuous interest in this area.

On the other hand, it seems almost certain that in the field of suicide prevention the "match" between means and goals is a crucial problem. For one thing, suicide and attempted suicide are phenomena with a very complex etiology or causation. The search for one single responsible agent, a "suicidococcus," has proven to be unfruitful. Every suicidal act grows from an array of societal, psychological, and biological variables, and although there are well-defined subgroups of suicidal persons, the larger part of the "landscape" has not yet been satisfactorily mapped. One of the reasons for this is the fact that the real number of persons engaging in any form of deliberate self-harm is unknown, but is probably much greater than the figures that are presently available because in many cases suicidal deaths are not recorded as such especially in the elderly, while for most suicide attempts no contact is established with services. In a recent survey of 200 medical examiners in the USA, more than half felt that the reported number of suicides is probably less than half the true number [312a]. The limited accuracy and reliability of suicide statistics are, in part, attributable to the lack of a commonly accepted and applied definition of suicide also (see Chapter 12). In addition to variability in the criteria for the classification of suicide as cause of death, personal biases, incomplete information, cultural resistance, and pressure from the family and community probably contribute to a marked underreporting of suicide. The same applies a fortiori for nonfatal suicide attempts. Nowhere in the world are national records kept on attempted suicide. Healthcare institutions that deal with suicide attempters may or may not register such cases. Those that routinely record cases of suicide attempt(ers) show a wide variability in operational criteria for the classification of a behavior as a suicide attempt. The few population sample surveys carried out in this area indicate that, on average, only one in four cases of attempted suicide or parasuicide that meet the definition and criteria set in a recent publication by the World Health Organization ([182a], see also Chapter 12) lead to contact with medical or other professional health care services.

Consequently, it may well be the case that our present knowledge regarding suicidal behavior and current preventive approaches are based on samples that are not representative of the total population of suicidal persons.

This having been said, in the following we briefly describe strategies and approaches in dealing with suicidal elderly, based on "clinical wisdom."

CRISIS INTERVENTION

One of the most important requirements made on a professional helper in a crisis situation with the elderly is availability. In view of the serious nature of a crisis situation, professional workers who are in contact with the person should always be reachable, either by phone or directly. A helper who cannot meet these demands better refrains from interfering in a suicidal crisis.

This direct availability has two important functions: First, the suicidal persons know that there will always be someone to answer their questions or react to their cries for help. For people who have felt helpless and powerless for a long time, this is certainly an important form of support. Second, through the availability of the helper, suicidal persons can break the pattern of social isolation they have fallen into, and communication with other people can begin again, which means they then have a way of testing out (and receiving feedback on) their own feelings and ideas.

Sometimes, with suicidal persons who have no place of residence, it might be impossible for the helper to be constantly available. This might be a reason for suggesting they be taken into the hospital. If the person concerned refuses, and if there are no proper grounds for involuntary commitment (as there very rarely are), then all the helper can do is offer the suicidal person what can feasibly be carried out. Offering or implying that one can do more than one in fact can is extremely dangerous: This may be the next disappointment in a long series of disappointments the suicidal person has already encountered, and it may actually encourage him or her to go ahead and commit the act.

Intervention in a suicidal crisis means talk, talk, and more talk, and also listen, listen, and listen yet again. Communication and building up a relationship, however frail in the beginning, may be of vital importance. One of the things a helper can achieve is to convince the suicidal person that he or she should not make a definitive decision about suicide during a crisis situation, but should wait until things have calmed down and alternatives can be examined in a tranquil fashion. For suicidal people, communication with others often gives them a chance to release their pent-up aggression, anger, or sorrow. A suicide attempt or threat is very often an expression of aggression toward others, such as parents, partners, and the like. By offering alternative methods of expressing aggression, one may reduce suicidal tendencies.

It is also important to solve the problems of intense anxiety and sleeplessness, should they arise. A good night's sleep may sometimes reduce the risk of suicide for a while, and in an emergency it is sometimes advisable to give (through the proper channels) sleeping pills. A tranquilizer can sometimes help ease both sleeplessness and anxiety (which is often the reason for the lack of sleep). This type of medical treatment, however, must be seen as a temporary measure and should not take the place of personal attention.

Another important goal is to help the person restore social relations, or if they no longer exist, to make new ones. In the case of the former, this may mean that the helpers should arrange or encourage meetings with members of the family, parents, partners, or children as soon as possible, and and even "run" such meetings themselves if necessary.

The greater part of counseling a suicidal person is concerned with talking about and exploring (alternative) solutions for the person's problems. Activities like offering information, getting in touch with public authorities (social services, etc.), if necessary going to these services with the person concerned, and helping them fill out forms are all part of this. Inasmuch as long-term help is called for, it may fall upon the person who acted as a crisis worker, but this is not always the case. If this is not the case, it is important that the crisis worker only hand over the patient when other helpers are able to take on the job immediately. If the time-lag between crisis intervention and long-term help is too great, the suicidal person may easily give up, and a new disappointment is registered.

This fact, along with the other points mentioned in this section, are also of great importance when helping people who have already made an attempt on their lives and who cannot, strictly speaking, be included under crisis intervention because they have already alleviated the crisis by their attempt.

When someone has attempted suicide, it is of great importance that nonmedical help be available as soon as possible. If one waits too long, the motivation often disappears. Bearing this in mind, it is important that anyone treated in a hospital after a suicide attempt—whether as inpatient or not—be offered nonmedical help as well, or at least made aware of the possibilities, unless they are already receiving aid. If they are already being helped, there may still be a need to look into the nature of the assistance offered, because quite often suicide attempts are related to problems with helpers, such as a crisis in a psychotherapeutic relationship.

Crisis intervention need not necessarily result in long-term assistance. Sometimes suicide threats, suicide attempts, and other related crisis interventions prove to be sufficiently powerful in themselves to generate solutions for the problems that led to this behavior. But the opposite is more often the case, and suicidal tendencies appear to be the expression of severe personal or social disruption—or both—for which long-term help is required.

LONG-TERM TREATMENT

From the above one may conclude that the problems and processes leading to suicidal behavior are extremely diverse. There is no case for assuming a certain suicidal personality profile, nor for specific social profiles leading to suicidal behavior. While it is true that suicidal behavior is more likely to occur under the influence of certain personality traits or social conditions than others, the same traits and conditions often also increase the probability of certain other types of deviant behavior, like physical abuse of others, chronic alcohol abuse, and mental disturbance. The specific factors that lead a person to suicidal rather than other behavior in stressful circumstances should be looked for in the learning history or in the behavioral repertoire of the person concerned.

Long-term treatment of suicidal subjects should, on the whole, concentrate on two aspects: First, it should help to reduce or resolve the psychological or social problems that led to the suicidal behavior; second, alternative problem-solving strategies should be taught for use in future crisis situations.

Many people incorrectly believe that the first-mentioned measure is enough to prevent suicidal behavior from occurring. But solving immediate problems is no guarantee that they will never return. If similar problems arise in the future, and if the patient has not learned any other problem-solving strategies in the meantime, chances are the patient will react in the same way as before—with suicidal behavior.

One implication of this is that long-term treatment of suicidal elderly is hardly any different from the treatment of psychological or psychotherapeutic problems in general. The current approaches and strategies in these fields are, for the most part, relevant in helping suicidal people, always bearing in mind certain provisions. First, if the threat of suicide constantly permeates the discussions and interaction between patient and helper, the helping relationship will be threatened and disorientated. Of major importance here is the way in which and the reason why the patient does this and what he or she gets out of it—if anything. These themes need to be explored and brought out into the open. Once this has taken place, the helper can, whenever the threat arises again, point out this interaction pattern to the client, thereby diminishing the probability of its occurrence and eventually making it disappear altogether.

This method is only likely to work if helper and client have carefully defined the therapeutic goals. In this case, important questions to put to a suicidal patient are: "What do you want to do with your life?" and "Does the way suicide attracts you help you to achieve those ends?" Letting patients formulate their own goals is not an easy task at all and is by itself an important part of the therapeutic work. Suicidal patients are very often extremely ambivalent as to their desires and find it very difficult to commit themselves to them and "to work on them." It is important, wherever possible, to talk about these difficulties with suicidal patients, in order to find out if and when such ambivalent positions cause them to founder. If patients can made aware of this, they may be able to change their attitude.

Quite a few suicidal clients are "yes, but" thinkers. Ideas and activities directed toward a more sane relationship with themselves or with life are first accepted, but then almost always watered down with a "but . . ."

Summarizing the points mentioned above, Diekstra [179] formulated five general objectives for psychosocial or psychotherapeutic intervention with suicidal patients, particularly elderly patients. These are as follows:

1) To help de-escalate or reduce psychological/emotional problems due to interpersonal conflicts and social isolation.

2) To help improve, or build a better, self-image.

3) To develop satisfactory social relations.

4) To develop problem-solving strategies other than suicidal behaviour.

5) To develop long-term objectives.

The way in which the objectives are attained—by what therapeutic methods or modalities—may vary greatly from patient to patient. However, every intervention that fails to attain one or more of these objectives is bound to suffer from lack of any long-term effects on suicide risk.

Thus far, however, it has often proved to be difficult to meet these objectives when working with elderly suicidal patients. One of the main reasons may well be that long-term individual interventions that are not embedded in community-based or community-supported, large-scale, mental-health programs are doomed to remain relatively ineffective in populations such as the elderly, where well-being is so intimately dependent upon community support.

There is clearly then a need for comprehensive, community-based programs in this area. We conclude this chapter, therefore, with a set of guidelines for such programs.

TOWARD A COMPREHENSIVE PROGRAM FOR THE PREVENTION OF SUICIDE

There are several important implications to be drawn from the information presented in this chapter for the development of general prevention programs that aim at a substantial reduction of national suicide rates. First, programs for the prevention of suicide are not feasible and are in fact doomed to be ineffective if they are not cast within the framework of large-scale programs for the prevention of deliberate self-harm in general. Second, given the complex interplay of social, psychological-psychiatric, and possibly biological factors in the causation of deliberate self-harm, the search for a major breakthrough or intervention that will wipe out suicide is necessarily in vain.

Breakthroughs are exceedingly rare and less and less likely as the complexity of the problem increases. Simply put, one would assert that complex problems only yield to complex solutions. Every suicidal or self-harming act has multiple causes, so that large-scale prevention programs should be "multimodal."

The call for complex solutions in this area has gone out from national task forces on suicide that were recently established in three countries (Canada, the United States, and The Netherlands) to advise the government, health-care planners as well as health-care workers on how to deal as effectively as possible with suicidal problems.

The reports and recommendations of these task forces appear to have a significance that is much greater than just the national situation for which they were originally produced [181, 212, 615].

Although the US task force was explicitly restricted to the problem of suicide among the young, its recommendations are nevertheless very similar to those of the other two task forces dealing with all age groups.

The explicit and implicit recommendations made by the task force of The Netherlands are described below in detail. They can be summarized into four categories: the design and implementation of research (I), the improvement of services (II), the provision of information and/or training to relevant organizations and groups and the general public (III), and special risk groups (IV).

The task force has abstained from making recommendations at the macro level that might help prevent suicide. Although its report clearly shows that there is a link between factors at the macro level and suicidal behavior, it did not deem it part of its mandate to make concrete proposals at that level.

In drawing up its recommendations, the task force seems to have constantly borne in mind their financial implications. Although a certain degree of investment is necessary to implement some of the recommendations, notably those concerning research, many of them can be put into a practice with a limited amount of (short-term) investment.

Although the recommendations of the task force do not exclusively address the elderly, most of the recommendations also have direct implications for the prevention of suicidal behaviors among this age group. We therefore present these recommendations here in their complete original wording.

Research and Information

There is an urgent need for more and better information concerning the cause of suicidal behavior, risk factors involved, and methods of prevention. Compared with other health problems, the amount of knowledge available in this field is extremely limited. The information that is necessary if effective prevention programs are to be set up must be collected by means of a carefully designed and implemented national research program.

The essential components of such a program are as follows:

1) The collection at national level of valid and up-to-date data concerning the incidence of suicide and suicide attempts and the characteristics of individuals who make suicide attempts, whether with a fatal or nonfatal outcome. For this it is necessary that
   – the classification/certification of suicidal behavior be im-

proved through the adoption of uniform definitions and operational criteria for suicide and suicide attempts;
– efforts be made to ensure that the authorities or persons whose responsibility it is to establish suicide as the cause of death do in fact apply the criteria referred to above;
– different sets of national statistics, regardless of where they are presently being kept (e.g., suicide as a category both in mortality and criminal statistics), be replaced or merged to make one statistical record in which duplication is avoided;
– data collection at national level be developed in such a way that the information can be used for analytical-epidemiological studies of the characteristics of high-risk groups and the changes in those characteristics that take place over time;
– data collection be done such that the effects of local and regional prevention or intervention programs can be tested;
– general hospital and other medical and social services treating attempted suicides be encouraged to keep a record of such cases which are regularly reviewed by a regional or local body, and in which duplication is avoided.

2) The findings of a carefully designed multidisciplinary research program in which a range of relevant risk factors for suicidal behavior are investigated. The program must be planned and directed in such a way that existing research projects and available knowledge are employed, and so that it provides the information necessary for effective prevention or intervention programs. It should also study, among other things, the interaction between multiple risk factors, such as emotional disturbance and alcohol and drug abuse, as well as the question as to whether there is a casual relation between biological factors and suicidal behavior.

3) The carrying out of well-planned studies using control groups of methods of treating attempted suicides and of prevention programs for high-risk groups, the latter specifically to include the relatives and close friends of people who have committed suicide.

4) The carrying out of carefully planned studies into the most effective way of informing the public about suicide, and into the positive and negative effects the media can produce in this context.

5) To implement steps 1) to 4), national program committees should be set up to supervise all research projects. These

should include representatives of the ministries involved, health-care agencies, and university research institutes.

Improving Services

It is of great importance that available services designed to help people with a high risk of suicidal behavior, within the public mental health services, the welfare and social services, and the judicial/law enforcement agencies, be expanded and improved. Pending the results of research into the effectiveness of methods of prevention and intervention, improvements can be made in a number of areas:

1) The competence of professionals in the health and mental health services to identify and treat depression must be increased.

2) Their ability to identify and treat people with a high risk of suicidal behavior must likewise be enhanced. This means that the training for general practitioners, doctors of internal medicine, psychiatrists, clinical and health psychologists, psychotherapists, social workers, and general and social/psychiatric nurses must include the following (obligatory) components:
   − information on the epidemiology of suicide and attempted suicide, and on acute and chronic risk factors of suicidal behavior;
   − information on and training in the skills necessary to identify people with a high risk of suicidal behavior;
   − training in interview techniques, treatment, and aftercare of suicidal people, relatives of those who have committed suicide, and the families of friends of people who have made a suicide attempt;
   − training in the appropriate referral of suicidal people to (other) health care workers.

3) Models or scenarios should be developed to assist institutions and staff within the health and mental health services to give more specific and better coordinated assistance and aftercare to suicidal people and their relatives.
   One of the ways of achieving this is to make community mental health centers (CMHC) responsible in each region for the coordination of care/treatment of suicidal persons, and for

developing a model that ensure that the following tasks are fulfilled:
– the provision of direct and specific assistance or intervention in crisis situations;
– making thorough assessment of suicide risk and appropriate plans for treatment and counseling;
– referral and transfer of suicidal people to other services and the provision of appropriate help and aftercare by the various services;
– the provision of consultation facilities for dealing with suicidal persons and their relatives to the health services and health-care workers;
– the keeping of records to monitor the extent of the problem and to evaluate the care provided.

The implications of the above are that the CMHC assume a coordinating role in creating expertise and sufficient access to services within each region. Each CMHC must establish contact with other relevant services available in the region (police, general practitioners, emergency telephone services, social health services, ambulance services, etc.) and ensure collaboration with health-care institutions (general hospitals, psychiatric units in general hospitals, general psychiatric hospitals, crisis and walk-in centers, [university] psychiatric clinics). Every effort must be made to ensure that a single address and telephone number in a region becomes so well known and so accessible that the CMHC operates as the central point from whence immediate assistance in case of emergencies can be obtained.

Measures should be taken to ensure that the following be provided:

1) In every general hospital providing medical (emergency) treatment for attempted suicides, a formal policy should be established with regard to psychiatric psychological assessment, treatment, and referral of the attempted suicides and their relatives.

2) The help given attempted suicides in general hospitals should be organized so that clinical psychological knowledge and skills as well as expertise in crisis intervention can be fully utilized.

3) Facilities should be established for prolonged observation of suicidal persons in general hospitals, even when physical treatment has ended.

4) Formal arrangements should be made between the CMHC and psychiatric institutions for the referral and aftercare of attempted suicides and their relatives (see above).

5) In order to further improve the care and help provided in general psychiatric hospital
   − research be carried out into the short- and long-term factors that have contributed to the rise in the suicide rate in such hospitals;
   − greater emphasis should be put on training people who work in psychiatric hospitals in dealing with suicidal patients. More attention should be devoted to care workers' own attitudes toward suicide. In this connection, research into affective treatment methods for patients who repeatedly attempt suicide is of great importance.

Training and Information Regarding the Problem of Suicide

The provision of appropriate information and training to relevant organizations or groups and the general public is essential if one is to reduce the number of suicides substantially and to mitigate their aftereffects. The following points are worthy of particular consideration:

1) The curricula of primary and secondary teachers, school counselors, and career teachers should include information and training on assessing severe depression and the risk of suicide and appropriate referral of suicidal pupils. Relevant curricula models must include
   − information concerning the acute and chronic risk factors governing suicidal behavior;
   − information on the characteristic signs and symptoms of depression and other psychological disturbances within the school context;
   − information on criteria and methods for referral of pupils who are clearly at risk and the institutions to which they may be referred;
   − training in interpersonal and communication skills necessary to approach and entertain an understanding relationship with such pupils;
   − information on how schools can best deal with and respond to suicide or attempted suicide by pupils through contacts with the mental health services.

2) With regard to the role of the police, the following recommendations seem to be relevant:
   – Senior police officials should ensure that in the event of suicide or attempted suicide, police duties be carried out, wherever possible, by officers who have the necessary social skills and aptitudes.
   – It is important that a set of rules be drawn up, based on police experience, that can be followed in cases of suicide and attempted suicide. These might include the wearing of civilian clothes, not leaving relatives alone before other helpers have arrived, getting in touch with the family doctor where necessary, etc.
   – Arrangements must be made to ensure that items seized at the time of a suicide, such as suicide notes, diaries, and other materials of a personal nature be returned to the family as soon as investigations have been completed.

3) In order to assess the role of emergency telephone services and their potential in suicide prevention, research should be undertaken aimed
   – to investigate how the role of emergency telephone services can be used to best advantage in preventing suicide. The focus should be on aspects such as the training of voluntary workers and the relationship of the services with other bodies providing help or assistance, and on the involvement of professional care workers.
   – to study suicidal persons who have contacted emergency telephone services and to assess what happens to these people afterwards. The information obtained should help to clarify the role of the telephone services and ensure that receive better support from government than is at present the case.

4) With regard to the general public, measures must be taken to increase awareness of the symptoms of depression and other signs indicating a suicide risk. In addition, more publicity should be given to organizations that can offer confidential and professional advice and/or help and assistance in cases of suicidal threats or acts.

5) In the opinion of the task force, although the role of the media with regard to the above-mentioned (1–4) can be a very significant one, but on the other hand they may also indeed sometimes provoke or encourage suicidal behavior. In fact, a

substantial problem in using television and newspapers in suicide prevention is the possible imitation effect, as demonstrated by Phillips [520], Phillips and Carstensen [521], and Schmidtke and Häfner [597]. This imitation or so-called Werther effect appears to be stronger for the young and for those observers or readers who resemble the portrayed model. Therefore, in the interests of suicide prevention, the media should exercise great prudence and restraint in news items concerning suicide and in publishing articles or broadcasting programs concerning cases of suicidal behavior [336]. It should be the rule that such materials/series are discussed with experts in suicidal behavior and prevention before being made public.

Special Groups

For certain special groups the following provisions must be made or measures taken:

1) Provisions for identifying and preventing suicidal behavior among adolescents should be clearly organized and should take the form of collaboration between schools and the mental health services within each region; where possible, parents should also be involved. Furthermore, it should be possible for pupils with severe emotional problems to call upon a professional, such as a psychologist, to provide counselling on school premises. This type of assistance should be made available not only in secondary schools, but also in institutes for higher (vocational) education and at universities.

2) As far as care for potential suicidal elderly is concerned, an active outreach program directed at elderly living alone, in particular those who have recently experienced the death of their partner, must be available in each districts. Efforts must be made both to make regular checks on the physical condition of the widow or widower, which often deteriorates rapidly after the death of the partner, and to encourage the person in question not to isolate him- or herself socially. Such an approach is of particular importance with regard to childless couples and should be continued until at least a year after the death of the partner. The various agencies concerned must (under coordination of CMHCs) establish clear policies at regional levels regarding such activities. Those in-

volved in the provision of this type of help, particularly family practitioners, should pay special attention to the "anniversary" phenomenon (birthday of the deceased or the anniversary of his or her death). Such occasions can cause deep depression in the surviving partners, and getting in touch with them on these days can often help them overcome the crisis. Another recommendation is the provision of better information both to the person providing the help or assistance, and to the elderly person concerning depressive disorders and how they can be treated. It should be the responsibility of the regional geriatric services to provide such information on a regular basis, backed up with written material, to both professional health-care workers and the elderly themselves.

3) There is a need for further research into suicidal behavior in correctional institutions and prisons, for training in identifying and dealing with such behavior by prison staff, and for assembling information on methods of preventing such behavior in those settings.

4) Those involved in caring for the chronically ill should be trained to identify and be able to communicate about suicidal thoughts and plans, to assess the risk of suicidal behavior, to evaluate the degree to which suicidal wishes are related to acceptance of illness or disability. They must also be trained in counseling such patients, or where this is not part of their job, in referring them appropriately.

5) Agencies and individuals involved in treating alcoholics and drug addicts should be alert to the risk of suicide among their patients/clients, and should be trained to identify and deal with suicidal behavior. From the point of view of prevention in general, it is important that national measures be taken to combat alcohol and drug (ab)use.

6) Survivors of those who have committed suicide should be considered a high-risk group and therefore an important target for preventive measures. Given that they do not often ask for help themselves, an active approach must be used to contact and assist them. It is an important responsibility of the (primary) mental health services to establish contact with relatives of persons who have committed suicide as soon as possible thereafter, to offer help and assistance, and to repeat this offer in follow-up contacts. This should continue until at least a year after the suicide has taken place.

Assistance should take the form of both individual help and of treating or counseling surviving family members as a group. It should also be possible in every region for survivors of those who have committed suicide to participate in grief work groups in order to come to terms with their bereavement. Organizing such groups is a suitable task for CMHCs. Information, for example, in the form of leaflets, should also be made available immediately to survivors, describing in simple terms the process of coming to terms with one's grief and loss, the feelings that one may be expected to experience, social consequences, and ways of dealing with them, as well as way of seeking help from others.

CHAPTER 14
Concluding Remarks

Geriatric psychiatry is today one of the fastest growing and most exciting branches of psychiatry. A powerful thrust in this direction was undoubtedly lent by the rapid population increases, especially among persons over 65, of recent years. The attention that has (finally) been addressed to this stage in life has resulted in a good deal of research and often the revision of much conventional wisdom on the clinical aspects of this age group (in this context we may point, for example, to questions centering around involutive melancholy and pseudodementia). A major concern of this volume has been mood disorders and suicide, that tragic event that is all too often a consequence of these problems. But it should not be forgotten that dementia, a pathology of great socioeconomic importance, has also undergone a profound cultural revision. Largely thanks to new noninvasive diagnostic techniques, it has been possible to acquire new and revolutionary insights into this disorder, and it may be hoped that these will prove to be a prelude to the development of an effective treatment.

PREVALENCE OF DEPRESSION IN THE ELDERLY

The theme of affective disorders was addressed in part because they represent the most frequent psychiatric pathology in this age group, as in others. As we have seen, much of the relevant literature reports a higher frequency of depression in the later stages of life [476]. Very recently, however, some North American authors have suggested, on the basis of epidemiological data, that depression is far less widespread than commonly believed, and that it may even be more common in the young than in the elderly [47]. This affirmation is, naturally, based on different diagnostic interpretations and, above all, on epidemiological data, such as that of the Epidemiologic Catchment Area Project, gathered through clinical interviews [482]. Certain critical observations have already been made in relation to this project in Chapter 1 of this volume.

Certain points should also be emphasized with regard to the need for a correct and standardized diagnosis in relation to the same patient (a problem of major concern for modern scientific psychiatry). First, there is no longer any doubt that the prevalence of the major mood disorders does not undergo modification with advancing age; elderly people are subject to major mood disorders with the same frequency as younger subjects (at present there appears to be no convincing evidence for a lower prevalence). The issue of the uncertain definitions of "dysphoria," "transitory—or situational—depressive states," and "depressive temperaments" is more complex. None of these conditions, when they may be differentiated, seem to have much to do with a clinical pathology. Bearing in mind that the boundary between "sadness" and "depression" remains to some extent a matter of opinion, this debate seems likely to remain inconclusive for the foreseeable future.

However, the higher prevalence of "organic" mood disorders—those conditions relating to a well-defined etiological event—is, in our opinion, an indisputable fact. As is well known, the elderly generally do not enjoy the good health of younger subjects. This, in turn, exposes them to a higher risk of untoward side effects of drugs, iatrogenic disease, systemic diseases, and disorders of the CNS. These aspects of aging were discussed at some length elsewhere in this volume (Chapter 2). Furthermore, particular attention was focused on the controversial aspects of depression arising in the course of Parkinson's disease (Chapter 6) and cerebrovascular accident (Chapter 5). But besides these particular diagnostic categories, other forms of depression (dysthymia, atypical depressions, adjustment disorder with depressed mood) also seem to be more frequent in the elderly. A very recent survey conducted by ourselves over 6 years of activity in a geriatric hospital [174] has provided further scientific support for this affirmation. The reason for this higher prevalence of "minor" (but clinically significant) depressions among the elderly may well lie in the greater frequency of the biological and psychosocial changes inevitably involved in getting older. Of all the possible etiologies, perhaps the biological factors are the most controversial—not so much in terms of the age-related deterioration in physical and sensorial performance (although this is important), but in the modifications occurring in the receptor synthesis, turnover, and binding regulating synaptic neurotransmission. This last field of enquiry was addressed in depth in Chapter 4. Bearing in mind that a definitive interpretation of these modifications is still being awaited, it may only be hypothesized that the reduced presence of certain neurotransmitters in the CNS of elderly subjects may lead to an increased receptorial sensitivity and hence a prompter depressive response to life events, whether loss or disease. Or, again, it may be speculated that the above-mentioned neurochemical modifications could give rise to a substantial reduction in the "elasticity" of the transmission system, thus implying a slower reorganization of an altered emotional balance and hence a certain tendency to chronicity of depressive life experience.

TREATMENT OF MOOD DISORDERS IN THE ELDERLY

As already mentioned in the Introduction, one of the most striking problems in the treatment of depression by physicians is a general failure to act incisively. This attitude may be attributed to a series of factors already examined. Its immediate consequences are, on the one hand, a tendency toward underdosage of psychotropic drugs and, on the other hand, a very low rate of referral to psychotherapy. The pharmacological and psychotherapeutic approaches have been discussed (Chapters 8–10); here, we limit ourselves to stressing the need for the study of new molecules that may increase the range of antidepressant agents available for the treatment of the elderly. Nor is it superfluous to recommend that clinical experimentation be carried out with evaluative instruments that are purpose designed or calibrated for use in elderly populations. The use of rating scales designed for use with young and young adult populations and containing too many "somatic" items—often leading to an overestimation of depressive symptoms in the elderly—is not, in fact, an infrequent occurrence and has obvious implications for the interpretation of trial results. On the other hand, it is also true that the majority of the available scales fail to assess some very important items for the elderly, for example, situations such as loss of self-esteem (*Hamilton's Rating Scale for Depression, Geriatric Depression Scale*), feelings of helplessness (*Hamilton RSD, Zung Self-Rating Depression Scale, Beck's Depression Scale*), or perception of cognitive deficits (*Hamilton RSD, Beck Depression Scale*). All these situations are typically related to elderly depressions, and their absence may lead to considerable underestimation. Therefore, the need for a new scale that has been validated on an elderly population is quite clear [681].

The insufficiency of data on the psychotherapeutic treatment of the elderly should also be noted at this juncture. Very few controlled trials are reported in the literature, and attempts to design theoretical-technical models specifically for use with the elderly are even rarer. Even for such widely used forms as cognitive and behavioral therapy, rigorously conducted trials with the elderly may be counted on the fingers of one hand (see Chapter 10). There is thus an urgent need for further research into psychotherapy of the elderly, a field offering a rich potential for this age group. It, furthermore, goes without saying that the possibility of effective, nonpharmacological treatment in a population already heavily exposed to the risks of polypharmacy cannot but justify the necessary investment of research energy and funds.

SUICIDE

Even though suicide is only about the 10th most frequent cause of death in subjects over the age of 65 years [483] (compared with the 2nd or 3rd place in adolescents of various Western countries [178]), the toll paid in numbers of deaths is much heavier in the elderly, as was amply reported in Chapter 12. It follows that advanced age alone is an important risk factor. Unfortunately, suicide is an extremely complex phenomenon: Risk factor study has failed to identify a homogeneous population, and the concomitant presence of a number of risk factors is likewise not a valid index of the danger experienced by any one individual. Our enquiry into attitude toward suicide did permit the verification of a phenomenon well known in epidemiology, namely, that increasing age corresponds to an increasing risk of death by suicide in male subjects, while the curve of female subjects tends to drop after the end of menopause. This trend is also confirmed in the curves expressing attitude [172]. Unfortunately, reliable epidemiological data were not available to support the findings of this Italian investigation. There is, however, convincing evidence pointing to the existence in Italy of a trend similar to that found in other European countries, as shown in Table 28, Chapter 12 [151].

In any case, it should be borne in mind that many of the most important risk factors for suicide tend to be particularly present in the experience of the elderly person: retirement, frequent loss events (including the very important experience of widowhood), depression, diminishing social support networks, a chronic disease. Of all these factors, the affective disturbances appear to play the most significant role, as in all stages of life [63]. In any case, it should be stressed that clinical diagnosis (in Axis I of the DSM-III) should be accompanied at least by a personality diagnosis (Axis II), in which particular attention should be paid to antisocial and borderline situations. Furthermore, as suggested by Blumenthal and Kupfer [63], the enquiry should not be limited to the definition of Axes I and II, but should extend to all personality traits and styles (for example, impulsiveness, aggression, hopelessness). Axis III of the DSM-III should also be formulated, especially in the elderly, as concomitant medical diseases are also held to be an important risk factor (552).

We feel that the most effective strategy for suicide prevention today, in the elderly as in younger subjects, lies in early identification and treatment of depression. This despite the fact that, as we have noted, "the absence of suicide generates no data. Thus, we can never prove what has been accomplished. Yet we can hardly doubt that it occurs" [480].

In conclusion, we feel that the best strategy for prevention must include a reevaluation of the view of old age that salvages its cultural content and rejects the notion of economic productivity as the only index of the importance of a role. While awaiting this reevaluation, however, it is our duty to do what we can to encourage the training and sensitization of people working in close contact with the elderly: general practitioners, geriatricians, psychiatrists, the doctors and staff of homes for the elderly, social workers, etc. Their capacity to listen for and hear possibly suicidal messages as well as to identify correctly depression or other risk factors may consent early and effective intervention in the case of potential suicidal crises.

REFERENCES

1) ABRAHAM K. The applicability of psychoanalytic treatment to patients at an advanced age. In *Selected Papers on Psychoanalysis*. John & Hogart Press, London 1949.

2) ABRAHAM G, SIMEONE J. La psychotherapie brève dans l'âge avancée. *Psychol Med (Paris)* 12: 597–600, 1980.

3) ABRAMS R, ESSMAN W B. *Electroconvulsive Therapy: Biological Foundation and Clinical Applications*. MTP Press, Lancaster, 1982.

4) ABRAMS R, TAYLOR M A. Unipolar mania. A preliminary report. *Arch Gen Psychiatry* 30: 441–443, 1974.

5) ADOLFSSON R, GOTTFRIES C G, ROOS B E, et al. Change in the brain catecholamines in patients with dementia of Alzheimer type. *Br J Psychiatry* 135: 216–223, 1979.

6) ALDRICH C J, MENDKOFFE J. Relocation of the aged and disabled: A morbidity study. *JAGS* 11: 35–41, 1977.

7) AKISKAL H S. Diagnosis and classification of affective disorders. *Psychiat Develop* 2: 123–160, 1983.

8) AKISKAL H S, BITAR A H, PUNZANTIAN V R, et al. The nosological status of neurotic depression. *Arch Gen Psychiatry* 35: 756–766, 1978.

9) AMBELAS A. Psychologically stressful events in the precipitation of manic episodes. *Br J Psychiatry* 133: 21–25, 1979.

10) AMERICAN PSYCHIATRIC ASSOCIATION. *Diagnostic and Statistical Manual of Mental Disorders* (3rd ed). A.P.A. Press, Washington DC, 1980.

11) AMERICAN PSYCHIATRIC ASSOCIATION. *Diagnostic and Statistical Manual of Mental Disorders* (3rd ed., rev.). APA Press, Washington, DC, 1987.

12) AMSTERDAM J, BRUNSWICK D, MENDELS J. Clinical application of tricyclic antidepressant pharmacokinetics and plasma levels. *Am J Psychiatry* 137: 653–662, 1980.

13) ANANTH J F, SOHN J H, BAN T A, et al. Doxepin in geriatric patients. *Curr Ther Res* 25: 133–138, 1979.

14) ANGST J. Discussion. In *Classification and Prediction of Outcome of Depression*. J Angst (Ed.). Simposia Medica, Hoechst and F.K. Schattaner Verlag, New York, 1974.

15) ANGST J, BAASTRUP P, GROF P. The course of monopolar depression and bipolar psychoses. *Psychiatr Neurol Neurochir* 76: 489–500, 1973.

16) ANONYMOUS. Benzodiazepines use, over-use, misuse, abuse? (Editorial). *Lancet* 1: 1101–1102, 1973.

17) ASBERG M, BERTILSSON L, MARTENSSON B. CSF monoamine metabolites, depression, and suicide. In *Frontiers in Biochemical and Pharmacological Research in Depression*. E Usdin, M Asberg, L Bertilsson et al. (Eds). Raven Press, New York, 1984.

18) ASBERG M, THOREN P, TRAKSMAN L, et al. Serotinin depression—A biochemical subgroup within the affective disorders. *Science* 191: 478–80, 1976.

19) ASBERG M, TRASKMAN L. Studies of CSF 5-HIAA in depression and suicidal behaviour. In *Serotinin*. B Haber, S Gabay, M R Issidovides, et al. (Eds). Plenum Press, New York, 1981.

20) ASHER C C. The impact of social support networks on adult health. *Med Care* 22: 349, 1984.

21) ASHFORD W, FORD C V. Use of MAO inhibitors in elderly patients. *Am J Psychiatry* 136: 1466–1470, 1979.

22) ASHTON H. Benzodiazepines withdrawal: An unfinished story. *Br Med J* 288: 1135–1140, 1984.

23) ASTRUP J, SIEJO B K, SYMON L. Thresolds in cerebral ischemia. The ischemic penumbra. *Stroke* 12: 723–725, 1981.

24) ATCHLEY R C. *The Sociology of Retirement.* New York, Healstead Press, 1976.

25) AVERY D, WINOKUR G. Suicide, attempted suicide, and relapse rates in depression. *Arch Gen Psychiatry* 35: 749–753, 1978.

25a) BABIGIAN H M, GUTTMACHER, L B. Epidemiological considerations in electroconvulsive therapy. *Arch General Psychiatr* 41: 246–253, 1984.

26) BALDESSARINI R J. *Biomedical Aspects of Depression.* American Pyschiatric Press, Washington, DC, 1983.

27) BALDWIN R C, JOLLEY D G. The prognosis of depression in old age. *Br J Psychiatry* 149: 571–583, 1986.

28) BALDWIN R C. Delusional and non-delusional depression in late life. *Br J Psychiatry* 152: 111–119, 1988.

29) BALL J. *L'Encephale.* Vol. 2. 22–32, 1882.

30) BANDURA, A. Self-efficacy: Toward a unifying theory of behavioral change. *Psychol Review* 84: 191–215, 1977.

31) BANERJEE S P, KUNG L S, RIGGI S J, et al. Development of alpha-adrenergic receptor subsensitivity by antidepressants. *Nature* 268: 455–459, 1977.

32) BARBEAU A. L-dopa therapy in Parkinson's desease. A central review of nine years experience. *Can Med Ass J* 101: 791–800, 1969.

33) BARON J C. New perspectives in functional imaging of the aging human brain. *Mod. Trends Aging Res* 147: 459–467, 1986.

34) BARRACLOUGH B M. Suicide in the elderly. In *Recent Development in Psychogeriatrics.* D W K Kay & A Walk (Eds). *Br J Psychiatry*, Special Publication No. 6, 87–97, 1971.

35) BARTUS R T, DEAN R L, BEER B, et al. The cholinergic hypothesis of geriatric memory disfunction. *Science* 217: 408–417, 1982.

36) BARTROP R W, LAZARUS L, LUCKHURST E, et al. Depressed lymphocyte function after bereavement. *Lancet* 1: 834–836, 1977.

37) BAXTER L R Jr, PHELPS M E, MAZZIOTTA J C, et al. Cerebral metabolic rates for glucose in mood disorders: Studies with positron emission tomography and fluorodeoxyglucose F 18. *Arch Gen Psychiatry* 40: 1018–1020, 1977.

38) BECH P, GJERRIS A, ANDERSEN J, et al. The melancholia scale and the Newcastle scales item conbinations and iter-observer reliability. *Br J Psychiatry 143:* 58–63, 1983.

39) BECK A T, KOVACS M, WEISSMAN A. Hopelessness and suicidal behaviour. An overview. *J Am Med Assoc* 234: 1146–1148, 1975.

40) BECK A T, RUSH J, SHAW B, EMERY G. *Cognitive Therapy of Depression.* Guilford, New York, 1979.

41) BECK A T, STEER R A, McELROY M G. Relationship of hopelessness, depression and previous suicide attempts to suicidal ideation in alcoholics. *J Stud Alcohol* 43: 1042–1046, 1982.

42) BECK A T, WARD C, MELDELSOM M, et al. An inventory for measuring depression. *Arch Gen Psychiatry 4:* 53–63, 1961.

43) BECKER GS. *The Economic Approach to Human Behaviour*. University of Chicago Press, Chicago, 1986.

44) BEDNAR R, KAULT T. Experiential group research. Current perspectives. In *Handbook of Psychotherapy and Behaviour Change*. S Garfield & A Bergin (Eds). Wiley, New York, 1978.

45) BEL A, GIRARD D. Hepatitis, cholestasis and amineptine. *Sem Hop Paris* 57: 1992–1995, 1981.

46) BELLAK L, SMALL L. *Emergency Psychotherapy and Brief Phychotherapy*. Grune & Stratton, New York, 1978.

47) BEREZIN M A, LIPTZIN B, SALZMAN C. The elderly person. In *The New Harward Guide to Psychiatry*. A Nicholi (Ed). Harvard Univ Press, Cambridge, 1988.

48) BERGONZI P, CHIARULLA C, GAMBI D, et al. L-dopa plus decarboxylase inhibitor sleep organization in Parkinson's syndrome before and after treatment. *Acta Neurol Belg* 75: 6, 1975.

49) BERKMAN L F, SYME S L. Social networks, host resistance and mortality: A nine-year follow-up study of Alameda county residents. *Am J Epidemiol* 109: 186–204, 1979.

50) BERNHEIMER H, BIRKMAYER W, HORNYKIEWICZ O, et al. Brain dopamine and the syndromes of Parkinson and Huntington. *J Neurol Sci* 20: 415–455, 1973.

51) BERTLER A, FALCK B, OWMAN C, ROSENGREEN E. The localization of monoaminergic blood-brain barrier mechanism. *Pharmacol Rev* 18: 369–385, 1986.

52) BERTLER A. Occurrence and localization of catecholamine in the human brain. *Acta Physiol Scand* 51: 97–107, 1961.

53) BESSON J A, CORRIGAN F M, FOREMAN E I, et al. Nuclear magnetic resonance (NMR). II. Imaging in dementia. *Br J Psychiatry* 146: 31–35, 1985.

54) BIELSKI R J, FRIEDEL R O. Depressive subtypes defined by response to pharmacotherapy. *Psychiatr Clin North Am* 2: 483–489, 1979.

55) BIRD J M, LEVY R, JACOBY R J. Computer tomography in the elderly changes over time in the normal population. *Br J Psychiatry* 148: 80–86, 1986.

56) BIRKMAYER W, RIEDERER P. Biochemical postmortem findings in depressed patients. *J Neural Transm.* 37: 95–109, 1975.

57) BLACKWELL B. Adverse effects of antidepressant drugs. Part 2. *Drugs* 21: 273–292, 1981.

58) BLAU D, BEREZIN M A. Neuroses and character disorders. *J Gen Psychiatry* 15: 55–97, 1982.

59) BLAZER D G. Social support and mortality in elderly community population. *Am J Epidemiol* 115: 684–694, 1982.

60) BLAZER D. The epidemiology of late life depression. *JAGS* 30: 587–592, 1982.

61) BLAZER D, WILLIAMS C D. Epidemiology of disphoria and depression in an elderly population. *Am J Psychiatry* 137: 439–444, 1980.

62) BLESSED G, WILSON I D. The contemporary natural history of mental disorders in old age. *Br J Psychiatry* 141: 59–67, 1982.

63) BLUMENTHAL S J, KUPFER D J. Generalizable treatment strategies for suicidal behavior. *Am N Y Acad Sci* 487: 327–340, 1986.

64) BLYTHY R. *The View in Winter*. Harcourt, Brace Jovanovich, New York, 1979.

65) BOCK E W. Aging and suicide the significance of marital, Kinship and alternative relations. *Family Coordinator* 21: 71–79, 1972.

66) BOJANOWSKY J. Wann droht der Selbstmord bei Verwitweten? *Schweizer Arch Neurol Neurochir Psychiatrie* 127: 99–103, 1980.

67) BOLLERUP T. Prevalence of mental illness among 70-year-old domicilied in nine Copenhagen suburbs. *Acta Psychiat Scand* 51: 327–339, 1975.

68) BOSTON COLLABORATIVE SURVEILLANCE DRUG PROGRAM. Clinical depression of the central nervous system due to diazepam and chlordiazepoxide in relation to cigarette smoking and age. *N Engl J Med* 228: 207–208, 1973.

69) BOTWINICK J. *Aging and Behaviour* (2nd ed.). Springer, New York, 1979.

70) BOURESTON N, TARS S. Alteration in life patterns following nursing home relocation. *Gerontologist* 14: 506–510, 1974.

71) BOWEN D M. Biochemical evidence for selective vulnerability in Alzheimer's disease. In *Biochemistry of Dementia*. P J Roberts (Ed). Wiley, Chichester, 1980.

72) BOYD J H, WEISSMAN M N. Epidemiology. In *Handbook of Affective Disorders*. E S Paykel (Ed.). Churchill Livingstone, Edimburgh, 1982.

73) BRACONNIER R J, COLE J O, GHAZVINIAN S. The therapeutic profile of mianserine in mild elderly depressives. *Psychopharmacolol Bull* 17: 129–131, 1981.

74) BRADLEY W G, WALUCH V, BRANT-ZAWADSKI M, et al. Patchy periventricular white matter lesions in the elderly: A common observation during NMR imaging. *Non-Invasive Med Imag* 1: 35–41, 1984.

75) BRECKENRIDGE J N, GALLAGHER D, THOMPSON L W, et al. Characteristic depressive symptoms of bereaved elders. *J Gerontology* 41: 163–168, 1986.

76) BRIDGES P. The drugs treatment of depression in old age. In *Affective Disorders in the Elderly*. E. Murphy (Ed). Churchill Livingstone, Edinburgh, 1986.

77) BROWN G L, WILSON W P. Parkinsonism and depression. *South Med J* 65: 540–545, 1972.

78) BROWN GW, HARRIS T. *Social Origins of Depression*. Tavistock, London, 1978.

79) BROWN G W, HARRIS T, COPELAND J R. Depression and loss. *Br J Psychiatry* 130: 1–18, 1977.

80) BROWN J H, PARASKEVAS F. Cancer and depression. Cancer presenting with depressive illness an autoimmune disease? *Br J Psychiatry* 141: 227–232, 1982.

81) BROWN L G, EBERT M H, GOYER P F, et al. Aggression, suicide and serotinin. Relationship to CSF amine metabolites. *Am J Psychiatry* 139: 741–746, 1982.

82) BROWN L G, GOODWIN F K, BALLENGER J C, et al. Aggression in humans correlates with CSF amine metabolites. *Psychiatry Res* 1: 131–139, 1979.

83) BROWN R G, MARSDEN C D, QUINN N, et al. Alterations in cognitive performance and affect-arousal state during fluctuations in motor function in Parkinson's disease. *J Neurol Neurosurg Psychiatry* 47: 454–465, 1984.

84) BROWN R P, SWEENEY J, LOUTSCH E A, et al. Involutional melancholia revisited. *Am J Psychiatry* 141: 24–28, 1984.

85) BROWN W A. Effect of age on DST results. *Am J Psychiatry* 139: 1376–1377, 1982.

86) BUCHSBAUM M S, CAPPELETTI J, BALL R, et al. Positron emission tomographic image measurement in schizophrenia and affective disorders. *Ann Neurol* 15 (suppl.): S157–S165, 1984.

87) BUCHSBAUM M S, COURSEY R D, MURPHY D L. The biochemical high-risk paradigm: Behavioral and familial correlates of low platelet monoamine oxidase activity. *Science* 194: 339–341, 1976.

88) BULBENA A, BERRIOS G. Pseudodementia: Facts and figures. *Br J Psychiatry* 148: 87–94, 1986.

89) BUNCH J. Recent bereavement in relation to suicide. *J Psychosom Res* 16: 361–366, 1972.

90) BUNCH J, BARRACLOUGH B M, NELSON B. The influence of parenthal death anniversaries upon suicide dates. *Br J Psychiatry* 118: 621–626, 1971.

91) BURCH E A Jr, GOLDSCHIMDT T J. Depression in the elderly: A beta-adrenergic receptor dysfunction? *Intl J Psychiat Med* 13: 207–213, 1983/1984.

92) BURVILL P W, STAMPFER H, HALL W. Does depressive illness in the elderly have a poor prognosis? *Aust. N Z J Psychiatry* 20: 422–427, 1986.

93) BUSSE E W, BARNES R M, SILVERMAN AJ, THALER T, FROST L L. Studies of the processes of aging. The strength and weaknesses of psychic functioning in the aged. *Am J Psychiatry* 11: 896–901, 1955.

94) BUSSE E W, PFEIFFER E. *Behaviour and Adaptation in Late Life.* Little Brown & Co., Boston, 1969.

95) BUTLER R M, LEWIS M I. Suicide in old age. In *Aging and Mental Health Positive Psychosocial Approaches.* C.V. Mosby, St. Louis, 61–63, 1973.

96) BUTLER R N. Psychiatry and elderly. An overview. *Am J Psychiatry* 132: 893–900, 1975.

97) CAIRD F I, ANDREWS G R, KENNEDY R D. Effect of posture on blood pressure in the elderly. *Br Heart J* 35: 527–530, 1973.

98) CANEVA A, DE LEO D, MARAZZITI D, et al. *3-H-Imipramine Binding Sites in Suicidal Behaviour.* Paper read at the XVth IASP Meeting, Brussels, June 11th–14th, 1989.

99) CARANASOS G J, STEWART R B, CLUFF L E. Drug-induced illness leading to hospitalization. *JAMA* 228: 713–717, 1974.

100) CARLSON G M, DAVENPORT Y B, JAMISON K. A comparison of outcome in adolescent and late-onset bipolar manic-depressive illness. *Am J Psychiatry* 143: 919–922, 1977.

101) CARLSSON A. Neurotrasmitters in old age and dementia. In *Mental Health in the Elderly.* H. Hafner et al. (Eds) Springer-Verlag, Berlin Heidelberg, 1986.

102) CARLSSON A. Brain neurotrasmitters in aging and dementia: Similar changes across diagnostic dementia groups. *Gerontology* 33: 159–167, 1987.

103) CARLSSON A, WINBLAD B. Influence of age and time interval beetwen death and autopsy on dopamine and 3-methoxytyramine levels in human basal ganglia. *J Neural Transmission* 38: 271–276, 1976.

104) CARROLL B J, FEINBERG M, GREDEN J F, et al. A specific laboratory test for the diagnosis of melancholia. *Arch Gen Psychiatry* 38: 15–22, 1981.

105) CATALAN J, GATH D, BOND A. The effects of non-prescribing of anxiolytics in general practice. II. Factors associated with outcome. *Br J Psychiatry* 144: 603–610, 1984.

106) CATALAN J, GATH D, EDMONDS G. The effects of non-prescribing of anxiolytics in general practice. I. Controlled evaluation of psychiatric and social outcome. *Br J Psychiatry* 144: 593–602, 1984.

107) CAZZULLO C L, ALTAMURA A C. Bioavailability of some atypical antidepressant and therapeutic management of late life depressive states. *Integr Psychiatry* 3: 50S–57S, 1985.

108) CELESIA G G, WANAMAKER W M. Psychiatric disturbances in Parkinson's diseases. *Dis Nerv System* 33: 577–583, 1972.

109) CHABROL H, GUELL A, BARRERE M, et al. Etude du débit sanguin cérébral chez 20 adolescent déprimés. *Encephale* 11: 207–208, 1985.

110) CHARATAN F B. The aged. In *Suicide Theory and Clinical Aspects*. L D Hankoff (Ed). PSG Publishing Co., Littleton, 1979.

111) CHARCOT J M. *Leçons sur les maladies du système nerveux*. Delahaye, Paris, 1875.

112) CHIODO L A, ANTELMON S M. Repeated tricyclics induce a progressive dopamine autoreceptor subsensitivity independent of daily drug treatment. *Nature* 287: 451–454, 1980.

113) CHRISTENSEN A L. *Luria's Neuropsychological Investigation*. Munksgaard, Copenhagen, 1974.

113) CHRISTIE A B. Changing patterns in mental illness in the elderly. *Br J Psychiatry* 140: 154–159, 1982.

114) CHURCH M. Psychological therapy with elderly people. *Bull Br Psychol Soc* 36: 110–112, 1983.

115) CHYNOWETH R. Suicide in the elderly. *Crisis* 2: 106–116, 1981.

116) CLAMAN A D. Introduction to panel discussion "Sexual difficulties after 50." *Can Med Ass J* 94: 207, 1966.

117) CLAYTON P J. Mortality and morbility of the first year of widowhood. *Arch Gen Psychiatry* 30: 747–750, 1974.

118) CLAYTON P J, DARVISH H S. Course of depressive symptoms following the stress of bereavement. In *Stress and Mental Disorder*. J E Barrett et al. (Eds). Raven Press, New York, 1979.

119) CLAYTON P J. The epidemiology of bipolar affective disorder. *Compreh Psychiatry* 22: 31–43, 1981.

120) COHEN N A. On loneliness and the ageing process. *Int. J Psychoanalysis* 63: 149–156, 1982.

121) COHEN R M, SEMPLE W E, GROSS M. Positron emission tomography. *Psychiat Clin North Amer* 9: 63–79, 1986.

122) COLE M G. Age, age of onset and course of primary depressive illness in the elderly. *Can J Psychiatry* 28: 102–104, 1983.

123) COLE M G. Frequency and significance of minor organic signs in elderly depressive. *Can Psychiatry Assoc. J* 21: 7–12, 1976.

124) COLE M G. The course of elderly depressed outpatients. *Can J Psychiatry* 30: 217–230, 1985.

125) COLE M G, MULLER H F. Sleep deprivation in the treatment of elderly depressed patients. *JAGS* 24: 308–313, 1976.

126) COMMISSION OF THE EUROPEAN COMMUNITY. *Social Indicators for the European Comunity 1960–1978*. Brussels, 1979.

127) COMMITTEE ON THE REVIEW OF MEDICINES. Systematic review of the benzodiazepines. Guidelines for data sheets on diazepam, chlordiazepoxide, medazepam, chlorazepate, lorazepam, oxazepam, temazepam, nitrazepam, and flurazepam. *Br Med J* 280: 910–912, 1980.

126) COOPER A, MURPHY E. Psychological approaches to depression in the aged. In *Affective Disorders in the Elderly*. E Murphy (Ed). Churchill-Livingstone, Edinburgh, 1986.

129) COOPER A J, DATTA S R. A placebo controlled evaluation of L-triptophan in depression in the elderly. *Can J Psychiatry* 25: 386–390, 1980.

130) CORBY N H. Assertion training with aged populations. *Consult Psychol* 5: 69–73, 1975.

131) COSTELLO J P, TANAKA G M. Mortality and morbidity in longterm institutional care of the aged. *JAGS* 9: 959–963, 1961.

132) COTÉ L J, KREMZNER L T. Changes in neurotransmitter system with increasing age in human brain. *Trans Am Soc Neurochem* 5: 83, 1974.

133) CRAIG T, VAN NATTA P A. Disability and depressive symptoms in two communities. *Am J Psychiatry* 140: 598–602, 1983.

134) CROOKS J, SHEPHERO A M, STEVENSON. Drugs and the elderly. The nature of the problem. *Health Bulletin* 35: 222–227, 1975.

135) CUTLER N R, NARANG P K. Implication of dosing tricyclic antidepressants and benzodiapezines in geriatrics. *Psychiat Clin North Amer* 7: 845–861, 1984.

136) CUTLER N R, ZAVADIL, LINNOILA M, et al. Effects of chronic desipramine on plasma norepinephrine concentrations and cardiovascular parameters in elderly depressed women. A preliminary report. *Biol Psychiatry* 19: 549–556, 1984.

137) DALEN P. Family history, the electroencephalogram, and perinatal factors in manic conditions. *Acta Psychiat Scan* 41: 527–563, 1965.

138) DASBERG H, VAN PRAAG H M. The therapeutic effect of short term oral diazepam treatment on acute clinical anxiety in a crisis centre. *Acta Psychiat Scand* 50: 326–340, 1974.

139) DAUMER J. Amineptine et manifestations depressive liées aux phénomènes involutifs de la senescence. *Psychol Med* (Paris) 13: 1091–1106, 1981.

140) DAVIS K L, YAMAMURA H I. Cholinergic underactivity in human memory disorders. *Life Sci* 23: 1729–1734, 1978.

141) DAWLING S, CROME P, BRAITHWAITE R A, et al. Nortriptyline therapy in elderly patients. Dosage prediction after single dose pharmacokinetic study. *Eur J Clin Pharmacol* 18: 147–150, 1980.

142) DE LEO D. Le psicoterapie. In *Argomenti di Clinica Psichiatrica*. L Pavan (Ed.). Cleup, Padova, 1982.

142a) DE LEO D. S-adenosyl-L-methionine in clinical practice: Preliminary repo on 75 minor depressives. *Curr Ther Res* 37: 658–661, 1985.

143) DE LEO D. SAMe as antidepressant. A double-blind study versus placebo. *Curr Ther Res* 41: 865–870, 1987.

144) DE LEO D. *What Therapy for Elderly Minor Depression? A Comparison among Different Treatments.* Paper read at the International Symposium "Normal Aging and Clinical Problems in the Elderly," Montreaux, March 30–April 2, 1987.

145) DE LEO D. Treatment of adjustment disorders. A comparative evaluation. *Psychol Rep* 64: 51–54, 1989.

146) DE LEO D, BANON D, SCHIFANO F, et al. *Suicidal Drive in Urban and Rural Communities of North Italy. A Comparison.* In *Current Research on Suicide and Parasuicide.* S. Platt & N. Kreitman (Eds.). University Press, Edinburgh, 1989.

147) DE LEO D, CEOLA A, MAGNI G. Sintomi psicosessuali da sindromi depressive. In *Diagnosi e Classificazione dei Disturbi Affettivi in Rapporto al DSM III.* Geigy, Milano, 1985.

148) DE LEO D, CEOLA A, MAGNI G. Viloxazine against placebo in a double-blind study in depressed elderly patients. *Curr Ther Res* 36: 239–244, 1984.

149) DE LEO D, DALLA BARBA G F, DALLA BARBA G P. Amineptine versus amitriptyline effects on depression, sex drive and prolactin levels. Preliminary observations. *Curr Ther Res* 40: 124–132, 1986.

150) DE LEO D, DALLA BARBA G F, DAM M, et al. *La depressione nel morbo di Parkinson.* Paper read at the 13th Congress of the Italian League against Parkinson Disease, Perugia, October 10–11 1986.

151) DE LEO D, DALLA BARBA G F, ZANCHIN G. Seizures following the withdrawal of long-term treatment with mianserin. *Italian J Neurol Sci* 9: 167–169, 1988.

152) DE LEO D, FRANCESCHI L, CUTRONE F, et al. *Neuropsychological Performances, Depressive Symptoms and Quality of Life Before and After Carotid Endarterectomy.* 3rd Meeting of the European Chapter of International Union of Angiology, Tours, France, 10–12 October 1984.

153) DE LEO D, FRANCESCHI L, MAGNI G, et al. Modificazioni del tono dell'umore e della qualità della vita dopo endarteriectomia carotidea. *Proceedings of the 33th Congress of the Italian Psychiatric Association,* Milan, October 21–26, 1985.

154) DE LEO D, FRANCESCHI L, SERRAIOTTO L, et al. *Does Asymptomatic Carotid Stenosis Really Exist?* International Congress of Angiology, Athens, Greece, June 9–14, 1985.

155) DE LEO D, MAGNI G. Antidepressants side effects. *Psychosomatics* 25: 919–920, 1984.

156) DE LEO D, MAGNI G. La depressione nella terza età. Identificazione, trattamento, prognosi. *Federazione Medica* 38: 364–377, 1984.

157) DE LEO D, MAGNI G. *Disturbi Affettivi nella Terza Età.* Masson, Milano, 1987.

158) DE LEO D, MAGNI G. Does viloxazine really improve sex drive? *Br J Psychiatry* 148: 597–599, 1986.

159) DE LEO D, MAGNI G. Problemi sessuali nella depressione e nella terapia con antidepressivi. *Medico & Paziente* 10: 475–484, 1984.

160) DE LEO D, MAGNI G. Quando trattare farmacologicamente i disturbi affettivi minori degli anziani. *Medico & Paziente* 13: 33–40, 1987.

161) DE LEO D, MAGNI G. Sexual side-effects of antidepressant drugs. *Psychosomatics* 24: 1976–1082, 1983.

162) DE LEO D, MAGNI G, PAVAN L. Modifications of libido and sex drive during treatment of minor depression with viloxazine. *Int J Clin Pharmacol Ther Toxicol* 21: 176–177, 1983.

163) DE LEO D, MAGNI G, VALLERINI A, et al. Assessment of anxiety and depression in general and psychiatric nurses. *Psychol Rep* 52: 335–337, 1983.

164) DE LEO D, PELLEGRINI C, SERRAIOTTO L. Adjustment disorders and suicidality. *Psychol Rep* 59: 355–358, 1986.

165) DE LEO D, PELLEGRINI C, SERRAIOTTO L, et al. Assessment of severity of suicide attempts. *Psychopathology* 19: 186–191, 1986.

166) DE LEO D, SERRAIOTTO L, FRANCESCHI L, et al. *Intellectual Functions after Carotid Endarterectomy. Long Term Follow-Up.* International Congress of Angiology, Athens, Greece, June 9–14, 1985.

167) DE LEO D, SERRAIOTTO L, FRANCESCHI L, et al. *Who Benefits More from Carotid Endarterectomy? The Young-Old or the Old-Old People? A Controlled Evaluation.* Paper read at the International Symposium "Normal Aging and Clinical Problems in the Elderly," Montreux, March 30– April 2, 1987.

168) DE LEO D, SERRAIOTTO L, PELLEGRINI C, et al. Does carotid endarterectomy really improve mental functions? *Proceedings of the 14th World Congress of Angiology.* Munich, July 6–11, 1986.

169) DE LEO D, SERRAIOTTO L, PELLEGRINI C, et al. Outcome from carotid endarterectomy: Neuropsychological performances, depressive symptoms and quality of life. *Int. J Psychiat Med* 17: 317–325, 1987.

170) DE LEO D, VILLA, A. *Crisis as Adjustment Disorder: Two Forms of Drug Therapy versus Supportive Psychotherapy.* Paper read at the XIIIth International

Congress on Suicide Prevention and Crisis Intervention, Wien, July 11–13, 1985.

171) DE LEO D, BANON D, CITRON P, et al. *The Search for Reliable Epidemiologic Data on Suicide. The Padua Sample.* Joint Meeting AAS-IASP, San Francisco, May 1987.

172) DE LEO D. *Sunset Depression.* Leiden University, Department of Clinical, Health, and Personality Psychology. Ph.D. Dissertation, 1988.

173) DE LEO D, MARAZZITI D. Biological prediction of suicide: The role of serotonin. *Crisis* 9: 109–118, 1988.

174) DE LEO D, BAIOCCHI A, CIPOLLONE B, et al. Psychogeriatric consultation within a geriatric hospital. A six-year experience. *Int J Geriat Psychiatry* 4: 135–142, 1989.

175) DE PAULO R. Lithium. *Psychiatr Clin North Am* 7: 587–599, 1984.

175a) DEW M A, BROMET E J, BRENT D, GREENHOUSE J B. A quantitative literature review of the effectiveness of Suicide Prevention Centers. *Journal of Consulting and Clinical Psychology* 55: 239–244, 1987.

176) DIDIEU-ANGLADE G. Psychotherapie des troubles psychoneurotiques au cours du vieullissement. *Enc Méd Chir Psychiatrie* 2: 37541, A10, 1981.

177) DIEKSTRA R F W. *Crisis en Gedragskenze.* Swets & Zeitlinger, Lisse, 1973.

178) DIEKSTRA R F W. Il comportamento suicidario tra gli adolescenti. Caratteristiche generali. In *Il Suicidio nel Mondo Contemporaneo.* L Pavan & D De Leo (Eds.). Liviana Editrice, Padova, 1988.

179) DIEKSTRA R F W. *Over suicide.* Samson, Alphen ad Rijn, 1981.

180) DIEKSTRA R F W. Suicide and suicide attempts in the European Community: An analysis of trends with special emphasis upon trends among the young. *Suicide Life Threat Behav* 15: 27–42, 1985.

181) DIEKSTRA R F W, ENGELS, G I. Cognitive therapy of depression. *Hexagon Roche* 14: 1–7, 1986.

181) DIEKSTRA R F W. *Rapport inzake suicide* (Report on suicide). Health Council of The Netherlands, The Hague, December 1986.

182) DIEKSTRA R F W, WINNUBST I, EVERAERD W. *Introduction to Health Psychology.* AMBO, Baan, 1989.

182a) DIEKSTRA, R F W, MARIS, R, PLATT, S, SCHMIDTKE, A, SONNECK, G. *Suicide and Its Prevention: The Role of Attitude and Imitation.* Brill, New York/ Leiden & WHO, Geneva (copublication), 1989.

182b) DIEKSTRA, RFW, VAN EGMOND, M. Suicide and attempted suicide in general practice, 1979–1986. *Acta Ostchiatr Scand* 79: 268–275, 1989.

182c) DIEKSTRA, R F W, HAWTON, K. *Suicide in Adolescence.* Kluwer Academic Publisher, Boston/Dordrecht, 1987.

182d) DIEKSTRA, R F W. Suicide and attempted suicide: An international perspective. Acta Psychiatr Scand 80 (Suppl. 354): 1–24, 1989.

182e) DIEKSTRA, R F W. *The Prevention of Suicidal Behaviour: A Review of Evidence for the Efficacy of Clinical and Community Based Programmes.* World Health Organization, Division of Mental Health, Geneva, 1989.

182f) DIEKSTRA, R F W. Suicide, unemployment and economic recession. In *Did the Crisis Really Hurt? Effects after 1980–1982 Economic Recession on Satisfaction, Mental Health and Mortality.* R Veenhoven (Ed.). Rotterdam, EUPR. 1989.

183) DIENER H C, DICHGANS J, HAMSTER W. Neuropsychological functions before and after carotid endarterectomy. In *Basis for a Classification of Cerebral Arterial Diseases.* R Couhier (Ed.). Excerpta Medica, Amsterdam, 1985.

184) DI MASCIO A. The effects of benzodiazepines on aggression: Reduced or increased? In *The Benzodiazepines*. S Garattini, E Mussini, LO Randall (Eds.). Raven Press, London, 1973.

185) DOLAN R J, CALLOWAY S P, MANN A H. Cerebral ventricular size in depressed subjects. *Psychol Med* 15: 873–878, 1985.

186) DOMINO E F, DREN A T, GIARDINA W J. Biochemical and neurotransmitter changes in the aging brain. In *Psychopharmacology: A Generation of Progress*. M A Lipton, A Di Mascio, K F Killam (Eds.). Raven Press, New York, 1978.

187) DORPAT L, ANDERSON W F, RIPLEY H R. The relationship of physical illness to suicide. In *Suicidal Behavioral Diagnosis and Management*. H P L Resnik (Ed). Little, Brown & Co., Boston, 1968.

188) DUCKWORTH G S, ROSS H. Diagnostic differences in psychogeriatrics patients in Toronto, New York and London, England. *Can Med Ass J* 112: 847–885, 1975.

189) EAGLES J M, WHALLEY L J. Aging and affective disorders the age at first onset of affective disorders in Scotland, 1969–1978. *Br J Psychiatry* 147: 180–187, 1985.

190) EGELAND J A, SUSSEX J N. Suicide and family loading for affective disorders. *JAMA* 254: 915–918, 1985.

191) ENGELS G I, DIEKSTRA R F W. Meta-analysis of rational-emotive therapy outcome. In *Behavioral Therapy Beyond the Conditioning Frame-Work*. P Eelen & O Fontaine (Eds.). Erlbaum, New Jersey, 1986.

192) EKERDT D, BOSSE R, LOCASTRO J. Claims that retirement improves health. *J Gerontology* 38: 231–236, 1983.

193) EKERDT D, BOSSE R, LOCASTRO J. The effect of retirement on physical health. *Am J Publ Health* 73: 779–783, 1983.

194) ELINSON L, GOETTLER F, KUHL D. Epidemiologic characteristics of suicide in the city of Toronto. *Can J Publ Health* 74: 422–426, 1983.

195) ENZELL K. Psychiatric study of 69-year-old health examinees in Stockholm. *Acta Psychiat Scand* 67: 21–31, 1983.

196) FANN W E. Pharmacotherapy in older depressed patients. *J Gerontology* 31: 304–308, 1976.

197) FARBEROW N L, MORIWAKI S Y. Self-destructive crises in the older person. *Gerontologist* 15: 333–337, 1975.

198) FEIGHNER J, ROBINS E, GUZE S, et al. Diagnostic criteria for use in psychiatric research. *Arch Gen Psychiatry* 26: 57–73, 1972.

199) FELTON B J, REVENSON T A. Coping with chronic illness: A study of illness controllability and the influence of coping strategies on psychological adjustment. *J Consult Clin Psychol* 52: 343–353, 1984.

200) FENICHEL O. *Trattato di Psicoanalisi*. Astrolabio, Roma, 1951.

201) FERRARI N A. Freedom of choice. *Social Worker* 8: 105–106, 1963.

202) FIBIGER H C. The neurobiological substrates of depression in Parkinson's disease: A hypothesis. *Can J Neurol Sci.* 11 (Suppl 17): 105–107, 1984.

203) FINCH C E. Catecholamine metabolism in the brains of ageing male mice. *Brain Res* 52: 261–276, 1973.

204) FINCH C E. Neuroendocrine and automatic aspects of aging. In *Handbook of the Biology of Aging*. C E Finch, L Hayflick (Eds.). Van Nostrand, New York, 1977.

205) FINKLESTEIN S, BENOWITZ L I, BALDESSARINI R J, et al. Mood, vegetative disturbance, and dexamethasone suppression test after stroke. *Ann Neurol* 12: 463–468, 1982.

206) FINLAYSON R E, MARTIN L M. Recognition and management of depression in the elderly. *Mayo Clin Proc* 57: 115–120, 1982.

207) FOLSTEIN M F, MAIBERGER R, McHUGH P R. Mood disorder as a specific complication of stroke. *J Neurol Neurosurg Psychiatry* 40: 1016–1020, 1977.

208) FOLSTEIN S E, McHUGH P R. Mini-mental state. A practical method for grading the cognitive state of patients for the clinician. *J Psychiat Res* 12: 189–198, 1975.

209) FORMAN B F. Cancer and suicide. *Gen Hosp Psychiatry* 108–114, 1979.

210) FRASER R M. *ECT. A Clinical Guide*. Wiley, Chichester, 1982.

211) FRASER R M, GLASS I B. Unilateral and bilateral ECT in the elderly. *Acta Psychiat Scand* 62: 13–31, 1980.

212) FRAZIER S H. *US Taskforce on Youth Suicide*. Paper read at WHO meeting on Preventive Strategies in Suicidal Behaviour. Geneva, October 4th, 1986.

213) FRERICHS R R, ANESHENSEL C S, CLARCK V A. Prevalence of depression in Los Angeles County. *Am J Epidemiol* 117: 173–185, 1981.

214) FRERICHS R R, ANESHENSEL C S, YOKOPENIC P A, et al. Physical health and depression. An epidemiologic survey. *Prev Med* 11: 639–646, 1982.

215) FREUD S. *Collected Papers*. Institute of Psychoanalysis and Hogarth Press, London, I, 20, 23, 1924.

216) FRY P S. Structured and unstructured reminiscence training and depression among the elderly. *Clin Gerontologist* 1: 15–37, 1983.

217) GAGNE A, METAFIOT M, DELOMIER Y. Etude clinique de l'amineptine dans la dépression du subject âgé. *Psychol Med* (Paris) 10: 1595–1602, 1982.

218) GAINOTTI G. Emotional behaviour and hemispheric side of the lesion. *Cortex* 8: 41–55, 1972.

219) GALLAGHER D E, THOMPSON L W. Effectiveness of psychotherapy for both endogenous and nonendogenous depression in older adult outpatients. *J Gerontology* 38: 707–712, 1983.

220) GALLAGHER D E, THOMPSON L W. Treatment of major depressive disorder in older adult outpatients with brief psychotherapies. *Psychotherapy: Theory, Research and Practice* 19: 482–490, 1982.

221) GANONG W F. *Fisiologia Umana* (8th ed.). Piccin, Padova, 1979.

222) GANZEMBOOM H B G, DE HAAN D. Gepubliceerde zelfmoorden en verbhoging van sterfte door zelfmoord en ongelukken in Nederland 1972–1980. *Mens en Maatschappy* 57: 55–69, 1983.

223) GARBER H J, WEILBURG J B, BUONANNO F S, et al. Use of magnetic resonance imaging in Psychiatry. *Am J Psychiatry* 145: 166–171, 1988.

224) GARDNER E A, BAHN A K, MACK M. Suicide and psychiatric care in the aging. *Arch Gen Psychiatry* 10: 547–553, 1964.

225) GARDNER E A, BAHN A K, MACK M. The relationship between premature deaths and affective disorders. *Br J Psychiatry* 115: 1277–1282, 1964.

226) GERNER R H. Depression in the elderly. In *Psychopathology of Aging*. O J Kaplan (Ed.). Academic Press, New York, 1979.

227) GERNER R, EASTBROOK W, STEUER J, et al. Treatment of geriatric depression with trazodone, imipramine and placebo: A double-blind study. *J Clin Psychiatry* 41: 216–220, 1980.

228) GERNER R H, JARVIK L F. Antidepressant treatment in the elderly. In *Depression and Antidepressants*. E Friedman, J Mann, S Gherson (Eds.). Plenum, New York, 1981.

229) GERSHON S. Comparative side effect profiles of trazodone and imipramine: Special reference to the geriatric population. *Psychopathology* 17 (suppl 2): 39–50, 1984.

231) GIBERTI F. Psicoterapia e senilità. *Min Psicoger* 1: 41–45, 1986.

232) GILMAN A G, GOODMAN L S, GILMAN A. *The Pharmacological Basis of Therapeutics* (6th ed.). MacMillan, New York, 1980.

233) GITARAM N, NURNBERGER J I, GERSHON E S, et al. Faster cholinergic REM sleep induction in euthymic patients with primary affective illness. *Science* 208: 200, 1980.

234) GLASSER M, RABINS P. Mania in the elderly. *Age and Aging* 13: 210–213, 1984.

235) GOETZL U, GREEN R, WHIBROW P, et al. X-linkage revisited. *Arch Gen Psychiatry* 31: 665–672, 1974.

236) GOLD M S, POTTASH A C L, EXTEIN I. Diagnosis of depression in the 1980's. *JAMA* 245: 1562–1565, 1981.

237) GOLD M S, POTTASH A C L, RYAN N, et al. THR induced TSH response in unipolar, bipolar and secondary depression. Possible utility in clinical assessment and differential diagnosis. *Psychoneuroendocrinology* 5: 147–155, 1980.

238) GOLDBERG D, KAY C, THOMPSON L. Psychiatric morbidity in general practice and the comunity. *Psychol Med* 6: 565–569, 1976.

239) GOLDBERG E L, VAN NATTA P, COMSTOCK G W. Depressive symptoms, social network and social support of elderly women. *Am J Epidemiol* 121: 448–454, 1985.

240) GOLDE P, KOGAN N. A sentence completion procedure for assessing attitudes toward old people. *J Gerontology* 14: 355–363, 1959.

241) GOLDFARB A L The psychotherapy of elderly patients. In *Medical and Clinical Aspects of Aging*. H T Blumenthal (Ed.). Columbia Press, New York, 106–114, 1962.

242) GOLDSTEIN S G, KLEINKNECHT R A, GALLO A E. Neuropsychological changes associated with carotid endarterectomy. *Cortex* 28: 308–321, 1970.

243) GOODSTEIN R K. Individual psychotherapy and the elderly. *Psychotherapy* 19: 412–418, 1982.

244) GOODWIN D. Alcohol in suicide and homicide. *Quart J Alcohol* 34: 144–156, 1973.

244a) GORDON W F. Elderly depressives: Treatment and follow-up. *Can J Psychiatry* 26: 110–113, 1981.

245) GOTHAM A M, BROWN R G, MARSDEN C D. Depression in Parkinson's disease: A quantitative and qualitative analysis. *J Neurol Neurosurg Psychiatry* 49: 381–389, 1986.

246) GOTTFRIES C G, ADOLFSSON R, ORELAND R, et al. Monoamines and their metabolites and monoamine oxidase activity related to age and to some dementia disorders. In *Drugs and the Elderly*. J Crooks & IH Stevenson (Eds.). University Park Press, Baltimore, 1979.

247) GOTTFRIES C G, ORELAND L, WIBERG A, et al. Brain level of monoaminooxidase in depression. *Lancet* II: 360–361, 1974.

248) GOTTFRIES C G, ORELAND L, WIBERG A, et al. Lowered monoamine oxidase activity in brains from alcoholic suicides. *J Neurochem* 25: 667–673, 1975.

249) GOTTFRIES C G, VON KNORRING L, ORELAND L. Platelet monoamine oxidase activity in mental disorders, II. Affective psychoses and suicidal behaviour. *Prog Neuropsychopharmachol* 4: 185–192, 1980.

250) GOVE W R. Sex, marital status and mortality. *Am J Sociology* 79: 45–67, 1973.

251) GOVONI S, SPANO P F, TRABUCCHI M. (3H) haloperidol and (3H) spiroderidol binding in rat striatum during ageing. *J Pharm Pharmacol* 30: 448–449, 1978.

252) GREENBERG L H, WEISS B. Beta-adrenergic receptor in aged rat brain reduced number and capacity of pineal gland develop supersensitivity. *Science* 201: 61–63, 1978.

253) GREENBERG R, PEARLMAN C. L-dopa, parkinsonism and sleep. *Psychophysiol* 7: 314–317, 1970.

254) GREENBLATT D J, ALLEN M O. Toxicity of nitrazepam in the elderly: A report from the Boston Collaborative Drug Surveillance Program. *Br J Clin Pharmacol* 5: 407–413, 1978.

255) GREENBLATT D J, DIVALL M, ABERNETHY D R. Benzodiazepine kinetics: Implications for therapeutics and pharmacogeriatrics. *Drug Metab Rev* 14: 251–292, 1983.

256) GRIFFIN J P, D'ARCY P F. *A Manual of Adverse Drug Interaction* (2nd ed.). J Wright and Sons, Bristol, 1979.

257) GROTE S S, MOSES S G, ROBINS E, et al. A study of selected catecholamine metabolizing enzymes: A comparison of depressive suicides and alcoholic suicides with controls. *J Neurochem* 23: 791–802, 1974.

258) GROTJAHN M. Analytic psychotherapy with the elderly. *Psychoanal Rev* 42: 419–427, 1955.

259) GROTJAHN M. Group communication and group therapy with the aged. A promising project. In *Aging into the Twenty-First Century*. L F Jarvik (Ed.). Gardner Press, New York, 1978.

260) GUR R E, SKOLNICK B E, GUR R C, et al. Brain function in psychiatric disorders. II. Regional cerebral blood flow in medicated unipolar depressives. *Arch Gen Psychiatry* 14: 695–699, 1984.

261) GURLAND B J. The comparative frequency of depression in various adult age groups. *J Gerontology 31:* 283–292, 1976.

262) GURLAND B J, COPELAND J, KURIANSKY J, et al. *The Mind and Mood of Aging*. Croom Helm, London, 1983.

263) GURLAND B J, DEAN L, CROSS P, et al. The epidemiology of depression and dementia in the elderly: The use of multiple indicators of these conditions. In *Psychopathology in the Aged*. J O Cole & J E Barrett (Eds.). Raven Press, New York, 1980.

264) HACHINSKY V. Multiinfarct dementia. *Neurol Clinics* 1: 27–36, 1983.

265) HAFNER H, RIECHER A. Research report, Central Institute of Mental Health, Mannheim, West Germany. *Psychol Med 15:* 417–431, 1985.

266) HALARIS A. Antidepressant drug therapy in the elderly enhancing safety and compliance. *Intl J Psychiat Med* 16: 1–16, 1986/1987.

267) HALE W D. Correlates of depression in the elderly. Sex differences and similarities. *J Clin Psychol* 38: 253–257, 1982.

268) HALEY W E. Behavioural self-management application to a case of agitation in an elderly chronic psychiatric patient. *Clin Gerontologist* 1: 45–52, 1983.

269) HALL R C W, BERESFORD T P. Antidepressivi triciclici: Molte cautele nel paziente anziano. *Geriatrics* (ed. ital.) 2: 21–31, 1985.

270) HAMSTER W, DIENER H C. Neuropsychological changes associated with stenoses or occlusions of the carotid arteries: A comparative psycometric study . *Eur Arch Psychiatr Neurol Sci* 234: 69–73, 1984.

271) HANLEY I, BAIKE E. Understanding and treating depression in the elderly. In *Psychological Approaches to the Care of the Elderly.* I Hounley & Hodge (Eds.). Crom Helm, Beckenham, 1984.

272) HARBISON JJM, GRAHAM PJ, QUINN JT, MAC ALLISTER H, WOODWARD R. A questionnaire measure of sexual interest. *Arch Sex Behav* 3: 357–366, 1974.

273) HARMAN D. The free radical theory of aging. In *Modern Biological Theories of Aging.* H R Werner et al. (Eds.). Raven Press, New York, 1987.

274) HARKEY B, HYER L. Suicide among psychiatric inpatients of older ages. *Psychol Rep* 58: 775–782, 1986.

275) HASEGAWA K. The epidemiological study of depression in late life. *J Affect Dis* (Suppl 1): 93–96, 1985.

276) HAYNES C D, GIDEON D A, KING G D, et al. The improvement of cognition and personality after carotid endarterectomy. *Surgery* 80: 699–704, 1976.

277) HAYNES S G, McMICHAEL A J, TYROLER H A. Survival after early and normal retirement. *J Gerontology* 33: 269–278, 1978.

278) HAYS P. Etiological factors in manic-depressive pychoses. *Arch Gen Psychiatry* 33: 1187–1188, 1976.

279) HELGASON T. Epidemiology of mental disorders in Iceland. *Acta Psychiat Scand* (suppl.) 173: 1964.

280) HELSING K J, SZKLO M. Mortality after bereavement. *Am J Epidemiol* 114: 41–52, 1981.

281) HELZER J E. Bipolar affective disorder in black and white males: A comparison of symptoms and familial illness. *Arch Gen Psychiatry* 32: 1140–1143, 1975.

282) HELZER J E, WINOKUR G. A family interview study of male manic depressives. *Arch Gen Psychiatry* 31: 73–77, 1974.

283) HEMMINGSEN R, MEJSHOLM B, BOYSEN G, et al. Intellectual function in patient with transient ischaemic attack or minor stroke. *Acta Neurol Scand* 66: 145–159, 1982.

284) HENDRICKSON E, LEVY R, POST F. Averaged evoked responses in relationship to the cognitive and affective state of elderly psychiatric patients. *Br J Psychiatry* 134: 494–501, 1979.

285) HIMMELHOCH J M, NEIL J F, MAY S J, et al. Age, dementia, diskinesias and lithium response. *Am J psychiatry* 137: 941–945, 1980.

286) HIMMELHOCH J M, AUCHENBACH R, FUGHS C. The dilemma of depression in the elderly. *J Clin Psychiatry* 43: 26–34, 1982.

287) HOLAHAN C K, HOLAHAM C J. Self-efficancy, social support, and depression in aging. A longitudinal analysis. *J Gerontology* 42: 65–68, 1987.

288) HOLCOMB H H, BANNON M J, RROTH R H. Striatal dopamine autoreceptors uninfluenced by chronic administration of antidepressants. *Europ J Pharmacol* 82: 173–178, 19882.

289) HOLDING T A. Suicidal behaviour in the elderly. In *Handbook of Studies on Psychiatry and Old Age.* D W K Kay & G D Burrosws (Eds.). Elsevier, Amsterdam, 319–328, 1984.

290) HOLLENDER M H. Individualizing the aged. *Soc Casework* 33: 337–342, 1952.

291) HOPKINSON G. A genetic study of affective illness in patients over 50. *Br J Psychiatry* 110: 244–254, 1964.

292) HOPKINSON G, LEY P. A genetic study of affective disorder. *Br J Psychiatry* 115: 917–922, 1969.

293) HORN S. Some psychological factors in Parkinsomism. *J Neurol Neurosurg Psychiatry* 37: 27–31, 1974.

294) HORNYKIEWICZ O. Neurohumoral interactions and basal ganglia function and dysfunction. In *The Basal Ganglia*. M D Yahn (Ed.). Raven Press, New York, 1976.

295) HORNYKIEWCZ O. Brain neurotransmitter changes in Parkinson's disease. In *Movement Disorders*. C D Marsden, S Fahn (Eds.). Butterworths, London, 1982.

296) HOVAGUIMIAN T, HIRSCH E. *Psychosocial Problems and the Physical Health of the Elderly: A Review of Controlled Studies*. WHO, Internal Document, 1988.

297) ILINSKY I, JOUANDET M L, GOLDAAM-RAKIC P S. The place of prefrontal cortex in the extrapyramidal motor scheme Nigro-thalamo-cortical connections in the rhesus monkey. *Society for Neurosciences* (abstract) 10: 181, 1984.

298) INGVAR D H. "Hyperfrontal" distribution of the cerebral grey matter flow in resting wakefulness: On the fuctional anatomy of the conscius state. *Acta Neurol Scand* 60: 12–25, 1979.

299) IRWIN M. Depression and immune function. *Stress Medicine* 4: 95–103, 1988.

300) IRWIN M, DANIELS M, BLOOM E T, et al. Life events, depressive symptoms, and immune function. *Am J Psychiatry* 144: 436–441, 1987.

301) IVERSEN S D, IVERSEN L. *Behavioural Pharmacology*. Oxford University Press, Oxford, 1981.

302) JACOBS L A, GANJI S, SHIRLEY J G, et al. Cognitive improvement after extracranial reconstruction for the low flow-endangered brain. *Surgery* 93: 683–687, 1983.

303) JACOBY R J, BIRD J M. Computer tomography and the outcome of affective disorder: A follow-up study of elderly patients. *Br J Psychiatry* 143: 124–127, 1981.

304) JACOBY R J, LEVY R. Computer tomography in the elderly. Senile dementia diagnosis and functional impairment. *Br J Psychiatry* 136: 256–269, 1980.

305) JACOBY R J, LEVY R. Computer tomography in the elderly. 3. Affective disorders. *Br J Psychiatry* 136: 270–275, 1980.

306) JAFFE J H. Drug addiction and drug abuse. In *The Pharmacological Basis of Therapeutics* (6th ed.). A G Gilman, L S Goodman, A Gilman (Eds.). MacMillan, New York, 1980.

306) JAMES N M. Early and late onset bipolar affective disorders: A genetic study. *Arch Gen Psychiatry* 34: 715–717, 1977.

307) JANET P. *Neuroses et idées fixes*. Vol.12, Felix Alcan, Paris, 1924.

308) JANOWSKI D S, EL-YOUSEF M K, DAVIS J M. Acetylcholine and depression. *Psychosom Med* 36: 248–257, 1974.

309) JARVICK L F. Antidepressant therapy for the geriatric patient. *J Clin Psychopharmacol* 1: 55–619, 1981.

310) JAVOY-AGID F, AGID Y. Is the mesocortical dopaminergic system involved in Parkinson's disease? *Neurology* 30: 1326–1330, 1980.

311) JEFFERSON J W. A review of the cardiovascular effects and toxicity of tricyclic antidepressant. *Psychosom Med* 37: 160–179, 1975.

312) JENIKE M A. The use of monoamine oxidase inhibitors in the treatment of elderly, depressed patients. *JAGS* 32: 571–575, 1984.

312a) JOBES D A, BERMAN A L, JOSSELSEN A R. The impact of psychological autopsies on medical examiners' determination of manner of death. *J Forensic Sci* 31(1): 177–189, 1986.

313) JOHNSTONE E C, OWENS D C G, FRITH C D. Neurotic illness and its response to anxiolytic and antidepressant treatment. *Psychol Med* 10: 321–328, 1980.

314) JOLLEY D, ARIE T. Psychiatric service for the elderly. How many beds? *Br J Psychiatry* 129: 418–423, 1976.

315) JOSEPH J A, BERGER R E, ENGEL B T, ROTH G S. Age-related changes in the nigrostriatum: A behavioral and biochemical analysis. *J Gerontology* 33: 643–649, 1978.

316) JOYCE B R. Age of onset in bipolar affective disorders and misdiagnosis as schizophrenia. *Psychol Med* 14: 145–149, 1984.

317) KANTOR S J, BIGGER J, GLASSMAN A H, et al. Imipramine-induced heart block. A longitudinal case study. *JAMA* 231: 1361–1366, 1975.

318) KANTOR S J, GLASSMAN A H. The use of tricyclic antidepressant drugs in geriatric patients. In *Psychopharmaclogy of Aging*. C Eisdorfer & W E Fann (Eds.). Spectrum, New York, 1980.

319) KAPRIO J, KOSKENVUO M, RITA H. Mortality after bereavement: A prospective study. *Am J Publ Health* 77: 283–289, 1987.

320) KARKI N, KUNTZMAN R, BRODIE B B. Storage, synthesis and metabolism of monoamines in the developing brain. *J Neurochem* 9: 53–58, 1962.

321) KASHANI J H, FRANK R G, KASHANI S R, et al. Depression among amputees. *J Can Psychiatry* 44: 256–260, 1983.

322) KASL S. Effect of "involuntary" relocation on the health and behaviour of the elderly. In *Epidemiology of Aging*. S G Haynes & M Feinleib (Eds.). Bethesda, MD, National Institute of Health, 1977.

323) KASTELER J M, GRAY R M, CARRUTH M L. Involuntary relocation of the elderly. *Gerontologist* 8: 276–279, 1968.

324) KATON W, RASKIND M. Treatment of depression in the medically ill elderly with methylphenidate. *Am J Psychiatry* 137: 963–965, 1980.

325) KAUFMAN A, BRIKNER P W, WARNER R. Tranquillizer control. *JAMA* 221: 1504–1506, 1972.

326) KAUFMAN M R. Old age and aging: The psychoanalytic point of view. *Am J Orthopsychiatry* 10: 73–84, 1940.

327) KAY D W K, BEAMISH P, ROTH M. Old age mental disorders in New-Castle-upon-Tyne. I. A study of prevalence. *Br J Psychiatry* 110: 146–158, 1964.

327a) KAY D. Affective disorders arising in the senium: Their association with organic cerebral degeneration. *J Ment Sci* 101: 302–316, 1955.

328) KAY D W K. The depression and neuroses of later life. In *Recent Advanced in Clinical Psychiatry*. K Granville-Grossman (Ed.). Churchill Livingstone, Edinburgh, 1976.

329) KAY D W K, BERGMAN K. Epidemiology of mental disorders among the aged in the comunity. In *Handbook of Mental Health and Aging*. J E Birren & B Sloane (Eds.). Prentice Hall, Englewood Cliffs, 1980.

330) KAY D W K, BERGMAN K. Physical disability and mental health in old age. *J Psychosom Res* 10: 3–12, 1966.

331) KAY D W K, BURROWS G D. *Handbook of Study on Psychiatry and Old Age*. Elsevier, Amsterdam, 1984.

332) KAY D W K, HENDERSON A S, SCOTT R, et al. Dementia and depression among the elderly living in the Hobart community. The effect of the diagnostic criteria on the prevalence rates. *Psychol Med* 15: 771–788, 1985.

333) KEELER M H, McCURDY R L. Medical practice without antianxiety drugs. *Am J Psychiatry* 132: 654–655, 1975.

334) KELLY M P, GARRON D C, JAVID H. Carotid artery disease, carotid endarterectomy, and behaviour. *Arch Neurol* 37: 743–748, 1980.

335) KENNEDY S, THOMPSON R, STANCER H C, et al. Life events precipitating mania. *Br J Psychiatry* 142: 398–403, 1983.

336) KERKHOF A J F M, VISSER A P H, DIEKSTRA R F W. The prevention of suicide among older people. *Crisis*, in press.

337) KHAN A V. *Nomifensine in the Treatment of Depression in Geriatric Practice.* 13th CINP Congress, Jerusalem, 1982.

338) KIELHOLZ P. *Depression in Everyday Practice.* Huber, Berne, 1974.

339) KIELHOLZ P, POLDINGER W, ADAMS C. *Masked Depression.* Deutscher Ärzte-Verlag, Köln-Lovenich, 1982.

340) KIEVET J, KUYPERS H G J M. Organization of the thalamo-cortical connections to the frontal lobe in the rhesus monkey. *Exper Brain Res* 29: 299–322, 1977.

341) KILOH LG, GARSIDE RF. The independence of neurotic depression and endogenous depression. *Br J Psychiatry* 103: 451–463, 1963.

342) KILOH L G, ANDREWS G, NEILSON M. The long-term outcome of depressive illness. *Br J Psychiatry* 153: 752–757, 1988.

343) KING G D, GIDEON D A, HAYNES C D, et al. Intellectual and personality changes associated with carotid endarectomy. *J Clin Psychol* 33: 215–220, 1977.

344) KING P. Notes on the psychoanalysis of older patients. *J Anal Psychology* 19: 22–27, 1974.

345) KING P. The life cycle as indicated by the nature of the transference in the psychoanalysis of the middle-aged and elderly. *Int J Psychoanalysis* 61: 153–160, 1980.

346) KIRSLING R A. Review of suicide among elderly persons. *Psychol Rep* 59: 359–366, 1986.

347) KLEIN D F, GITTELMAN R, QUITKIN F, et al. Clinical management of affective disorders. In *Diagnosis and Drug Treatment of Psychiatry Disorders Adults and Children* (2nd ed.). Williams and Wilkins, Baltimore, 1980.

348) KLEIN M. A contribution to the psychogenesis of manic depressive states. In *Contribution to Psychoanalysis, 1921–1945.* J D Sutherland (Ed.). Hogarth Press, London, 1965.

349) KLERMAN G L. Long term outcomes of nevrotic depressions. In *Human Functioning in Longitudinal Perspective Studies of Normal and Psychopatic Populations.* S B Sells, R Crandall, M Roff, et al. (Eds.). Williams & Wilkins, Baltimore, 1980.

350) KRAEPELIN E. *Lehrbuch der Psychiatrie* (7th ed.). McMillan, New York, 1907.

351) KRAGH-SORENSON P, HANSEN C E, BAASTRUP B C, et al. Self-inhibiting action of nortriptyline antidepressant effect at high plasma levels. *Psychopharmacologia* 45: 305–312, 1976.

352) KRAL V A. Depressions in the aged and their treatment. *Psychiatr Digest* 33: 49–56, 1972.

353) KRAL VA Psychiatric problems in the aged: A reconsideration. *Can Med Assoc J* 108: 584–590, 1973.

354) KRAMER M, SCHOEN L S. Problems in the use of long-acting hypnotics in older patients. *J Clin Psychiatry* 45: 176–180, 1984.

355) KRAUSE N. Stress and sex differences in depressive symptoms among older adults. *J Gerontology* 41: 727–731, 1986.

356) KRAUTHAMMER C, KLERMAN G. Secondary mania. *Arch Gen Psychiatry* 35: 1333–1338, 1978.

357) KREITMAN N. Age and parasuicide. *Psychol Med* 6: 113–121, 1976.

358) KRIEGER J, TURLOT J C, MAGIN P, KURTZ D. Breathing during sleep in normal young and elderly subjects hypapneas and correlated factors. *Sleep* 6: 108–11, 1983.

359) KUA E H, TSOI W F. Suicide in the island of Singapore. *Acta Psychiat Scand* 71: 227–229, 1985.

360) KUHL D E, METTER E J, RIEGE W H, et al. The effect of normal aging on patterns of local cerebral glucose utilization. *Ann Neurol* 15 (suppl.): S133–S137, 1984.

361) KUKULL W A, KOEPSELL T D, INVIT S, et al. Depressive and physical illness among elderly general medical clinic patients. *J Affect Dis* 10: 153–162, 1986.

362) KUPFER D J. Application of EEG sleep for the differantial diagnosis and treatment of affective disorders. *Pharmakopsychiatr Neuropsychopharmacol* 11: 17–26, 1978.

363) KUPFER D J, FOSTER F G. Interval between onset of sleep and rapid eye movements. Sleep as an indicator of depression. *Lancet* 2: 684–686, 1972.

364) KUPFER D J, FOSTER F G, REICH L, THOMPSON K S, WEISS B. EEG Sleep change as predictors in depression. *Am J Psychiatry* 133: 622–626, 1976.

365) KUPFER D J, SPIKER D G, COBLE P A, NEIL J F, ULRICH R, SHAW D M. Sleep and treatment prediction in endogenous depression. *Am J Psychiatry* 138: 429–434, 1981.

366) KUZUYA H, NAGATS T. Flavins and monoamino-oxidase activity in the brain, liver and kidney of the developing rats. *J Neurochem* 16: 123–125, 1969.

367) LADER M. Benzodiazepines: The opium of the masses? *Neuroscience* 3: 159–165, 1978.

368) LAFFEY P A, PEYSTER R G, NATHAN R, et al. Computer tomography and aging results in a normal elderly population. *Neuroradiology* 26: 273–278, 1984.

369) LAFFONT F, AUTRET A, MINZ M, BEILLEVAIRE T, GILBERT A, CATHALA H P, CASTAIGNE P. Etude polygraphique du sommeil dans 9 cas de maladie de Steele-Richardson. *Rev Neurol* 135: 127–136, 1979.

370) LAL H, CARROL P T. Alterations in brain neurotrasmitter systems related to senescence. In *Geriatric Psychopharmacology*. K Nandy (Ed.). Elsevier, New York, 1979.

371) LANGER S Z, BRILLEY M S, RAAISMAN R. Specific 3H-imipramine binding in human platelets. Influence of age and sex. *Arch Pharmacol* 313: 189–194, 1980.

372) LARSEN B, SKINHOJ E, LASSEN N A. Variations in regional cortical blood flow in the right and left hemispheres during automatic speech. *Brain* 101: 193–209, 1978.

373) LA TORRE R P, KEAR K. Attitudes toward sex in the aged. *Arch Sex Behav* 6: 203–213, 1977.

374) LAZARUS L W, WEINBERG J. Psychosocial intervention with the aged. *Psychiat Clin North Amer* 5: 215–227, 1982.

375) LAWTON M P, YAFFE S. Mortality, morbidity and voluntary change of residence by older people. *JAGS* 18: 823–831, 1970.

376) LAWTON M P, COHEN J. The generality of housing impact on the well-being of old people. *J Gerontology* 29: 194–204, 1974.

377) LAWTON M P, BRODY E M, TURNER-MASSEY P. The relationship of environmental factors to changes in well-being. *Gerontologist* 18: 133–137, 1978.

378) LEAROYD B M. Psychotropic drugs and the elderly patient. *Med J Australia* 1: 1131–1133, 1972.

379) LEHMANN H E. Epidemiology of depressive disorders. In *Depression in the 1970's*. R R Fieve (Ed.). Excerpta Medica, The Hague, 21–30, 1971.

380) LESSER J, LAZARUS L W, FRANKEL R, HAVASY S. Reminiscence group therapy with psychotic geriatric inpatients. *J Gerontology* 21: 291–296, 1981.

381) LEVY N. The hemodialysis patient. *Hosp Physician* 11 21–25, 1975.

382) LEWINSOHN P, BIGLAN T, ZEISS A. Behavioral treatment of depression. In *Behavioral Management of Anxiety, Depression and Pain*. P Davidson (Ed.). Brunner/Mazel, New York, 1976.

383) LEWIS J M, JOHANSEN K H. Resistances to psychotherapy with the elderly. *Am J Psychotherapy* 36: 497–504, 1982.

384) LEWIS J M, BUTLER R N. Life review therapy: Putting memories to work in individual and group psychotherapy. *Geriatrics* 29: 165–173, 1974.

385) LIEBERMAN A, DZIATOLOWSKI M, COOPERSMITH M, et al. Dementia in Parkinson's disease. *Am Neurol* 6: 355–359, 1979.

386) LIEBERMAN M A. Relationship of mortality rates to entrance to a home for the aged. *Geriatrics* 16: 515–519, 1961.

387) LINDEN M E. Group psychotherapy with institutionalized women study in gerontological relations. *Internat J Group Psychotherapy* 3: 150–170, 1953.

388) LINN M, ENSEL W M, SIMEONE R S, et al. Social support, stressful life events and illness: A model and empirical test. *J Health Soc Behav* 20: 108–119, 1979.

389) LINN M, HUNTER K, HARRIS R. Symptoms of depression and recent life events in the community elderly. *J Clin Psychol* 36: 675–682, 1980.

390) LINN B S, LINN M W, JENSEN J. Degree of depression and immune responsiveness. *Psychosom Med 44*: 128–129, 1982.

391) LINDESAY J. Suicide and attempted suicide in old age. In *Affective Disorders in the Elderly*. E. Murphy (Ed.). Churchill Livingstone, Edinburgh, 1986.

392) LIPINSKI J F, COHEN B M, FRANKENBURG F, et al. Open trial of S-adenosylmethionine for treatment of depression. *Am J Psychiatry* 141: 448–450, 1984.

393) LIPPMANN S. Drug therapy for depression in the elderly. *Postgrad Med* 73: 159–173, 1983.

394) LIPSEY J R, ROBINSON R G, PEARLSON G D, et al. Mood change following bilateral hemispere brain injury. *Br J Psychiatry* 143: 266–273, 1983.

395) LIPSEY J R, ROBINSON R G, PEARLSON G D, et al. Nortriptyline treatment of post-stroke depression: A double-blind treatment trial. *Lancet* 1: 297–300, 1984.

396) LIPSEY J R, ROBINSON R G, PEARLSON G D, et al. The dexamethasone suppression test and mood following stroke. *Am J Psychiatry* 142: 318–323, 1985.

397) LIPSEY J R, SPENCER W C, RABINS P, et al. Phenomenological comparison of poststroke depression and functional depression. *Am J Psychiatry* 143: 527–529, 1986.

398) LIPTON M A. Age differentiation in depression. Biochemical aspects. *J Gerontology* 31: 300–303, 1976.

399) LLOYD K G, HORNY-KIEWICZ O. Occurrence and distribution of aromatic L-aminoacid (L-dopa) decarboxylase in the human brain. *J Neurochem* 19: 1549–1559, 1972.

400) LLOYD K J, FARLEY I J, DECK J H N, et al. Serotin and 5-HIAA in discrete areas of the brain stem in suicide victims and control patients. *Adv Biochem Psychopharmacol* 11: 387–397, 1974.

401) LLOYD K G, DREKSLER S. An analysis of gamma-aminobutyric acid (GABA) binding in the human brain. *Brain Res* 163: 77–82, 1979.

402) LOCK W. Comments on Dr. Norman A. Cohen's paper "On loneliness and ageing process." *Int J Psychoanalysis* 63: 267–273, 1982.

403) LOCKE S E, KRAUS L, LESERMAN J, et al. Life change stress, psychiatric symptoms, and natural killer cell activity. *Psychosom Med* 46: 441–453, 1984.

404) LOO H, DUFOUR H, COTTEREAU M.D. Antidepressant and disinhibitory drugs. *Psychiat J Univ Ottawa* 4: 176–182, 1979.

405) LOPEZ M A. Social skills training with institutionalized elderly effects of pre-counseling structuring and over learning on skill acquisition and transfer. *J Counsel Psychology* 27: 286–293, 1980.

406) LOPEZ M J. *Relationship Between Conjugal Bereavement and the Immune System: A Review*. WHO, Internal Document, 1988.

407) LORANGER A W, LEVINE P M. Age at onset of bipolar affective illness. *Arch Gen Psychiatry* 35: 1345–1348, 1978.

408) MAAS J W. Clinical implications of pharmacological differences among antidepressants. In *Psychopharmacology: A Generation of Progress*. M A Lipton, A Di Mascio, K F Killam (Eds.). Raven Press, New York, 1978.

409) MACHLIN L J, BENDICH A. Free radical tissue damage protective role of antioxidant nutrients. *Faseb J* 1: 441–445, 1987.

410) MACKAY A V P, YATES C M, WRIGHT A, et al. Regional distribution of monoamines and their metabolites in the human brain. *J Neurochem* 30: 841–848, 1978.

411) MAC LEAN P D. Brain evolution relating to family, play and separation call. *Arch Gen Psychiatry* 42: 405–417, 1985.

412) MADDISON D, VIOLA A. The health of widows in the year following bereavement. *J Psychosom Res* 12: 297–306, 1968.

413) MAGGINI C, GUAZZELLI M, CONTI L. Modelli di sonno e disturbi affettivi in età involutiva. In *Il Sonno nell'Età Senile*. A Muratorio, C Maggini, L Murri (Eds.). Pacini, Pisa, 1978.

414) MAGGINI C, GUAZZELLI M, PIERI M, LATTANZI L. *Il sonno notturno nei depressi di età senile*. Paper read at the Ist National Congress of the Italian Society of Psychogeriatrics, Idelson, Napoli, 25–32, 1986.

415) MAGNI G, DE BERTOLINI C. Chronic pain as a depressive equivalent. *Postgrad Med* 73: 79–85, 1983.

416) MAGNI G, DE LEO D. *Aspetti Psicologici del Dolore Cronico*. Piccin, Padova, 1986.

417) MAGNI G, DE LEO D. La depressione nell'anziano: Diagnosi e trattamento farmacologico. *Giornale di Gerontologia* 31: 291–301, 1983.

418) MAGNI G, DE LEO D, CANTON G, et al. Psychotropic drug use in an italian general hospital. *Pharmacopsychiat* 17: 116–121, 1984

419) MAGNI G, DE LEO D, SALMI A, et al. Trattamento dell'ulcera duodenale con trimipramina. Una terapia efficace perchè agisce sulla depressione? *Minerva Dietologica e Gastroenterologica* 29: 123–125, 1983.

420) MAGNI G, DE LEO D, SCHIFANO F. Depression in geriatric and adult medical inpatients. *J Clin Psychol* 41: 337–344, 1985.

421) MAGNI G, SCHIFANO F, DE LEO D. Assessment of depression in an elderly medical population. *J Affect Dis* 11: 121–124, 1986.

422) MAGNI G, SCHIFANO F, DE LEO D, et al. The dexamethasone suppression test in depressed and non depressed geriatric medical inpatients. *Acta Psychiat Scand* 73: 511–514, 1986.

423) MAGNI G, SCHIFANO F, DE LEO D, et al. Evaluation of use patterns of psychotropic drugs in an Italian geriatric hospital. *Neuropsychobiology* 13: 38–43, 1985.

424) MAGNI G, PALAZZOLO O, DE LEO D. La prognosi della depressione nell'anziano. In *Disturbi Affettivi nella Terza Età.* D. De Leo & G. Magni (Eds.). Masson, Milano, 1987.

425) MAITRE L, MOSER P, BAUMAN P A, et al. Amine uptake inhibitors. *Acta Psychiat Scand* (Suppl. 280): 97, 1980.

426) MAKINODAN T, KAY M M. Age influence on the immune system. *Adv Immunology* 29: 287–330, 1980.

427) MANN A, JENKINS R, BELSEY E. The twelve-month outcome of patients with neurotic illness in general practice. *Psychol Med* 11: 535–550, 1981.

428) MANN A H, GRAHAM N, ASHBY D. Psychiatric illness in residential homes for the elderly. *Age & Aging* 13: 257–265, 1984.

429) MANTON K G, BLAZER D G, WOODBURY M A. Suicide in middle age and later life sex and specific life table and cohort analyses. *J Gerontology* 42: 219–227, 1987.

430) MARCOTTE D B, LOGAN C. Medical sex education allowing attitude alteration. *Arch Sex Behav* 6: 155–162, 1977.

431) MARIS R W. *Social Forces in Urban Suicide.* The Dosey Press, Homewood, 1969.

432) MARMOR J. Recent trends in psychotherapy. *Am J Psychiatry* 137: 409, 1980.

433) MAROZZA M I, RUBINO I A. Indicazioni al trattamento psicoanalitico dell' anziano. *Proceedings of the 1st National Congress of the Italian Psychogeriatric Association,* St. Vincent, July 1984.

434) MARSHALL J R. Changes in aged white male suicide 1948–1972. *J Gerontology* 33: 763–768, 1978.

435) MARSH G G, MARKHAM C H. Does levodopa alter depression and psychopathology in Parkinsonism patients? *J Neurol Neurosurg Psychiatry* 36: 925–935, 1973.

437) MARTIN-IVERSON M T, LECHEVE J F, FIBIGER H C. Cholinergic-dopaminergic interaction and the mechanism of action of antidepressants. *Europ J Pharmacol* 94: 193–201, 1983.

438) MATHEW R J. Cerebral blood flow in depression. *Lancet* 14: 1308, 1980.

439) MATHEW R J, MEYER J S, FRANCIS D J et al. Cerebral blood flow in depression. *Am J Psychiatry* 137: 1449–1450, 1980.

440) MAULE M M, MILNE J S, WILLIAMSON J. Mental illness and physical health in older people. *Age & Aging* 13: 349–356, 1984.

439) MATHEW R J, MEYER J S, FRANCIS D J et al. Cerebral blood flow in depression. Am J Psychiatry 137: 1449–1450, 1980.

440) MAULE M M, MILNE J S, WILLIAMSON J. Mental illness and physical health in older people. Age & Aging 13: 349–356, 1984.

441) MAYEUX R, STERN Y, ROSEN J et al. Depression, intellectual impairment, and Parkinson's diseases. Neurology 31: 645–650, 1981.

442) MAYEUX R, STERN Y, COTE L, WILLIAMS B W. Altered serotonin metabolism in depressed patients with Parkinson's disease. Neurology 34: 642–646, 1984.

443) MAYEUX R, WILLIAMS J B W, STERN Y, et al. Depression and Parkinson's disease. In Advances in Neurology. R G Hassler & J F Christ (Eds.). Raven Press, New York, 1984.

444) McCARLEY R. REM sleep and depression: Common neurobiologic control mechanism. Am J Psychiatr 139: 565–570, 1982.

445) McCLURE G M. Suicide in England and Wales, 1975–1984. Br J Psychiatry 150: 309–314, 1987.

446) McGEER E G, McGEER P L. Age changes in the human for some enzymes. In Neurobiology of Aging. J M Ordy, K R Brezzee (Eds.). Plenum, New York, 1975.

447) McGEER E G, McGEER P L. Neurotransmitter metabolism in the aging brain. In Neurology of Aging, Vol. 3. R D Terry & S Gershon (Eds.). Raven Press, New York, 1976.

448) McGEER P L, McGEER E G. Aging and neurotransmitter systems. In Parkinson's Disease. C E Finch, D E Potter, A D Keny (Eds.). Plenum Press, New York, 1978.

449) McGHIE A, RUSSEL S. The subjective assessment of normal sleep patterns. J Ment. Sci. 8: 642–654, 1962.

450) McKEITH I G, MARSHALL E F, FERRIER I N. 5-HT receptor binding in postmortem brain from patient with affective disorders. J Affect Dis 13: 64–74, 1987.

451) McINTOSH J, SANTOS J F. Methods of suicide by age sex and race differences among the young and old. Int J Aging Human Developm 22: 122–139, 1985–1986.

452) MEERLOO J A M. Transference and resistance in geriatric psychotherapy. Psychoanal Rev 42: 72–82, 1955.

453) MELAMED E, LAVY S, BENTIN S, et al. Reduction in regional cerebral blood flow during normal aging in man. Stroke 11: 31–35, 1980.

454) MELLSTROM D, et al. Morbidity among the widowed in Sweden. Scand J Soc Med 10: 31–41, 1982.

455) MENDLEWICZ J, FIEVE R R, RAINER J D, FLEISS J L. Manic-depressive illness: A comparative study of patients with and without a family history. Br J Psychiatry 120: 523–530, 1972.

456) MENDELS J, SCHLESS A P. Comparative efficacy of alprazolam, imipramine, and placebo administred once a day in treating depressed patients. J Clin Psychiatry 47: 357–361, 1986.

457) MEYER J S, SHAW T. Cerebral blood flow in ageing, the dementias and depression. In Handbook of Studies on Psychiatry and Old Age. D W K Kay & G D Burrows (Eds.). Elsevier, Amsterdam, 1984.

458) MICCOLI L, PORRO V, BERTOLINO A. Comparison between the antidepressant activity of S-adenosylmethinine (SAMe) and that of some tricyclic drugs. Acta Neurol 33: 243–255, 1978.

459) MILLER M. Geriatric suicide. The Arizona Study. *Gerontologist* 18: 488–495, 1978.

460) MILLER M. *Suicide After Sixty*. Springer, New York, 1979.

460a) MILLER H L, COOMBS D W, LEEPER J D, BARTON S N. An analysis of the effects of suicide prevention facilities on suicide rates in the United States. *Amer J Public Health* 74: 340–343, 1984.

461) MINDHAM R H S, MARSDEN C D, PARKES J D. Psychiatric symptoms during L-dopa therapy for Parkinson's diseases and their relationship to physical disability. *Psychol Med* 6: 23–33, 1976.

462) MINTZ J, STEUER J, JARVICK L. Psychotherapy. *Am J Psychiatry* 137: 409, 1980.

463) MITSCHERLICH M. The psychic state of patients suffering from parkinsonism. *Adv Psychosom Med* 1: 317–324, 1960.

464) MJONES H. Paralysis agitans. *Acta Psychiat Neurol* (suppl. 54): 1–195, 1949.

465) MOFFIC H S, PAIKEL E S. Depression in medical inpatients. *Br J Psychiatry* 126: 346–353, 1975.

466) MOLINARI V A, CHACKO R C, ROSEMBERG S D. Bipolar disorders in the elderly. *J Psychiat Treat Evaluation* 5: 325–330, 1983.

467) MOLLER M, THEVSSEN P, KRAGH-SORENSEN P, et al. Miaserin cardiovascular effects in elderly patients. *Psychopharmacology* 80: 174–177, 1983.

468) MOLLER S E, KIRK L, FREMMING K H. Plasma aminoacids as an index for subgruops in manic depressive psychosis Correlation to effect of triptophan. *Psychopharmacologia* 49: 205–211, 1976.

469) MOSS L M, HAMILTON D M. Psychotherapy of the suicidal patient. *Am J Psychiatry* 112: 814–820, 1956.

470) MOURET J. Differences in sleep in patients with Parkinson's disease. *Electroenceph Clin Neurophysiol* 38: 653–657, 1975.

471) MOUREN P, POINSO Y, OPPENHEIM G, et al. La personnalité du parkinsonien. Approche clinique et psychometrique. *Ann Med-Psychol.* 141: 153–167, 1983.

472) MULLER H F. Physiological and clinical sleep studies and implications for psychogeriatrics. In *Handbook of Studies on Psychiatry and Old Age*. D W K Kay & G D Burrows (Eds.). Elsevier, Amsterdam, 1984.

473) MUNIJAYA M. Epidemiological characteristics of psychoses in involutive and senile age in Belgrade, 1966–1969. Am Zav. *Men Z Drav* 5: 21–28, 1973.

474) MURATORIO A, MAGGINI C, MURRI L. Il sonno nelle sindromi depressive. Studio poligrafo di 35 casi. *Noopsichiatria* 33: 397, 1967.

475) MURPHY E. The prognosis of depression in old age. *Br J Psychiatry* 142: 111–119, 1983.

476) MURPHY E. The impact of depression in old age on close social relationships. *Am J Psychiatry* 142: 323–327, 1985.

477) MURPHY E. *Affective Disorders in the Elderly*. Churchill Livingstone, Edinburgh, 1986.

478) MURPHY E, SMITH R, LINDSAY J, et al. Increased mortality rates in late life depression. *Br J Psychiatry* 152: 347–353, 1988.

479) MURPHY GE The physician's responsibility for suicide. *Ann Internal Med* 82: I 300–304; II 305–309, 1975.

480) MURPHY G E. The prediction of suicide. Why is it so difficult? *Am J Psychotherapy* 38: 341–349, 1984.

481) MURREL S A, HIMMELFARBS, WRIGHT K. Prevalence of depression and its correlates in older adults. *Am J Epidemiol* 117: 173–185, 1983.

482) MYERS J K, WEISSMAN M M, TISCHLER G L, et al. Six month prevalance of psychiatric disorders in three communities 1980–1982. *Arch Gen Psychiatry* 41: 959–967, 1984.

483) NATIONAL CENTER FOR HEALTH STATISTICS. *Vital Statistics of the United States 1980, Vol 2: Mortality (Part B)*. DHHS publication (Phs) 85–1102, 1985.

484) NAUTA W J H. The problem of the frontal lobe: A reintepretation. *J Psychiat Res* 8: 167–187, 1971.

485) NIELSEN J. Geronto-psychiatric, period-prevalence investigation in a geographically delimited population. *Acta Psychiat Scan* 38: 307–330, 1962.

486) NIES A. Relationship between age and tricyclic plasma levels. *Am J Psychiatry* 134: 790–793, 1977.

487) NIES A, ROBINSON D S, DAVIS J M, et al. Change in monoamine oxidase with aging. In *Psychopharmacology and Aging*. C Eisdorfer & W E Farm (Eds.). Plenum, New York, 1973.

488) NIES A, ROBINSON D S, LAMBORN K R, et al. Genetic control of platelet and plasma monoamine oxidase activity. *Arch Gen Psychiatry* 26: 834–838, 1973.

489) NORBERG A, WILBLAND B. Cholinergic receptors in humans Hippocampus, regional distribution and variance with age. *Life Sci* 29: 1937–1942, 1981.

490) NORRIS F H, MURRELL S A. Older adult family stress and adaptation before and after bereavement. *J Gerontology* 42: 606–612, 1987.

491) NOVAK L P. Aging, total body potassium, fat free mass, and cell mass in males and females, between ages 18 and 85 years. *J Gerontology* 27: 438–443, 1972.

492) OBRIST W D, THOMPSON H K, WANG H S, et al. Regional cerebral blood flow estimated by xenon inhalation. *Stroke* 6: 245–256, 1975.

493) OESTERREICH K. Sexualverhalten alterer Menschen: Gerontopsychiatrische aspekte. *Z Gerontol* 15: 228–233, 1982.

494) OGREN S O, FUXE K, AGNATI L F, et al. Reevaluation of the indolamine hypothesis of depression. Evidence for a reduction of functional activity of central 5-HT system by antidepressant drugs. *J Neural Trasm* 46: 85–91, 1979.

495) OKIMOTO JT, BARNNES RF, VEITH RC, et al. Screening for depression in geriatric medical patients. *Am J Psychiatry* 139: 799–802, 1982.

496) OLLAT H, SEBBAN C. Lesions histologique et modifications des systèmes de neurotrasmetteurs du cerveau âgé. (Discussion de leur rôle pathogénique). *Presse Medicale* 12: 809–814, 1983.

497) OSGOOD N J. The alcohol suicide connection in late life. *Postgrad Med* 81: 379–384, 1987.

498) OSWALD I. Benzodiazepines and sleep. In *Benzodiazepines Divided*. M R Trimble (Ed.). Wiley, London, 1983.

499) OULES J, BOSCREDON J. Amineptine versus imipramine, étude contrôlée à double insu. *Press Med* 12: 2243–2248, 1983.

500) OUSLANDER J G. Drug therapy in the elderly. *Ann Int Med* 95: 711–722, 1981.

501) PARDES H. Neuroscience and psychiatry: Marriage or coexistence? *Am J Psychiatry* 143: 1205–1212, 1986.

502) PARENT A, SMITH Y, BOUCHARD C. Differential connections of caudate nucleus and putamen in monkey (abstract). *Society for Neuroscience* 10: 79, 1984.

503) PARIKH R M, LIPSEY J R, ROBINSON R G, et al. Two years longitudinal study of post-stroke mood disorders dynamic changes in correlates of depression at one and two years. *Stroke* 18: 579–584, 1987.

504) PARKER J C, GRANBERG B W, NICHOLS W K, et al. Mental status outcomes following carotid endarterectomy: A six-month analysis. *J Clin Neuropsychol* 5: 345–353, 1983.

505) PARKES C M. Effects of bereavement on physical and mental health: A study of medical records of widows. *Br Med J* 2: 274–279, 1964.

506) PARKINSON J. *Medical Classics, Vol. 2.* 964–997, 1938.

507) PATRICK H T, LEVY D M. Parkinson's disease: A clinical study of 146 cases. *Arch Neurol Psychiatry* 7: 711–720, 1922

508) PEDERSON A M, BARRY D J, BABIGON H M. Epidemiological consideration of psychotic depression. *Arch Gen Psychiatry* 27: 193–197, 1972.

509) PERRIS C. Abnormality on paternal and maternal side. Observation in bipolar (manic-depressive) and unipolar depressive psychoses. *Br J Psychiatry* 118: 207–210, 1971.

510) PERRIS C. The separation of bipolar (manic-depressive) from unipolar reccurrent depressive psychoses. *Behav Neuropsychiatry* 1: 17–24, 1969.

511) PERRY E K, PERRY R H, GIBSON P H, et al. A cholinergic connection between normal aging and dementia in the human hippocampus. *Neurosci Letters* 6: 85–89, 1977.

512) PERRY P M, DRINKWATER J E, TAYLOR G W. Cerebral function before and after carotid endarterectomy. *Br Med J* 4: 215–216, 1975.

513) PERSSON G. Prevalence of mental disorders in a 70-year-old urban population. *Acta Psychiat Scand* 62: 119–139, 1980.

514) PETTERSON U. Manic-depressive illness. A clinical, social and genetic study. *Acta Psychiat Scand* (suppl) 269: 1977.

515) PFEFFER E, DAVIS G C. Determinants of sexual behaviour in middle and old age. *J Am Soc* 10: 753–758, 1972.

516) PFEFFER E. Psychotherapy of the elderly. *NAPPHJ* 10: 41–46, 1978.

517) PFLUG B, TOLLE R. Therapie endogener Depressionen durch Schlafentzung: Praktische und theroretische Konsequenzen. *Der Nervenarzt* 42: 117–124, 1971.

518) PHARAM I A, PRIDDY T V, M C GOVERN, et al. Group psychotherapy with the elderly: Problems and prospects. *Psychotherapy* 19: 437–443, 1982.

519) PHELPS M E, MAZZIOTTA J C, BAXTER L, et al. Positron emission tomographic study of affective disorders: Problems and strategies. *Ann Neurol* 15 (suppl.): S149–S156, 1984.

520) PHILLIPS D P. The influence of suggestion on suicide: Substantive and theoretical implications of the Werther effect. *Am Soc Rev* 39: 340–354, 1974.

521) PHILLIPS D P, CARSTENSEN L L. Clustering teenage suicides after television news stories about suicide. *N Engl J Med* 315: 685–689, 1986.

522) PHILOT M P. Biological factors in depression in the elderly. In *Affective Disorders in the Elderly.* E Murphy (Ed.). Churchill Livingstone, Edinburgh, 1986.

523) PITT B. *Psychogeriatrics.* Churchill Livingstone, Edinburgh, 1974.

524) POEWE W, GERSTENBRAND F, RANSMAYR G, PLORER S. Premorbid personality of Parkinson's patient. *J Neural Transm* (Suppl 19): 215–224, 1983.

525) POLDINGER W J. Suicide and attempted suicide in the elderly. *Crisis* 2: 117–121, 1981.

526) POLLOCK G H. On ageing and psychopathology. *Int J Psychoanalysis* 63: 275–281, 1982.

527) POPKIN S J, GALLAGHER D, THOMPSON L W, et al. Memory complaint and performance in normal and depressed older adults. *Exper Aging Res 8:* 141–145, 1982.

528) POST F. *The Significance of Affective Symptoms in Old Age.* Maudsley Monographs 10, Oxford University Press, 1962.

529) POST F. The management and nature of depressive illnesses in late life. A follow-through study. *Br J Psychiatry* 121: 393–404, 1972.

530) POST F. Use of anticonvulsant carbamazepine in primary and secondary affective illness: Clinical and theoretical implications. *Psychol Med* 12: 701–704, 1982.

531) POST F. Affective psychoses. In *Handbook of Studies on Psychiatry and Old Age.* D W K Kay & G D Burrows (Eds.). Elsevier, Amsterdam, 1984.

532) PRADHAN S. Minireview: Central neurotransmitters and aging. *Life Sci* 26: 1643–1656, 1980.

533) PRANGE A J Jr, WHITE J E, LIPTON M A, et al. Influence of age on monoamino-oxidase and catechol-O-metyltransferase in rat tissue. *Life Sci* 6: 581–586, 1967.

534) PRYOR W A. The free radical theory of aging revisited: A critique and a suggested disease-specific theory. In *Modern Biological Theories of Aging.* H R Warner et al. (Eds.). Raven Press, New York, 1987.

535) RANDRUP A, MUNKRAD I, FOG R, et al. Mania, depression, and brain dopamine. In *Current Developments in Psychopharmacology.* W B Essman & L Vanzelli (Eds.). Spectrum, New York, 1979.

536) RECHTSCHAFFEN A. Psychotherapy with geriatric patients: A review of the literature. *J Gerontology* 14: 73–84, 1959.

537) REES W D C, LUTKINS S G. Mortality of bereavement. *Br Med J* 4: 13–16, 1967.

538) REGIER D A, MYERS J K KRAMER M, et al. The NIMH Epidemiologic Catchment Area (ECA) program historical context, major objectives, and study population charateristics. *Arch Gen Psychiatry* 41: 934–941, 1984.

539) REGIS E. *Précis de Psychiatrie.* Octave Doin, Paris, 1906.

540) REHAVI M, PAUL S M, SKOLNICK P, et al. Demonstration of high affinity binding sites for SH-imipramine in human brain. *Life Sci* 26: 2273–2279, 1980.

541) REIS D J, ROSS R A, JOH T H. Changes in the activity and amounts of enzymes synthesizing cathecholamines and acetylcholine in brain, andrenal medulla, and sympathetic ganglia of aged rat and mouse. *Brain Res* 136: 465–474, 1977.

542) REISBY N, GRAM L F, BECH P, et al. Imipramine: Clinical effects and pharmacokinetic variability. *Psychopharmacology* 54: 263–272, 1977.

543) REYNOLDS C F, SPIKER D G, HANIN I, KUPFER D J. Electroencephalographic sleep, aging and psychopathology: New data and state of the art. *Biol Psychiat* 18: 139–154, 1983.

544) RICKELS K, FEIGHNER J P, SMITH W T. Alprazolam, amitriptyline, doxepin and placebo in the treatment of depression. *Arch Gen Psychiatry* 42: 134–141, 1985.

545) RICKELS K, GINGRICH R L Jr, MCLAUGHLIN F W, et al. Methylphenidate in mildly depressed outpatients. *Clin Pharmacol Ther* 13: 595–601, 1972

546) RICHELSON E. Psychotropics and the elderly: Interactions to watch for. *Geriatrics* 39: 30–42, 1984.

547) RIPECKYJ A J, LAZARUS L W. Management of the old age. Psychotherapy: Individual, group, and family. In *Handbook of Studies on Psychiatry and Old Age.* D W K Kay & G D Burrows (Eds.). Elsevier, Amsterdam, 1984.

548) RISBERG J. Regional cerebral blood flow in Neuropsychology. *Neuropsychologia* 24: 135–140, 1986.

549) RISBERG J, HALSEY J H, WILLS E L, et al. Hemishepric specialization in normal man studied by bilateral measurements of the regional cerebral blood flow. *Brain* 96: 511–524, 1975.

550) RISCH S C. Beta-endorphin hypersecretion in depression: Possible cholinergic mechanism. *Biol Psychiatry* 17: 1071–1077, 1982.

551) ROBINS A H. Depression in patients with Parkinsonism. *Br J Psychiatry* 128: 141–145, 1976.

552) ROBINS E. *The Final Months.* Oxford Univ Press, New York, 1981.

553) ROBINS E, MURPHY GE, WILKINSON RH, et al. The communication of suicidal intent: A study of 134 consecutive cases of successful (completed) suicide. *Am J Psychiatry* 115: 724–733, 1959.

554) ROBINS E, WEST P A, MURPHY G E. The high rate of suicide in older white men: A study testing ten hypotheses. *Soc Psychiatry* 12: 1–20, 1977.

555) ROBINS LN, HELTZER JE, CROUGHAN J, et al. *The Diagnostic Interview Schedule, Version III.* National Institute of Mental Health, Division of Biometry and Epidemiology, Washington, 1981.

556) ROBINSON D S, DAVIS J M, NIES A A, et al. Relation of sex and aging to monoamine-oxidase activity of human brain, plasma, and platelets. *Arch Gen Psychiatry* 24: 536–539, 1971.

557) ROBINSON D S, NIES A A, DAVIS J M, et al. Ageing monoamines and mono-amine-oxidase levels. *Lancet* I: 290, 1972.

558) ROBINSON D S, SOURKES T L, NIES A, et al. Monoamine metabolism in human brain. *Arch Gen Psychiatry* 34: 89–92, 1977.

559) ROBINSON R G, KUBOS K L, STARR L B, et al. Mood changes in stroke patients: Relationship to lesion location. *Compr Psychiatry* 24: 555–566, 1983.

560) ROBINSON R G, KUBOS K L, STARR L B, et al. Mood disorders in storke patients (importance of location of lesion). *Brain* 107: 81–93, 1984.

561) ROBINSON RG, BOLLA-WILSON K, KAPLAN E, et al. Depression influences intellectual impairment in stroke patients. *Br J Psychiatry* 148: 541–547, 1986.

562) ROBINSON R G, LIPSEY J R, BOLLA-WILSON K, et al. Mood disorders in left-handed stroke patients. *Am J Psychiatry* 142: 1424–1429, 1985.

563) ROBINSON R G, LIPSEY J R, PRICE T R. Diagnosis and clinical management of post-stroke depression. *Psycosomatics* 26: 769–778, 1985.

564) ROBINSON R G, LIPSEY J R, RAO K, et al. Two-year longitudinal study of poststroke mood disorders: Comparison of acute-onset with delayed-onset depression. *Am J Psychiatry* 143: 1238–1244, 1986.

565) ROBINSON R G, PRICE T H R. Post-stroke depressive disorders: A follow-up study of 103 patients. *Stroke* 13: 635–641, 1982.

566) ROBINSON R G, STARR L B, KUBOS K L, et al. A two-year longitudinal study of post-stroke mood disorders: Findings during the initial evaluation. *Stroke* 14: 736–741, 1983.

567) ROBINSON R G, STARR L B, LIPSEY J R, et al. A two-year longitudinal study of post-stroke mood disorders: Dynamic changes in associated variables over the first six months of follow-up. *Stroke* 15: 510–517, 1984.

568) ROBINSON R G, STARR L B, PRICE T H R. A two-year longitudinal study of mood disorders following stroke: Prevalence and duration at six months follow-up. *Br J Psychiatry* 144: 256–262, 1984.

569) ROBINSON R G, SZETELA B. Mood change following left hemispheric brain injury. *Ann Neurol* 9: 448–453, 1981.

570) RODIN J. Behavioural medicine beneficial effects of self-control training in aging. *Int Rev Appl Psychol* 32: 153–181, 1983.

571) ROGERS M P, DUBAY D, REICH P. The influence of the psyche and the brain on immunity and disease susceptibility: A critical review. *Psychosom Med* 41: 147–164, 1979.

572) ROOSE S P, GLASSMANN A H, WALSH T, et al. Depression, delusion, and suicide. *Am J Psychiatry* 140: 1159–1162, 1983.

573) ROSSE R B, CIOLINO C H P. Effects of cortical lesion location on psychiatric consultation referral for depressed stroke inpatients. *Intl J Psychiat Med* 15: 311–320, 1986.

574) ROTH M. The natural history of mental disorders in old age. *J Ment Sci* 101: 281–301, 1955.

575) ROTH M. The psychiatric disorders of later life. *Psychiat Ann* 9: 57–101, 1976.

576) ROTH M. Treatment of depression in the elderly. *Acta Psychiat Scand* (Suppl 290): 401–433, 1981.

577) RUSH J A, SCHLESSER M A, ERMAN M, et al. Alprazolam in bipolar-1 depressions. *Pharmacotherapy* 4: 40–42, 1984.

578) SAINSBURY P. *Suicide in London. An Ecological Study.* Maudsley Monographs, Chapman & Hall, London, 1955.

579) SAINSBURY P. Social and epidemiological aspects of suicide with special reference to the aged. In *Processes of Aging. Social and Psychological Perspectives.* R H Williams, O Tibbita, W Donahus (Eds.). Atherton Press, New York, 1963.

580) SAINSBURY P. Suicide in old age. *Proc R Soc Med* 54: 266–268, 1961.

581) SALZMAN C. *Clinical Geriatric Psychopharmacology.* McGraw-Hill, New York, 1984.

582) SALZMAN C, KOCHANSKY G E, SHADER R I. Chlordiazepoxide-induced hostility in a small group setting. *Arch Gen Psychiatry* 31: 401–405, 1974.

583) SALZMAN C, SHADER R I. Depression in the elderly. I. Relationship between depression, psychologic defense mechanism and physical illness. *JAGS* 26: 253–260, 1978.

583a) SALZMAN C, SHADER R I. Clinical evaluation of depression in the elderly. In *Psychiatric Symptoms and Cognitive Loss in the Elderly.* A Raskin & L F Jarvik (Eds.). Holstead Press, New York, 1979.

584) SAMANIN R, BERNASCONI S, GARATTINI S. The effect of nomifensine on the depletion of brain serotin and catecholamines induced respectively by fenfluramine and 6-hydroxydopamine in rats. *Europ J Pharmacol* 34: 377–380, 1975.

585) SAMANIN R, JORI A, BERNASCONI S, et al. Biochemical and pharmacological studies on amineptine (S1694) and (+) amphetamine in the rat. *J Pharm Pharmacol* 29: 555–561, 1977.

586) SAMORAJSKI T. Central neurotrasmitter substances and aging: A review. *JAGS 25:* 337–348, 1977.

587) SAMORAJSKI T, ROLSTEN C. Age and regional differences in the chemical composition of brain of mice, monkey and humans. *Prog. Brain Res 40:* 253–265, 1973.

588) SARTORIUS N, BAN T. *Assessment of depression.* Springer, Berlin Heidelberg, 1986.

589) SASKATCHEWAN ALCOHOLISM COMMISSION RESEARCH DIVISION. *Central Nervous System Prescription Drugs and Elderly People. An Overview of the Issue and a Saskatchewan Profile.* Final Report, 1981.

590) SCHAEFER C, COYNE J C, LAZARUS R S. The health–related functions of social support. *J Behav Med* 4: 381–406, 1981.

591) SCHATZBERG A F, ROTSCHILD A J, STHAL J S, et al. The dexamethasone suppression test: Identification of subtype of depression. *Am J Psychiatry* 140: 88–91, 1983.

592) SCHILDKRAUT J J. *Neuropsychopharmacology and the Affective Disorders.* Little, Brown & Co., Boston, 1970.

593) SCHILGEN B, TOLLE R. Partial sleep deprivation as therapy for depression. *Arch Gen Psychiatry* 37: 267–271, 1980.

594) SCHLEIFER S J, KELLER S E, CAMERINO M, et al. Suppresssion of lymphocyte stimulation following bereavement. *J A M A 259, 3:* 374–377, 1983.

595) SCHLEIFER S J, KELLER S E, MEYERSON A T, et al. Lymphocyte function in major depressive disorders. *Arch Gen Psychiatry: 41* 484–486, 1984.

596) SCHLEIFER S S, KELLER S E, SIRIS S G, et al. Depression and immunity. *Arch Gen Psychiatry* 42: 129–133, 1985.

597) SCHMIDTKE A, HAFNER H. The Werther effect after television films: New evidence for an old hypothesis. *Psychol Med* 18: 665–676, 1988.

598) SCHOCKER D D, ROTH G S. Reduced beta-adrenergic receptor concetrations in aging man. *Nature* 267: 856–858, 1977.

599) SCHOU M. Lithium as a prophylactic agent in unipolar affective illness. *Arch Gen Psychiatry* 36: 849–851, 1979.

600) SCHWARTZ J M, BAXTER L R, MAZZIOTTA J C, et al. The differential diagnosis of depression. *JAMA* 258: 1368–1374, 1987.

601) SCHWARTZ M F, KOLODAY R C, MASTERS W H. Plasma testoterone levels of sexuality functional and dysfunctional males. *Arch Sex Behav* 9: 355–366, 1980.

602) SEDVALL G, FRYO B, GULLBERG B, et al. Relationship in healthy volunteers between concentration of monoamine metabolites in CSF and family history of psychiatric morbidity. *Br J Psychiatry* 136: 366–374, 1980.

603) SENDBUEHELER J M. Suicide and attempted suicide among the aged. *Can Med Ass J* 117: 412–419, 1977.

604) SERRA G, ARGIOLAS A, FADDA F, et al. Hyposensitivity of dopamine "autoreceptors" induced by chronic administration of tricyclic antidepressants. *Pharmachol Res Comm* 12: 619–624, 1980.

605) SEVERSON J A, MARCUSSON J, WINBLAD B. Age-correlated loss of dopaminergic binding sites in human basal ganglia. *J Neurochem* 39: 1623–1631, 1982.

606) SHAMOIAN C A. Assessing depression in elderly patients. *Hosp Comm Psychiatry* 36: 338–339, 1985.

607) SHAW K M, LEES A J, STERN G M. The impact of treatment with levodopa on Parkinson's disease. *Q J Med.* 49: 283–293, 1980.

608) SHIH J C, YOUNG H. The alteration of serotonin binding sites in aged human brain. *Life Sci* 23: 1441–1448, 1978.

609) SHIRAHATA N, HENRIKSEN L, VORSTRUP S, et al. Regional cerebral blood flow assessed by 133 Xe inhalation and emission tomography normal values. *J Comput Assist Tomog* 9: 861–866, 1985.

610) SHOLOMSKAS M D. Short-term interpersonal therapy (I.P.T.) with the depressed elderly: Case reports and discussion. *Am J Psychotherapy* 37: 552–565, 1983.

611) SHULMAN K I. Mania in old age. In *Affective Disorders in the Elderly*. E Murphy (Ed.). Churchill-Livingstone, Edinburgh, 1986.

612) SHULMAN R, POST F. Bipolar affective disorders in old age. *Br J Psychiatry* 136: 26–32, 1980.

613) SILVER A. Group psychotherapy with senile psychotic patients. *Geriatrics* 5: 147–150, 1950.

614) SILVERMAN C. *The Epidemiology of Depression*. Johns Hopkins, Baltimore, 1968.

615) SIMMONS K. Task force to make recommendations for adolescent in terms of suicide risk. *JAMA* 257: 3330–3332, 1987.

616) SIMPKINS J W, MUELLER G P, HUANG H H, MEITES J. Evidence for depressed catecholamine and enhanced serotin metabolism in aging male rats possible relation to gonadotropin secretion. *Endocrinology* 100: 1672–1678, 1977.

617) SINYOR D, JACQUES P H, KALOUPEK D G, et al. Poststroke depression and lesion location. *Brain* 109: 537–546, 1986.

618) SJOSTROM R, ROOS B E. 5-hydroxyindoleacetic acid and homovanillic acid in cerebrospinal fluid in manic-depressive psychosis. *Eur J Clin Pharmacol* 4: 170–176, 1972.

619) SKEGG D C G, RICHARDS S M, DOLL R. Minor tranquillizers and road accidents. *Br Med J* i: 917–919, &979.

620) SKINNER B F, VAUGHAN M E. *Vivere bene la terza età*. Sperling & Kupfer, Milano, 1984.

621) SLATER E. The inheritance of manic-depressive insanity. *Proc R Soc Med* 29: 981–990, 1936.

622) SMITH C, EBRAHIM S, ARIE T. Drug trials, the elderly, and the very aged. *Lancet* 2: 1139–1140, 1983.

623) SNOW R, CRAP O. Emotional bondedness, subjective well-being and health in elderly medical patients. *J Gerontology* 37: 609–615, 1982.

624) SOLOMON K. The depressed patient: Social antecedents of psychopatologic changes in the elderly. *JAGS* 29: 14–18, 1981.

625) SORENSEN A, STROMGREN E. Frequency of depressive states within geographically delimited population groups. *Acta Psychiat Scand* (Suppl 162): 62–68, 1961.

626) SPAR J E, LA RUE A. Major depression in the elderly DSM III and the dexamathosone suppression test as predictors of treatment response. *Am J Psychiatry* 140: 844–847, 1983.

627) SPARACINO J. An attributional approach to psychotherapy with the aged. *JAGS* 26: 414–417, 1978.

628) SPICER C C, HARE E H, SLATER E. Neurotic and psychotic forms of depressive illness. Evidence from age-incidence in a national sample. *Br J Psychiatry* 123: 535–541, 1973.

629) SPIKER D G, PUGH D D. Combining tricyclic and monoamine oxidase inhibitor antidepressants. *Arch Gen Psychiatry* 33: 828–830, 1976.

630) SPITZER RL, ENDICOTT J. *Schedule for Affective Disorders and Schizophrenia.* New York State Department of Mental Hygiene, New York, 1973.

631) STANLEY M, VIRGILIO J, GERSHON S. Tritiated imipramine in the frontal cortex of suicides. *Science* 216: 1337–1338, 1982.

632) STEIN M, KELLER S, SCHLEIFER S. The hypothalamus and the immune response. In *Brain, Behaviour, and Bodily Disease.* H Weiner, M A Hofer, A J Stunkard (Eds.). Raven Press, New York, 1981.

633) STENBACK A. Research in geriatric psychiatry and care of the aged. *Compr Psychiatry 14:* 9–15, 1973.

634) STENSTEDT A. Involutional melancholia. *Acta Psychiat Neurol Scand* (suppl). 127, 1959.

635) STEVER J. Psychotherapy with the elderly. *Psychiat Clin North Amer* 5: 199–213, 1982.

636) STROEBE W, STROEBE M S. *Bereavement and Health.* Cambridge University Press, New York, 1987.

637) SUGRUE M F. Current concepts on the mechanism of action of antidepressant drugs. *Pharmac Ther* 13: 219–224, 1981.

638) SURTEES P G. Social support, residual adversity and depressive outcome. *Soc Psychiatry* 15: 71–80, 1980.

640) TALLMANN J F, HAMMER D W. *Receptor Mechanism in Depression and Anxiety.* Upjohn Company, Kalamazoo, 1983.

640a) TANNEY B L. Electroconclusive Therapy and Suicide. In *The Biology of Suicide.* R Maris (Ed.). Guilford Press, 116–140, 1986.

641) TAYLOR A E, SAINT CYR J A, LANG A E, et al. Parkinson's disease and depression. A critical re-evaluation. *Brain* 109: 279–292, 1986.

642) TAYLOR M, ABRAMS R. Manic state: A genetic study of early and late onset affective disorders. *Arch Gen Psychiatry* 28: 656–658, 1973.

643) THOMPSON L W, BRECKENRIDGE J N, THOMPSON L W, et al. Effects of bereavement on self-perceptions of physical health in elderly widows and widowers. *J Gerontology* 39: 309–314, 1984.

644) TIMIRAS P S, HUDSON D B, MILLER C. Developing and aging brain serotin systems. In *The Aging Brain Cellular and Molecular Mechanism of Aging in the Nervous System.* E Giacobini, G Filogamo, G Giacobini, et al. (Eds.). Raven Press, New York, 1982.

645) TITLEY W B. Prepsychotic personality of patients with involutional melancholia. *Arch Neurol Psychiatry* 7: 1–17, 1936.

646) TODES C J. Idiopatic Parkinson's disease and depression: A psychosomatic view. *J Neurol Neurosurg Psychiatry* 47: 298–301, 1984.

647) TODES C J, LEES A J. The premorbid personality of patients with Parkinson's disease. *J Neurol Neurosurg Psychiatry* 48: 97–100, 1985.

648) TRABUCCHI M, REGGIANI A. E' possibile una biochimica dell'invecchiamento cerebrale? In *Psichiatria Geriatrica.* Masson, Milano, 1981.

649) TRASKMAN L, ASBERG M, BERTILSSON L. Monoamine metabolites in CSF and suicidal behaviour. *Arch Gen Psychiatry* 38: 631–636, 1981.

650) TRETHOWAN W H. Pills for personal problems. *Br Med J* iii: 749–751, 1975.

651) TYRER P. Dependence on benzodiazepines. *Br J Psychiatry* 137: 576–577, 1980.

652) THURST J S, SALK L, KENNEDY M. Mortality, morbidity and retirement. *Am J Publ Health* 47: 1434–1444, 1957.

653) ULLMAN M. *Behavioral Changes in Patients Following Strokes.* C. C. Thomas, Springfield, 1986.

654) ULRICH R F, SHAW D W, KUPFER D J. Effects of aging on EEG sleep in depression. *Sleep* 3: 31–40, 1980.

655) US CONGRESS SENATE SPECIAL COMMITTEE ON AGING. *Development in Aging.* 95th Congress, 1st session, April 7, 1976. US Government Printing Office, 1976.

656) UYTDENHOEF P, PORTLANGE P, JACQUY, et al. Regional cerebral blood flow and lateralized hemishperic dysfunction in depression. *Br J Psychiatry* 143: 128–132, 1983.

657) VALZELLI L. *Psychobiology of Aggression and Violence.* Raven Press, New York, 1981.

658) VAN DER HOOFDAKKER R H, ELSENGA S. Clinical effects of sleep deprivation in endogenous depression. In *Sleep 1980.* W P Koella (Ed.). Karger, Basel, 1981.

659) VAN PRAAG H M. Amine hypotheses of affective disorders. In *Handbook of Psychopharmacology.* L L Iversen, S D Iversen, S H Snyder (Eds.). Plenum, New York, 1978.

660) VAN PRAAG H M. Depression. *Lancet* 2: 1259–1264, 1982.

661) VAN PRAAG H M, DE HAAN S. Central serotonin metabolism and the frequency of depression. *Psychiatry Res* 1: 219–224, 1979.

662) VAN PRAAG H M, DE HAAN S. Depression vulnerability and 5-ydroxytryptophan prophylaxis. *Psychiatry Res* 3: 75–83, 1980.

663) VEITH R C, RASKIND M A, CALDWELL J H, et al. Cardiovascular effect of tricyclic antidepressants in depressed patients with chronic heart disease. *N Engl J Med* 306: 954–959, 1982.

664) VEITH R C, RASKIND M A. The neurobiology of aging: Does it predispose to depression? *Neurobiol Aging* 9: 101–117, 1988.

665) VERWOERDT A, PFEIFFER E, WANG H S. Sexual behaviour in senescence. *Geriatrics* 24: 137–154, 1969.

666) VESTAL R E, WOOD A J, SHAND D G. Reduced beta-adrenoreceptor sensitivity in the elderly. *Clin Pharmacol Ther* 26: 181–186, 1979.

667) VESTERGAARD P, AMDISEN A. Lithium treatment and kidney function. A follow-up study of 237 patients in long-term treatment. *Acta Psychiat Scan* 63: 333–345, 1981.

668) VOGEL G W. The relationship between endogenous depression and REM sleep. *Psychiat Annals* 11: 21–26, 1981.

669) VOGEL H P. Symptoms of depression in Parkinson's disease. *Pharmacopsychiatry* 15: 192–196, 1982.

670) VON AMMON CAVANOUGH S. The prevalence of emotional and cognitive dysfunction in a general medical population using the MMSE, GHQ and BDI. *Gen Hosp Psychiatry* 5: 15–24, 1983.

671) VON KNORRING L. A double blind trial Vivalan against placebo in depressed elderly patients. *J Int Med Res* 8: 18–21, 1980.

672) WALLACE S, WHITNEY B. Factors affecting drug binding in plasma of elderly patients. *Br J Clin Pharmacol* 3: 327–330, 1976.

673) WARBURTON J W. Depressive symptoms in Parkinson patients referred for thalamotomy. *J Neurol Neurosurg Psychiatry* 30: 368–370, 1967.

674) WARREN L R, BUTLER R W, KATHOLI C H R, et al. Focal changes in cerebral blood flow produced by monetary incentive during a mental mathematics task in normal and depressed subjects. *Brain Cognit* 3: 71–85, 1984.

675) WARREN L R, BUTLER R W, KATHOLI C H R, et al. Age differences in cerebral blood flow during rest and during mental activation measurements with and without monetary incentive. *J Gerontology* 40: 53–59, 1985.

676) WARVICK R, WILLIAMS P L. *Anatomia del Gray*. Zanichelli, Bologna, 1980.

677) WAYNE G J. Psychotherapy in senescence. *Am West Med Surg* 6: 88–91, 1952.

678) WEBB W B, SWINBURNE H. An observational study of sleep of the aged. *Percept Motor Skills* 32: 845–848, 1971.

679) WESTCOTT N A. Application of the structured life-review technique in counselling elders. *Personnel Guid J* 62: 180–181, 1983.

680) WEINBEG J. Geriatric psychiatry. In *Comprehensive Textbook of Psychiatry (II)* (3rd ed.). H I Kaplan, A M Friedman & B J Sadocil (Eds.). Williams & Wilkins, Baltimore, 1980.

681) WEISS I K, NAGEL C L, ARONSON M K. Applicability of depression scales to the old old person. *JAGS* 34: 215–218, 1986.

682) WEISSMAN M M. The myth of involutional melancholia. *JAMA* 242: 742–744, 1979.

683) WEISSMAN M M, FOX K, LERMAN G L. Hostility and depression associated with suicide attempts. *Am J Psychiatry* 130: 450–455, 1973.

684) WEISSMAN M M, KLERMAN G L. Epidemiology of mental disorders. *Arch Gen Psychiatry* 35: 705–712, 1978.

685) WEISSMAN M M, KLERMAN G L. The chronic depressive in the community unrecognized and poorly treated. *Compr Psychiatry* 18: 523–532, 1977.

686) WEISSMAN M M, MYERS J K. Affective disorders in a US community. The use of research diagnostic criteria in an epidemioloical survey. *Arch Gen Psychiatry* 35: 1304–1311, 1978.

687) WEISSMAN M M, MYERS J K, TISCHLER G L, et al. Psychiatric disorders (DSM-III) and cognitive impairment among the elderly in a US urban community. *Acta Psychiat Scand* 72: 382–388, 1985.

688) WELLS C E. Pseudo-dementia. *Am J Psychiatry* 136: 895–900, 1979.

689) WELZ R. Suicidal areas cluster analysis profile of urban environment. *Acta Psychiat Scand* (Suppl 285): 372–381, 1980.

690) WELZ R. *Drogen, Alkohol und Suizid—Strukturelle und individuelle Aspekte abweichenden Verhaltens*. Enke, Stuttgart, 1983.

691) WERTHAM F I. A group of benign chronic psychoses prolonged manic excitements with a statistical study of age, duration and frequency in 2000 manic attacks. *Am J Psychiatry* 9: 17–78, 1929.

692) WHITE F J, WANG R Y. Differential effects of classical and atypical antipsychotic drugs on Ag and A10 dopamine neurons. *Science* 221: 1054–1057, 1983.

693) WHITE P, HILEY C R, GOODHART M J, et al. Neocortical cholinergic neurons in elderly people. *Lancet* I: 668, 1977.

694) WHITTEN R H, GEE W, KAUPP H A, et al. Extracranial surgery for low flow endangered brain. *Arch Surg* 116: 1165–1169, 1981.

695) WHO. *Health in Crisis*. Heinemann, London, 1983.

696) WILLIAMS M, McGEE T H F. Psychological study of carotid occlusion and endarterectomy. *Arch Neurol* 10: 293–297, 1964.

697) WILLIAMS R, KARACAN I, HURSCH C. *Eletroencephalography of Human Sleep Clinical Applications*. Wiley, New York, 1970.

698) WILLNER M. Individual and group psychotherapy with the depressed geriatric patient: A rewarding approach. *Long Term Care Health Serv Admin Quart* 308, 1978.

699) WILSON M A, ROY E J. Age alters the observed response of imipramine binding sites to chronic antidepressant treatment in female rats. *Europ J Pharmacol* 106: 391, 1983.

700) WINEFIELD H R. The nature and elicitation of social support: Some implications for the helping professions. *Behav Psychother* 12: 318–330, 1984.

701) WINOKUR G. The Iowa 500: Heterogeneity and course in manic-depressive illness (bipolar). *Compr Psychiatry* 16: 125–131, 1975.

702) WINOKUR G, BELAR D, SCHLESSER M. Clinical and biological aspects of depression in the elderly. In *Psychopathology in the Aged.* J Cole & J E Barrett (Eds.). Raven Press, New York, 1980.

703) WINOKUR G, CLAYTON P, REICH T. *Manic-depressive Illness.* Mosby, St. Louis, 1969.

704) WINOKUR G, MORRISON J. The IOWA 500: Follow-up of 22 depressives. *Br J Psychiatry* 123: 543–548, 1983.

705) WIRZ-JUSTICE A, PUHRINGER W, HOLE G. Response to sleep deprivation as a predictor of therapeutic result with antidepressant drugs. *Am J Psychiatry* 136: 1222–1223, 1979.

706) WOLFF K. Depression and suicide in the geriatric patient. *JAGS* 17: 668–673, 1969.

707) WOLFF K. Group psychotherapy with geriatric patients in a mental hospital. *JAGS* 5: 13, 1957.

708) WORTMAN C B Social support and the cancer patient: Conceptual and methodologic issues. *Cancer,* May 15, (suppl.) 2339–2362, 1984.

709) YAHR M D, DUVOISIN R C, SCHEAR M J, et al. Treatment of parkinsonism with levodopa. *Arch Neurol* 21: 343–354, 1969.

710) YALOM I D. *The Theory and Practice of Group Psychotherapy.* Basic Books, New York, 1975.

711) YESAVAGE J A S, BRINK T L, ROSE T L, et al. Development and validaton of a geriatric depression screening scale. A preliminary report. *J Psychiat Res* 17: 37–49, 1983.

712) YOUNG M, BENJAMIN B, WALLIS G. The mortality of widowers. *Lancet* 2: 452–456, 1963.

713) ZEVON M A, KARUZA J, BRICKMAN P. Responsibility and the elderly application to psychotherapy. *Psychotherapy* 19: 405–411, 1982.

714) ZISOOK S. *Biopsychosocial Aspects of Bereavement.* American Psychiatric Press, Washington, DC, 1987.

715) ZUNG W W K. A self-rating depression scale. *Arch Gen Psychiatry* 12: 63–70, 1965.

716) ZUNG W W K. Affective disorders. In *Handbook of Geriatric Psychiatry.* E W Busse & D G Blazer (Eds.). Van Nostrand Reinhold, New York, 1980.

717) ZWEIG J P, CSANK J Z. Mortality fluctuations among chronically ill medical geriatric patients as an indicator of stress before and after relocation. *JAGS* 24: 264–277, 1976.

SUBJECT INDEX